HINCHLEY WOOD:

THE ORIGINS OF A 1930s SETTLEMENT

With best wishes

BY

HOWARD MALLINSON

Howard Mallinson

First published 2002 by
Howard Mallinson
22 Gordon Road
Claygate
Surrey
KT10 0PQ

British Library Cataloguing-in-Publication Data
A catalogue record for this book is available from the British Library

ISBN 0-9543934-0-6

Printed in Great Britain by BAS Printers Ltd, Over Wallop, Stockbridge, Hampshire

Dedication

This book is dedicated to the memory of two men, both of whose community work was pivotal to the origins of Hinchley Wood: to one, Edgar Royston Pike, goes tribute to his leadership in civic affairs: to the other, less well known, Bishop Cyril Golding-Bird, goes tribute to his constancy and clear vision which ensured that the ecclesiastical development of the new settlement kept pace with the civil: the man who ensured, in spite of many obstacles, that we had a spiritual life, and a Church, housed temporarily for 20 years, but which ultimately, by the consecration of St Christopher's in 1953, saw the monument to his leadership for all the generations that follow.

Esher Filling Station at the junction of Manor Road and the Kingston by-pass (from a photograph published in the Garage and Motor Agent *on 29 September 1929). This picture is the only one known to exist showing the fields where Hinchley Wood was developed from 1930.*

Photo: Courtesy of British Library

CONTENTS

ACKNOWLEDGEMENTS

In the course of researching and writing this book I have become indebted to many kind people, to whom I will record my gratitude and thanks here. There are two people who have to be thanked first and well: both of them former workmates with intimate knowledge over many years of my shortcomings and peccadilloes, who, with the most generous application of skill and care went out of their way to help me. Alec Bogie and I both underwent the same training process, and learned (or were supposed to) clear and economical writing. That process, working with much better material in Alec than with me, produced in him a fine professional, much loved by his clients for his gentle, unassertive, incisive mind. Alec read the first typescript of this book. The over-arching result of his wise suggestions, has been a book which is better focused. By his suggestions I have been able to edit out or re-order material which interrupted the flow or was digressive or gratuitous: these deletions, the reader will not notice. Through helpful suggestions about the balance of the book; by encouragement for some and questioning of other material, the reader will, I think, find a better presentation than existed before Alec's conscientious effort. He has no responsibility for what the reader sees, nor for the style, which is mine; but I will for ever be grateful to him.

Jan Griffiths, having had the chance of being done with me, helped with patient typing of about 120% of what you see, much of it from careless manuscript, yet more from obscure copies of old archives; all of it cheerfully in her helpful way; in her time which could have been consumed more agreeably, and more deservedly, in pursuing her new leisure without frequent bulky parcels arriving to derange her own life. It is not just that she allowed me to keep to the timetable: for without her work there was no sensible time-frame in which the book could have been produced at all.

In researching historical records, I have developed a very high regard for the archivists who make it possible. Most of this activity is funded with public money, and may it remain so: the activity is uneconomic but it is central to the sustainability of our culture. I have received a welcome, and much valuable guidance from: Surrey History Centre in Woking; the Local History Room (in Richmond Road) of Kingston Museum; and from Elmbridge Museum in Weybridge. I am very grateful to all those who helped me there, and to those unseen who made it possible.

Many parishioners of St Chrisopher's have been enthusiastic with their help with archives, photos and facts remembered: Mary Taylor, Hilda Williams, Ann Ashby, Christopher and Candida Gill; others have in great numbers given suggestions which have led to good discoveries. I am specially grateful in one direction: Audrey Phillips told me of the existence of the log of Hinchley Wood school: solely through the persistence of a resident, Michael Beaney, I was able to get access to it; without both of them my account of school life during the war would not exist. Margaret Lamb introduced me to Anita Littler (neé Witten) who had covered some of the ground I wished to tread, and had written it up in an unpublished dissertation: her willingness to allow me to borrow this was particularly generous. I had help in another unexpected direction. Although I have known Mrs Pat Gregory of the Dorritt House in Esher for a long time; even long enough to know she had been Pat Jordan, I did not know that she was the daughter of Mr John Jordan who was a Churchwarden at a critical point in the history of St Christopher's. She helped me both with mementoes and recollections to give more colour to the natal years of the Church in Hinchley Wood.

The research to support the chapters on St Christopher's Church has been eased immeasurably by two separate efforts to record facts relating to its history, each about 35 years or more apart. The most recent was the work done by the late Will Vaughan Williams, a former Churchwarden, and kindly lent to me by his widow, Hilda. Mr. Williams compiled some notes in 1987, about the history of St Christopher's which he called 'a brief guide': it is a modestly compiled source of studied historical composition of facts about our Church: it is included as an appendix to the book.

Equally, a great debt is owed to that immediate post war generation of parishioners who made an attempt, collectively, at a definitive history of St Christopher's Church. Sadly, the work wasn't finished but much of its efforts are retained at the Surrey History Centre in Woking. A sub-committee was appointed by the Parochial Church Council; its terms of reference were to 'set down the history of the Church in Hinchley Wood for the reference of future generations'. The sub-committee took its task very seriously and advertised in the parish magazine and in the Esher News for material and recollections. In addition, it took eye-witness accounts from the participants from the 1930s period: I am pleased to acknowledge the value of that generation's work in producing my own account.

Bill Gibson (always Uncle Bill to the kids in my road), a community stalwart of the Royston Pike mould, helped me in a special way. Beverley and Hilary Abbey of Semaphore House were very kind; they allowed me into the oldest house in Hinchley Wood, and an important one on any basis, and generously allowed me to share with readers some of its intimate details. Other residents have helped me: Gerry and Janet Hall told me about Hinchley Wood before I ever knew it, and gave me some useful photos. Geoffrey Tregaskes, a friend from my earliest days in Hinchley Wood: and a fellow miscreant on Telegraph Hill; helped with photos and recollections.

Roger Allen, a former resident, gave me useful information about the Milk Marketing Board and other tips. Jeff Jefferies, another resident gave me first hand information from when the Surtax Office opened on "the land between the railway lines". Councillor Janet Turner gave me encouragement and access to the archive of the Hinchley Wood Residents' Association which allowed colour to be added to the story.

Malcolm Peebles gave me several tips on the whole process of writing, producing and marketing a book of this nature; it was helpful to me, treading new ground, to talk to someone who had done it before.

Photographs have been a nightmare: my thanks go to every-one who has helped me with them; along with my hope that I have given proper attribution. Where photographs are not attributed, they are mine.

My wife Irene was at all times enthusiastic for my task, and even if not incredulous of the extent of it, then praising: more, she was uncomplaining as my working method meant first the occupation of all flat ground in one room of our home, only to see me advance again to take another as well: and finally a third! Sufficiently, she was an encourager and auxiliary typist, for me to regard her as a collaborator. My son, Dudley, helped with the charts and other graphics: to him, and Irene and to everyone else: my thanks.

FOREWORD BY IAN TAYLOR, MBE, MP

In my Esher and Walton Constituency, there are many communities that feel proud of their separate identity and character. This book offers an interesting and detailed account of the history of one of them, Hinchley Wood. Although the 'village' may not be of national renown, in my judgment the people living in Hinchley Wood have a strong sense of community values and are prepared to stand up for them when necessary. We should be grateful to the book's author, who has worked hard to give a comprehensive account of all the vital influences on Hinchley Wood's creation. He has cast a critical but affectionate eye.

The rapid pre-war growth of Hinchley Wood was, as the author writes, crucial to the development of a sustainable community since building was largely stopped during the war. The speed at which the development grew was attributable to eager property developers providing affordable new housing in the green belt attractive to the London commuter. Also, with Southern Railway's active promotion of their new electric train service, which was fast, clean and straight into the capital, it is not surprising Hinchley Wood became a popular place to live.

The author provides background to the early housing boom; the growth, year by year, of the new residents; the interesting key role of the Council and town planning in the new settlement and how Telegraph Hill became a public space. As the local Member of Parliament, I have enjoyed several visits to local schools in Hinchley Wood

and so was fascinated by the sensitive account of how the war impacted on school life.

The Council, as in today's Hinchley Wood, played a fundamental role in determining the housing densities, transport routes and shopping provisions (with guidance from the county and national administrations of the day). However, the author is not without a critical view, which history and the benefit of hindsight allows, of what he regards as failures in the town plan leading to the lack of provision of public facilities.

From a political perspective, I particularly noted the author's research and findings into the origins of the Hinchley Wood Residents' Association and about key local leaders such as Edgar Royston Pike who contributed massively to the community. It was interesting to think the sense of community spirit, which rallied residents in Hinchley Wood to battle with McDonald's in recent years, has been evident since the settlement developed with residents actively wishing to protect their community

'Hinchley Wood: The Origins of a 1930s Settlement' is a thorough account of local history. How scientific and technological invention stimulated development; how national and global circumstances influenced everyday life and how a sense of community spirit developed and flourished. It is a book for those who live, know or are familiar with Hinchley Wood, but also one for historians who will find of interest the detailed account of social history.

PREFACE

The origins of this book can be traced to a conversation with the new Vicar of St Christopher's Church, Hinchley Wood, the Rev Trevor Donnolley, who was inducted as incumbent of the parish in February 2001. It would take someone new to spot that the 50th anniversary of the consecration of the Church (on 7 February 1953) was up-coming soon: although the foundation stone on the front wall of the church announces boldly that it had been laid a year earlier, in 1952, familiarity had prevented many from noticing that the jubilee was imminent.

The new vicar wanted to celebrate the jubilee, but being new to Hinchley Wood, needed a source for local history to mark the occasion in its historical context. My mind went to Royston Pike, whom I remembered as being an author and lecturer on local affairs in the 1950s and 1960s, and I volunteered to try and trace what had been written up. I discovered that at the Surrey History Centre, the official repository in Woking, there was indeed some high quality material which would form a good basis for a history of how the Church came into being. I was to find out later that several parishioners had good archive material as well.

By the time I had established that there was sufficient material to attempt a book, it was January 2002 and I volunteered to write this work. The character of the book has changed since its first conception. Even in the beginning, it was clear that a history of St Christopher's, without the story of Hinchley Wood being told as well, would be incomplete. At first, however, I had in mind a chronological account, taking the reader from the earliest times to the present day. I had to reject this notion because I soon realised that there was just too much material, or potential material, to be handled: as the notable historian, A J P Taylor, said. 'History gets thicker as it approaches recent times: more people: more events: more …' Moreover, if I had embarked on a big round of eye-witness interviews, the task of assembling all this succinctly, and keeping the text interesting, might have overwhelmed me. While many people have kindly helped me with their memories, this story is not built round anecdotal evidence: it has been sourced from official archives, contemporary newspaper reports and, with proper attribution, other authors' work.

In spending many hours engaged agreeably in research at several libraries; the Surrey History Centre; Elmbridge Museum and Kingston Heritage Centre, I discovered that there were a number of voids in the literature: for example, no historian had written up the history of the Kingston by-pass, a development which lies at the heart of the Hinchley Wood story. Although the history of the railways is very well documented, no author had, single-mindedly, looked at the history of the routes, whether branch or main, as they have evolved passing through Hinchley Wood; and, most notably, neither was there an account of how the relatively recent station at Hinchley Wood came to be built.

Moreover, although quite a bit of work has been done in a general sense on the phenomenon of the 1930s housing boom, no historian had ever published any work on how Hinchley Wood fitted into that scene; of how in the space of a few years, a new settlement arrived and was placed round an area where a new arterial road met a railway line which had already been running through the area for 45 years: a line on which commuters to London had no interruption to their journeys from Claygate and beyond, through the farmland that was from 1930 to be transformed before their eyes. No author had explained any of this. Certainly, some short works on Hinchley Wood and its Church have been written over the years: but such monographs that exist only deal with fragments; there had been no published attempt at a consolidated account of how Hinchley Wood happened. All this was true until I was introduced to Anita Littler (née Witten) who had actually covered the ground in writing a dissertation for her Master's degree in 1983. She kindly lent me her work which had been informed by sources which had much in common with mine.

As my research accumulated the title of the book spoke to describe the contents: **"Hinchley Wood: the origins of a 1930s settlement."** I have attempted to keep the content of the book faithful to its title: it is a history of how Hinchley Wood emerged: as a settlement with its notable 1930s imprint. Although the new settlement was substantially finished before war broke out in 1939, several key components in the story of its origins were deferred for completion later; an account of these matters is continued in the book until each reaches its own end: for example, the story of the Church starts early but can't be finished until 1953. I think readers will agree that although the war got in the way (both at the time with dreadful effect, and in telling the story), the post-war completion of several stories keeps faith with the title of the book: it contains nothing whose origin is not in the 1930s.

The reader will find in the text a scarcely veiled attachment for the subject of this book, born of an association with Hinchley Wood (as either a resident, or a churchgoer of more or less frequent habit, over the years), that is only a whisker short of the Church's jubilee itself. The reader will find, however, that where criticism of how Hinchley Wood developed is justified, my objectivity has overcome my fondness; I hope so anyway. I hope that the book has something to hold the interest of former residents as well as those either living there now or who may do so in the future.

Boundaries often cause difficulties in local histories. The ecclesiastical boundary of the parish is out of synchronisation with the civil boundary, but not many people know where either boundary is anyway. For my purposes, I haven't been too exercised about the issue for in the 1930s there was no official recognition of Hinchley Wood: it was all a part of Thames Ditton. As far as I am concerned, Hinchley Wood runs from Telegraph Hill in the south but never crosses the Portsmouth Road in the north; and from the Claygate end of Manor Road South to Angel Road in the east. The parish boundary does not include Couchmore Avenue or Westmont Road: nor Semaphore House on Telegraph Hill; but fortunately, they are captured by the civil boundary.

The book falls informally into three parts: in the first two chapters I discuss what may be described as the pre-history of Hinchley Wood in order to set the scene for the development explosion that was to take place from 1930. In Chapter 1, I discuss the history of the railway routes that run through Hinchley Wood, while in Chapter 2 the history of the Kingston by-pass is covered. (I have not dwelt at length on the Esher by-pass: it is an important subject, certainly, capable of a work all of its own, but it is diversionary from my theme of the origins of a 1930s settlement; in as far as it touches on this theme, it is discussed in Chapters 2 and 9.)

In Chapters 3 and 4 I review the background to the 1930s housing boom and how Hinchley Wood was planned. In Chapters 5 and 6 are the accounts of much of the building activity; a key part of the story. Chapter 7 gives an account of how civic life evolved and the role of the Residents' Association; while Chapter 8 is about Telegraph Hill. Although most of the story of the Kingston by-pass is in Chapter 2, those aspects which are particular to the 1930s are in Chapter 9.

The story of the land between the railway lines is in Chapter 10: schools are in Chapter 11 with a section on how air raids seriously disrupted school life. Chapter 12 contains an account of how Hinchley Wood was nearly swamped by a proposed huge development between it and Hook. In Chapter 13 I have brought together a discussion of the housing completions after the war and an overview of Hinchley Wood in retrospect.

Chapters 14 and 15 are dedicated to matters concerning the Church: the first of those two chapters deals with the early days of spiritual life, while the last chapter gives the story of the building of the permanent Church. In an Appendix is a brief guide to the fabric of the Church which was written in 1987 by the late Will Williams, a former Churchwarden: I can't add anything to it so it is presented here as he wrote it, save only for one additional fact and the photographs.

Some technical points: in the currency of the period of this book, there have been three local authorities for Hinchley Wood at the district level: I have not thought it helpful, generally, to distinguish between them and they are referred to as "the Council". Esher and the Dittons Council became part of Esher Urban District Council on 1 April 1933, when Cobham and Molesey were added: on 1 April 1974, Elmbridge Borough Council was formed to include Walton and Weybridge.

Spelling: the benefits of a computer "spell check" facility are not unalloyed; I have tried to stop it saying "realization" when I mean "realisation"; and "traveled" when I mean "travelled", and other unbending assertions which it makes, unless corrected.

Where I say "church" it means no particular building nor denomination: where I say "Church" it is either short for "The Church of England" or a particular consecrated Church. Holders of elective offices have capital letters, so we have Councillors and Churchwardens, but generally I have tried to avoid the use of capitals except for proper names: so we have the "Parish of St Christopher" but: "St Christopher's did not become a parish until…" In the contemporary records, the two first clergymen of the parish were referred to variously as "Priests-in-charge" and "Curate-in charge", sometimes with a capital, sometimes not; whether correctly or not, I have used "Curate-in-charge" for consistency. Technically, when the Rev Newton Jones came to the parish, he was "the Priest-in-charge": he became the Vicar, so I have avoided labouring the difference.

Footnotes: these can be tiresome for the reader: I have kept them to a minimum.

I have enjoyed researching and writing this book. Writing against a deadline, however, is for professionals – I don't recommend it to amateur writers, for it is not compatible with rhythmic life. On the other hand, authorship is conducive to indulgence of language and style – this has its reward. I will be rewarded also, if any reader were to intone: *I never knew that*: or *that's interesting*: or *I'd forgotten that*. I hope, equally, no reader has cause to say: *he's got that wrong*. I pray that any errors are minor ones: but whether errors are small or not, or if there are any omissions (please, none serious) I crave forgiveness.

Howard Mallinson
Claygate
October, 2002

Map of Hinchley Wood area : 1838 (when the railway came)

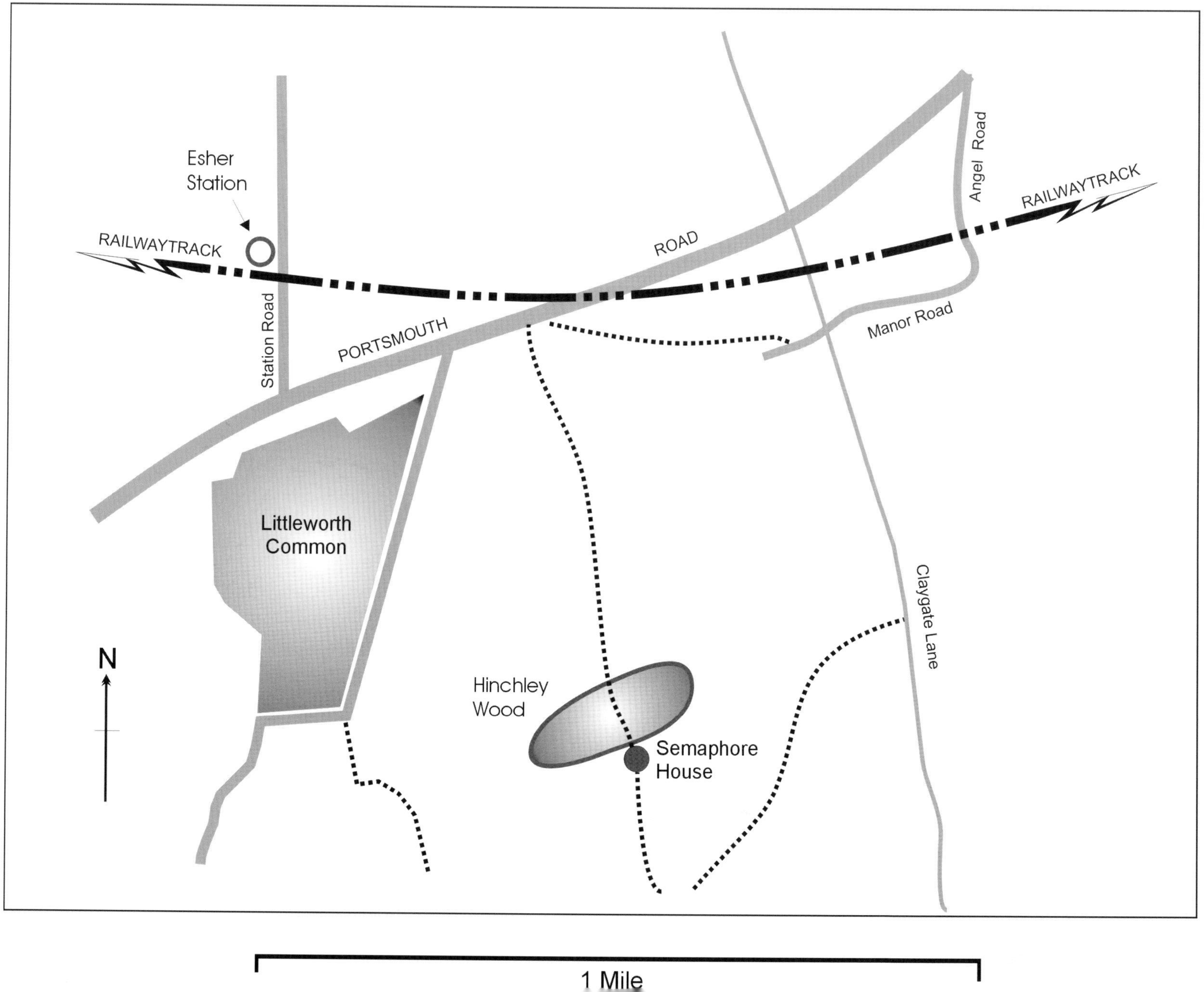

RAILWAYTRACK

Angel Road

Manor Road

Claygate Lane

ROAD

Semaphore House

Hinchley Wood

PORTSMOUTH

Littleworth Common

Esher Station

Station Road

RAILWAYTRACK

N

1 Mile

CHAPTER 1:
THE RAILWAYS

Construction of Hampton Court Junction fly-over: opened 1915.   Photo: Lens of Sutton

Just over 75 years ago a new road bridged a railway line at a place which had no name. It is here, where two arteries of London met: the Kingston by-pass and the 'New' railway line to Guildford (which opened 40 years earlier) that our story begins. Here was the place at which emerged a new settlement, built on farm land astride the new road and a new railway station: a settlement of the age in which it was built; the 1930s. In this chapter, we examine the origins of the railways which run through this new district of 'Hinchley Wood'. I trace the history of all the routes, main line and branch, which have made their way through our area: but because it is central to the story of Hinchley Wood itself, the development of its own station must wait for its proper place in Chapter 4. In this chapter we are concerned with that part of the railway story which preceded Hinchley Wood.

The main line

The railways came through the influence of Southampton with its docks and London. The main line through Esher (the station was called Ditton Marsh then) was opened in 1838 by the London and Southampton (later South Western) Railway after an Act of Parliament in 1834. On 12 May there was an experimental run from Nine Elms, which was then the London terminus, to

Woking which at that time was just a station on a heath, the nearest house being half a mile away; from that beginning Woking has grown into the present substantial town, every brick being laid since the railways came. That first train covered the 23½ miles in 45 minutes, an astonishing time for the period. This was just the beginning of an expansionary era which transformed life and which was totally unthreatened until the invention of the internal combustion engine some 50 years later.

The experimental run was followed quickly by the official opening of the line between Nine Elms and Woking on 21 May 1838. It was an immediate success with reports of over 7,500 passengers a week in its first summer. People in Guildford found that their best route to London was to forsake the stagecoach through Esher on the Portsmouth Road and take it to Woking instead and then on by train. A branch railway to Guildford, from Woking was opened in 1845, making Woking an important junction and contributing further to the stimulus for its growth.

By this time the main line had already been driven through to Southampton (11 May 1840) where a connection with the docks was soon added in 1843. This had a major impact on trade and traffic; a boat connection between Le Havre and Paris was opened and shipping movements were pulled towards Southampton from Falmouth and Weymouth. Portsmouth wanted to get in on this act but inter-company rivalries got in the way. The direct route to Portsmouth via Woking finally opened in 1859 by means of the Guildford branch (1845), its extension to Godalming (1849), then to Havant (1859) from where the route ran on the existing London, Brighton and South Coast Railway tracks from Brighton to Portsmouth. Those readers who have ever wondered about the bingo call for 59: 'five and nine, the Brighton line', may be interested to know that it comes from the LB&SCR exhortation to passengers arriving at Portsmouth Harbour station, to take their, longer, route to London for the cheaper price of 5/9d.

Beyond Woking, line extensions enabled stations to be opened in Farnham (1849), Alton (1852), Weymouth (1857) and Bournemouth (1870). All these routes ran through Esher and went their own ways after Woking. The branch to Thames Ditton and Hampton Court opened as early as 1 February 1849 and was very popular bringing a new influx of visitors to the Palace. Around the turn of the century the track was made quadruple to cope with the traffic. Of course, all these routes also went through Surbiton, creating the ignition for the urban expansion around its station.

Surbiton, not Kingston!

The curious fact is that the line was never intended to be in Surbiton in the first place. When the engineers designed the line, their quest for economy in construction costs by avoiding difficult gradients, kept the optimal route near to natural and other watercourses. The Thames valley would guide a route from London as the Basingstoke Canal guided it beyond Woking. The engineers, when faced with an unavoidable obstacle, and mindful of a maximum gradient imperative, would resort to embankments, cuttings, bridges and tunnels all of which, to a greater or lesser extent, cost money. The route across Ditton Marsh required a high embankment, reflecting the low level of the land there (and not, it should be noted, the need to clear the Hampton Court Way, which was not built until nearly 100 years later). A more economical route to this point, and on to Walton on Thames, would have taken a line not through Surbiton but much closer to Kingston, where the levels were entirely compatible with Walton.

The engineers of the London and Southampton Railway were, however, to meet in Kingston a blind refusal to recognise that the railway must inevitably supersede stagecoaches and barges. The Corporation roundly repudiated plans put forward by the railway company to run its line through the town. Instead, the company was forced to cut a deep and expensive cutting through St Mark's Hill in Surbiton. In fact the first station there, just below the Ewell Road bridge, was actually called 'Kingston' for Surbiton scarcely existed; it was to be 1863 before Kingston had its own station.

It is, of course, very easy to mock the lack of foresight of Kingston's leaders; it's the 19th century equivalent, if you like, of saying today: "the internet is fine but it won't catch on!" but some historians have said the blindness was much exaggerated and covered the railway company's difficulty with key landowners on the Kingston route. Anyway, 'Kingston' station was put in Surbiton which grew and prospered with commuters' favours which remain as strong today. This is in spite of its being mocked on account of its name which, although it sounds like a derivation of Suburbia is, quite innocently, the southern twin with its neighbour, Norbiton, on the other side of the Hogsmill river.

Nine Elms to Waterloo

The railway was extended eastwards from Nine Elms along a brick viaduct to a terminus that we now know as Waterloo, it being opened as Waterloo Bridge station in 1848. From this it can be seen that Waterloo station was not named after the 1815 battle, but after the bridge over the Thames and carried that name until it was shortened to 'Waterloo' in 1886. The bridge itself was renamed on the second anniversary of the battle: it started life as Strand Bridge. The development of Waterloo Bridge station took place in uncoordinated stages and for many years there were in fact two stations, a North and a South station. In 1903 work commenced on the rebuilding of the station into something which by 1922 remains recognisable today.

The 'New' Guildford Line

When Hinchley Wood station came, ultimately, to be built it was to be on the 'New' Guildford Line, now more commonly referred to as 'Guildford via Cobham': it ran south of the main line from Hampton Court Junction through, or near to, a number of very old country settlements on its own route to Guildford, with its connection to Portsmouth. This line, along with the Leatherhead to Effingham junction route, were among the last railways to be built in Surrey. Curiously the new line came to be built by the London and South Western Railway after an opportunistic attempt at expansion by the Metropolitan District Railway, which had a line terminating at Putney Bridge. They planned an extension of their line through Kingston, then striking out to Guildford to open up the county south of the main line and north of the North Downs.

Faced with a new competitor, with an obvious new market for rail travel to be tapped, the L&SWR was obliged to come up with its own scheme and the new line was now born; it opened on 2 February 1885. After Surbiton, the next station was Claygate: there was no thought of a station at Hinchley Wood because, until the Kingston by-pass was being built, no-one had thought of putting houses there. Effingham Junction station was opened some six years after the line opened and was a modest affair; the station at Hinchley Wood would not be built until 1930. All the stations on the line, bar Hinchley Wood and Effingham Junction, had handsome brick built structures of some style: neither of these two later stations follow the pleasing Victorian country station styles of the others on the line.

Fly-overs and fly-unders

Readers will be familiar with the system of a fly-over and a fly-under by which the Hampton Court branch and the new Guildford line are accommodated into the main Woking to Waterloo main line: it was not always so. When our line was built it joined the main line on the level: consequently, the up line had to cross over the down main line to get into position on its way to Surbiton. The Hampton Court branch down line had been doing the same since it was opened in 1849. This meant that for each down train to Hampton Court and each up train from Cobham, all traffic on the main line had to be halted to clear a path for the crossing train to join its proper track. As traffic increased this became untenable and, as with the Kingston by-pass 50 years later, the problem was solved in the same way by the use of fly-overs and fly-unders.

A train approaching Hinchley Wood station on the down line: until 1908, this was a double track, the space for which is still discernible.

To achieve this on the railway, the up Cobham line was deviated to the north (where Hinchley Wood station was to be built later): it was taken through the embankment by a new tunnel under the main line some three hundred yards west of its old route: then turning to run parallel to the main line and, quickly gaining its height, it joined the slow up line from Esher. From an engineering point of view, this was not unduly troublesome and the deviation was opened on 21 October 1908: but the separation of the two tracks created two matters of interest years later. The point of separation marked the most easterly place at which the Kingston by-pass could cross the railway with only one bridge to build and not two: this effectively determined the route which the road would take. The separation also created a railway locked triangle of land of nearly 30 acres which, because of access difficulties, was to be troublesome when Hinchley Wood was being developed in the 1930s, as we will see in Chapter 10.

Because the Hampton Court branch was carried on an embankment, the cheaper solution of a fly-under was not available: instead the long Hampton Court Junction

A train leaving Hinchley Wood station on the up line (re-routed 1908). "Hinchley Wood" (on Telegraph Hill) is in the background, while to the left is "the land between the railway lines".

viaduct that we see today had to be constructed to form a fly-over with its spectacular main girders carrying the down branch line over the main line. It was brought into use during the Great War on 4 July 1915.

Electrification

Familiar as we are with our electric trains, we have to remind ourselves that steam locomotives once worked the entire network. The over-working of the system during the Great War left a considerable back-log of maintenance and modernisation to make good. Post-war reorganisation of the railways found our London and South Western Railway forming the largest constituent of the new Southern Railway, formed in 1923. The main part of Southern's history is concerned with electrification, a process which only reached its final stages in 1967 when the Bournemouth line was electrified and, ultimately, Weymouth in 1988.

When my family moved from Guildford to Hinchley Wood in 1954, a prospective attraction for an eleven year old was being nearer to the main line, where everything going beyond Woking to the West Country was steam hauled: electric train sets never exhale; they have no charm or aggressive thrusting manifestations of power! Steam locos, having all these features were (and remain) endearing: many a moment was spent in Lynwood Road, on my way home from school, watching them steam by in their busy manner.

But, to go back to the story, by 1923 the London and South Western Railway had already electrified several lines with the third rail DC system. These included the line to Hampton Court and on our line, as far as Claygate, which were both electrified in 1916. There was a surprisingly large amount of electrification in the Southern Railway area when it was formed, but much of it was by incompatible systems and during the 1920s the London and South Western third rail system was adopted as the standard.

The big moment locally came on 12 July 1925 when the line, among others, was electrified from Claygate to

3

Guildford, along with the Leatherhead to Effingham junction line. Electrification work by the Southern Railway continued into the 1930s until 1939 when war brought it to a halt. But on 12 July 1925 the electrification of our line (remembering that Hinchley Wood station did not exist) brought a huge expansion in traffic and, ultimately, passengers as the general housing boom of the 1930s gathered pace.

The increase in train numbers from Guildford via Cobham, which started their new timetable on 12 July 1925, is astonishing; 39 steam trains a day replaced by an incredible 97 electric trains. Initially, the electric service was of three trains an hour each way but nowadays there are only two an hour outside the rush hour. Today there are 86 trains a day through Hinchley Wood. In their 1925 advertisement in the Surrey Comet, the Southern Railway trumpeted:

"After two and a half years of reconstruction and reorganisation, two more sections of the Southern Railway's suburban system are ready for the new electric trains.

To Guildford and Dorking, in rural Surrey, on the one hand, and to Orpington, in the countryside of Kent, the clean green trains will start to run on July 12, replacing to a large extent the older steam trains now maintaining the service.

It has been no small task to carry the "third rail" over 182 miles of track, while the steam trains were still running; to erect 27 sub-stations along the routes to regulate the current; to widen, rebuild and alter many of the stations and platforms on the system, while the public were using these stations and platforms; to install a new and ingenious "speedlight" signalling system, costing many thousands of pounds; and to instruct and test the steam-drivers and guards who will operate the new electric services. But the spade-work has been done, the tests made, and the timetables, after months of careful preparation, completed. The two sections of track now ready have cost £2,500,000 [An astonishing amount]; *and they have given employment, directly and indirectly, to thousands of workers all over Britain.* [A key theme of the period]

A change of the magnitude which will take place on July 12 can hardly be made with the certain knowledge that no adjustments will be needed, and that no delays, however small, will occur. Both staff and passengers will be new to the services, and each can help the other to a great degree.

We are sure the public will bear these things in mind, and so help us to establish the largest suburban electric railway in the world." [Which they certainly did.]

The introduction of electric trains, with their more frequent service with faster, cleaner journeys, was to play an important role in our story.

**How London was connected by rail with the major towns and cities:
All routes through Hampton Court Junction.**

Destination	Date of public opening	Date of electrification
Woking to Nine Elms*	21 May 1838	3 January 1937
Southampton	11 May 1840	3 April 1967
Guildford	5 May 1845	3 January 1937
Portsmouth	14 June 1847	4 July 1937
Hampton Court	1 February 1849	18 June 1916
Farnham	8 October 1849	3 January 1937
Alton	28 July 1852	4 July 1937
Weymouth	20 January 1857	May 1988
Exeter	18 July 1860	-
Bournemouth	14 March 1870	3 April 1967
Guildford New Line (via Cobham)	2 February 1885	12 July 1925

* Nine Elms was the original terminus; the extension to Waterloo opened on 11 July 1848

Source: History of the Southern Railway: C F Dendy Marshal, 1963
A century and a half of The Southern Railway: David St John Thomas & Patrick Whitehouse, 1988

CHAPTER 2:
THE KINGSTON BY-PASS

When the Kingston by-pass opened in 1927, Hinchley Wood station had not been built. This view is looking north towards "the land between the railway lines".

Photo: Surrey County Council

The Kingston by-pass, as well as the railway station, was to be of seminal importance to the development of the settlement of Hinchley Wood. As such, it is appropriate to consider in this chapter its own history as a means of understanding a part of the backdrop to Hinchley Wood's explosive development in the 1930s, once all the components of a sustainable development: roads; railway station; bus routes; shops; and an embryo church, were in place.

Traffic congestion in Kingston

The Kingston by-pass was opened on 28 October 1927: taking the trunk road number, A3, it ran for eight and a half miles from Robin Hood Gate to the Portsmouth Road at the Marquis of Granby where we now know the junction as 'the Scilly Isles'. Parts of the by-pass were opened in sections on the previous Good Friday but the official and actual opening had to wait for the three bridges over the railways to be completed. When Surrey County Council decided to go ahead and build the by-pass in 1923, we can easily surmise that they, and other good judges too, thought that they were creating an imaginative solution to two big problems of the day. These were traffic congestion in Kingston and unem-

ployment in the aftermath of the Great War. While Kingston may have benefited from a reduction in through traffic (for the time being), its by-pass, far from solving the problem of free movement of arterial traffic, actually created problems which were to tax traffic engineers and public bodies for the rest of the 20th century and beyond.

But the problems for the public authorities, intractable though they were to become, were not just in the future; even in the building of it, the Kingston by-pass took its toll of anguish. As the Surrey Comet reported at the time, it was probably true to say that of all the important works undertaken by Surrey County Council, none had given more trouble and anxiety than this new road. It was, therefore, with some relief on the part of the Council that the road was finally opened some four years after the decision to build it was made. But the opening of this new and at the time, fascinating, road by the Prime Minister, Stanley Baldwin, marked not the end of the anxiety but just a point in a long story in which each attempted increment in design and capacity standard was overtaken by underestimation of traffic growth which was to continue, inexorably except for the war years, until the present day.

The story begins in 1912, when a scheme was put forward by Surrey County Council to the Road Board (the

Traffic congestion in Kingston gave rise in 1912 to the planning of a by-pass.   Photo: Surrey Comet

national road planning body of the time) for a by-pass scheme. That Board urged consideration of the proposal as an arterial road from London to the south-west and Surrey County Council sanctioned expenditure on surveys and plans. Even before the Great War, traffic congestion in Kingston had become troublesome: this was not just about motor traffic volume; the roads, then, were being shared between horses (which could be frightened), pedal cycles and motor vehicles all with their different normal speeds and habits. They did not mix very well! The Great War intervened and it caused a postponement of civil projects. During the war the decision was made to recommend that the route should be included in any Town Planning Schemes that might emerge; when the war was over the planners picked up the previous design concept and found it had been given new urgency by the fact that traffic levels were growing fast. On the Portsmouth Road the increase, compared with the 1913 levels, was 70% by 1922 and 163% by 1925.

The task faced by the designers of the Kingston by-pass had no precedent to inform a design. The experience of the railway engineers wasn't helpful because the early 20th century road engineers had to work in a consensual way: always compromising with an existing network; having some respect for land ownership and current use and evolving the system into the modern world. Although the new road was driven through virgin land, the Kingston by-pass was not designed (as the Road Board had urged) as part of an arterial route to Portsmouth: it was designed as a by-pass of Kingston with no thought being given to the impact on Esher!

Some problems with the route

The problem addressed by the road engineers before the Great War; a problem which was not redefined when the old plans were taken back off the shelf after the war, was essentially conceived as a problem of how to by-pass Kingston. The engineers had to find a way of not only avoiding the streets of Kingston but had also to grapple with the bottleneck on the Portsmouth Road in Hinchley Wood (it was Thames Ditton then) caused by what we

call "the long arch"; that tunnel under the London to Southampton Railway, still there today mostly as built in 1838; a tunnel 170ft. long with a span of 23ft.8ins. and headroom ranging from 15ft.2ins at best to only 10ft. This tunnel, built in the stagecoach era, was a difficult problem. The land at that point is very low and liable to flooding so the road could not be lowered: the railway could scarcely be elevated because, for the gradient to be acceptable, the length of track to be raised would be so long as to be hopelessly uneconomic. The solution which was adopted was to by-pass both the long arch and Kingston with one road.

The engineers, having no brief to by-pass Esher, had to find a route which avoided Telegraph Hill, because, in engineering terms, its height was unacceptably great, while achieving a connection with the Portsmouth Road west of the long arch and which avoided violating Littleworth Common any more than was reasonable. To these restraints must be added a fourth; the railway tracks divide in Hinchley Wood in order to make a route to achieve a fly-under of the main line. This would mean that any by-pass crossing east of the railway track division would need two bridges, while a crossing of the railway where it was still dual tracked would need only one. Economics being what it is, the point at which the new road was to cross the new line to Guildford was effectively fixed by the reconciliation of all the restraints discussed above. This explains why the road swings sharply to the south, just after Claygate Lane, to skirt the base of Telegraph Hill and then swings north again in order in order to get across the railway in time to cut in to the Portsmouth Road to the east of Littleworth Common.

A 100 foot land corridor

In 1920, in conference with the Ministry of Transport and Surrey County Council, the by-pass route was settled with the Councils of Esher and the Dittons, Surbiton, Malden and Coombe and Merton and Morden, through whose areas the new road was to be driven. It is necessary to remind ourselves that all the land required for the eight and a half-mile route was undeveloped farmland. A 100 foot wide land corridor, exclusive of that occupied by the slopes of embankments and cuttings, had to be acquired using statutory powers granted by Parliament. From notices published in the Surrey Comet, we can see that the land required in Esher Council area formed part of the Couchmore Farm estate; a name which, as we shall see, was to be prominent when Hinchley Wood came to be developed nearly 10 years later. If a corridor of this width had not been acquired when it was, and building lines set accordingly, the post Second World War widening schemes would scarcely have been possible. A 100 foot corridor might have sounded generous for a road which was built as a 30 foot wide single track, but Surrey County Council at least got hold of the land which was to be needed 40 years later; it might easily not have been so!

Very early in the 1920s someone put his hand up, before it was too late, and said that the 50 feet of land which, until then was the design width being allowed to accommodate the road, was insufficient. A conference of local authorities agreed to widen this to 100 feet. By doubling the land corridor, the road designers, naïve though they proved to be in many other respects, at least avoided creating intractable problems for the future. Perversely, the bridges over the railways were built to a width of only 60 feet! Future generations would have to fund their widening, at the cost of millions of pounds.

Funding

Post Great War pressure to accommodate town planning and building programmes, not just in our area but radially from London, led to the government sponsoring from the early 1920s, until the Second World War halted it again, a massive road building programme by County Councils. It was not just traffic levels which were the imperative; providing work for the unemployed was an urgent concern of central government and the Kingston by-pass was hastened by the government for this purpose. Surrey County Council was to be the procuring authority but because these large schemes were quite unfundable by local government alone, a public funding arrangement was hammered out whereby, broadly, 50% was funded by central government, 25% by the London County Council and 25% by Surrey. As a quid pro quo for LCC financial support, and reflecting the imperative of the time, all the unskilled and a considerable number of skilled workers were recruited from London and transported daily to work.

The cost of the road works was estimated at £718,000 and the bridges at £77,000. From the earliest moments it is clear that the road was under-engineered due almost certainly to the hard reconciliation which had to be made between the government's need for speed in delivering their programme, and the long-run extra cost of remedying design and specification shortcomings at the beginning.

Specification

At this distance, the original design specification for the Kingston by-pass appears astonishingly naïve. Stretching as I am, in making this criticism, to avoid judgment with hindsight and by the standards of a different age, there was to be ample and quick demonstration of its validity. The road was conceived and built as a 30 foot wide single carriageway; dual carriageways were unknown at the time but, as we have seen, at least the land was acquired for the inevitable widening. Dual carriageways might have been unknown but fly-overs and fly-unders had been in use in railway engineering for decades. Their use had become endemic on busy routes because safety and high volume use of a junction demanded the separation of different traffic streams trying to use the same road. At any time from the 1950s the Kingston by-pass would have been built to motorway design standards. But this was the 1920s; money was scarce; no-one made (or more likely, I think, was allowed to make) any extrapolations of

traffic growth to show how inadequate were the junction designs. As the road was driven from Robin Hood Gate to the Marquis of Granby, it crossed no fewer than nine existing roads radiating out from Kingston, some of them busy trunk roads; no concession was made to traffic flow at any of them. Each junction was a plain crossroad with no provision of islands, roundabouts, traffic lights or any traffic management facility (save for policemen on point duty). This was on a road which, because of its comparative paucity of junctions, allowed vehicles to achieve speeds which were increasing at a much faster pace than was the braking power to stop them. As we shall see, early chaos, injury and loss of life resulted.

An 8 foot wide paved footway was constructed throughout the whole length of the road. In today's world this seems bizarre, but was it in 1927? For the greater part of its length the road was fenced with concrete post and wire fencing. In one important concession to modern road design, the gradients were easy, not exceeding 1 in 30 at any point. To achieve this, just like the railways, cuttings and embankments had to be built. The largest cutting is on the approach to Hinchley Wood, immediately to the west of Woodstock Lane, where 84,000 cubic yards of clay were removed and used to form the embankments. The total quantity of excavation amounted to about 220,000 cubic yards. In the construction of the carriageway, about 32,000 tons of gravel, 17,000 tons of sand, 8,500 tons of cement and 750 tons of steel were used.

For the technically minded, the original carriageway was built of reinforced concrete, laid 8 inches thick in alternate bays with joints at 15 foot intervals and at an angle of 60° to the centre line of the road. The foundations were clinker. This specification proved to be inadequate: little was known by road engineers of the loading created by fast traffic and the 1930s saw the need for more or less continuous repair!

Contractual difficulties

Three railway bridges were needed to take the new road over the railway: one over the main line near Raynes Park: one over the Epsom branch on the road to Merton, which was built as a spur of the by-pass as part of the original works and one, of course, at Hinchley Wood. The bridge contractors were Christiani & Nielson, who built the bridge at Hinchley Wood, and Holloway Bros (London) Ltd, who built the other two; although these three contracts were performed satisfactorily and more or less on budget they became out of phase with the civil works for the road which themselves had been delayed through a combination of the fault of the road contractor and difficulties endured by the inexperienced Council officers.

In road contracting terms, nothing had been done like this before. In making criticism we must remember that no-one in the public service knew from experience how to go about it in contracting terms. Considerable trouble was experienced, as it often is, at the six interfaces between the road and the bridge works. Many of these skills had existed with the railways but the great railway

Work in progress on Kingston by-pass: note the temporary light railway.
Photo: Surrey Comet

building programme had finished, substantially, about 50 years earlier and in any event they existed within the files and corporate know-how of the private railway companies, not public service road engineers.

The road contract gave difficulty from the start. Early tenders came in above the budget level. The Council reacted by chipping away at the specification. This is always dangerous. Although money was very tight in the period when this contract was let, better value would have been achieved if the budget had been raised and the specification held. In the event, after delay caused by the penny pinching, the road contract was let to Stewart & McDonnell and the work started, slowly, and it seems, in the adversarial manner which was to characterise the industry well into my own lifetime.

Work in progress on Kingston by-pass showing the temporary railway sidings.
Photo: Surrey Comet

We have already seen how much earth shifting was to be done to dig cuttings and make embankments. When the contractor became properly mobilised, steam shovels arrived and, reflecting the distances involved, the weight of material and the low carrying capacity of motor trucks in those days, a temporary railway was laid down to carry the muck.

But progress was slow. The weather was blamed; frustration increased. The delays became serious; the contractor lodged claims; relations became acrimonious. As already noted, the interfaces with the bridge contracts

became hot spots for difficulty. With each blaming the other, the Council was ultimately obliged to finish the approach roads off itself by direct action, a most unusual occurrence. The contractor was losing money, the client suffering from delay. Litigation was inevitable when the two sides were too far apart for a deal to be struck. The Council was warned to be prepared for a long and expensive legal battle. In fact, the case was settled in 1928, out of court, and the contractor was paid an additional sum of £50,000, a result which probably left everyone unhappy.

Inspection of the work in progress on the Kingston by-pass, on horseback.
Photo: Surrey Comet

The opening ceremony

The opening ceremony took place at the junction where the Merton spur joins the by-pass: it was clearly a big affair and was reported the next day in the national press and at length by the Surrey Comet according to whom it was fitting that the completion of "such an important undertaking" should be marked by a little "pomp and circumstance". They reported the opening remarks of the Surrey County Council chairman, who said that the enormous growth of motor traffic of all kinds constituted a big problem. He observed that it was no longer a question of road maintenance; it had become a question of widening, and of improving existing roads and bridges and constructing new ones to meet the demands that were being made. It was, he said a national problem, and in no county was that problem more pressing than in Surrey, with its great and increasing volume of traffic from London to the coast. "We were all motorists now, in one form or another", he claimed: "whether it was the lordly carriage or the plebeian omnibus, … depending in a great measure for all kinds of commodities to be brought to the doors by motor van." Clearly alive to the coming age of the motor car he touched on the question of bridges across the Thames having clearly in mind the decision soon to be made to build a new bridge at Hampton Court and to connect it to the Portsmouth Road.

The chairman of the Highways and Bridges Committee had his turn: he knew a thing or two about the problems and he was probably more anxious about the future than anyone else on the day. Clutching at a diversionary straw, he felt the need to reassure motorists that they would feel quite safe in passing over the new bridges because, he said: "they had recently sustained without a murmur a test of 70 tons"! In one small respect, he announced defensively, the road could not be considered complete – he referred to the unsatisfactory bottleneck at the London County Council boundary at the Hogsmill river bridge. Within hours he was proved right with the most fearful traffic jams!

The Prime Minister's speech

And so it fell to the Prime Minister to cut the ribbon, declare the road open and address the assembly. He achieved much laughter from the crowd when, after surveying in tranquil terms the scene before them, and congratulating all involved, he observed that: "There was only one thing he thought wanting to complete the picture and that would be a small cottage hospital on that spot". Was he joking? I am not sure he was! The carnage wrought by speeding motorists was to become almost a weekly affair as reported by the Surrey Comet. Road safety had not yet been made second nature!

Prime Minister, Stanley Baldwin at the opening ceremony, Kingston by-pass: 28 October 1927? Photo: Surrey Comet

> # KINGSTON BY-PASS OPEN.
>
> ---
>
> ### The Prime Minister on the Beautifying of London's Great Approach Roads.
>
> ---
>
> ## "ENGLAND AS A SANCTUARY AND A SHRINE"
>
> ---
>
> ### Mr. Baldwin's Plea for Good Roadside Manners and No Litter.

Surrey Comet: 27 October 1927

His remarks took a wider view by declaring that the project, which was started seven years, previously, of building the Greater London arterial roads, was rapidly approaching completion. Four-fifths of that work was now completed. He was proud, he said, of the results that had been achieved. "They were in process of seeing all round London these great roads one hundred feet wide, free from bottle-necks and from obstruction," he trumpeted. In this, of course, he was to be proved wrong: "bottlenecks and obstructions" were to become endemic, first because of design faults and then, as these were remedied, the inexorable rise in traffic caught up with each successive improvement.

The Surrey Comet reported the Prime Minister's speech in its entirety. Its only claim to foresight was the reference to the need for a cottage hospital close by. The Prime Minister expressed the hope that in time trees and grass might be seen along the new roads and he said: "Let us see if we cannot have upon these roads houses and gardens right up to the roads themselves". He got his wish; in the four years after it opened, the Kingston by-pass had 1300 houses and 57 shops along its route! It took 30 years to realise that by-passes are for vehicles and the co-existence of houses and settlements with them in contiguous format was an irredeemable blunder.

Chaos

When the Surrey Comet reported the scene on the first real day of opening of the by-pass, a Sunday when seemingly every car owner flocked to observe the purpose built fast road, its headlines caught the scene.

> # BY-PASS CONGESTION.
>
> ---
>
> ## Long Queues of Vehicles at Kingston Vale.
>
> ---
>
> ## BEVERLEY BRIDGE BOTTLE-NECK.

Surrey Comet: 27 October 1927

The report talked of the by-pass being "a snare and a delusion". It took about twice as long to reach the Portsmouth Road from Kingston Vale as it did when the journey is made through Kingston there being a gigantic jam at the Robin Hood bottle neck, lasting for hours.

A major design problem was that four streams of traffic were now meeting together at one junction: the by-pass, the entrance to Richmond Park, Kingston Hill and the road from London. The result, it said, was awe-inspiring. Obviously some quick work would be necessary on redesigning the junction. Sparing no detail, the report continued:

"As you gently coasted down the hill from Wimbledon Common you saw a line of cars in front of you as far as sight went. As you got near Kingston Vale cemetery the car

in front of you stopped, and you followed suit. Here you remained for the next quarter of an hour admiring the scenery, drinking in the beautiful oil-filled atmosphere, wondering why about twenty of the two hundred or more cars ahead of you did not stop their engines. Just as you were thinking of having a nice sleep, or a first bite of your luncheon, there was a cackle of exhausts, and, with sundry jerks, the flotilla of 250 or more cars moved a whole ten yards, only to stop again with much screeching of brakes. The journey would have made an excellent slow motion film – only there was no motion! Occasional passers by – cyclists grinning happily – would inform you that it was just the same in the other direction and that there was a line of vehicles three deep to the top of Kingston Hill. 'Buses and motor coaches were packed into the crowd, and some delicious samples of breezy humour of the drivers of the 'buses came wandering on the breeze. Several remarks about time-tables deserve publication, only the law would not allow them in cold print!"

The average speed during the late afternoon and evening at the London end of the by-pass was reported as "880 yards an hour"!

Cars try out the new single carriageway Kingston by-pass.
Photo: Surrey Comet

The chaos lasted into the night: "The police who were on duty at the various junctions had a most unenviable time, and stated later that the control of the traffic at lighting-up time was almost a nightmare, so thick was it and because so many motorists persisted in keeping their headlights on all the time." But not all the Surrey Comet's remarks were critical: "At all events, even if the entrance at Robin Hood is badly designed, there are many other things in favour of the road. With heavy rain skidding seems to be impossible, even in places where leaves have fallen thickly and where an attempt was made to skid a car on purpose, while the six-inch high kerbs are a valuable guide for night or fog driving."

The telephone lines must have been frantic on that Sunday because a conference was held on the following day, on site at the Robin Hood junction, between the County Surveyor and officials of the Ministry of Transport and the Police. What they discovered was that the main trouble during the week-end was caused by traffic which desired to turn right across the lines of traffic either

to or from the by-pass and Richmond Park. (It isn't easy, today, to understand how anyone could find this surprising.) The by-pass junction and the Robin Hood Gate are not exactly opposite each other, explained the Surrey Comet, so that four-road cross-over working was not possible, and a sergeant and two policemen found it impossible to clear the traffic, mainly because cars having come out of the park gates blocked much of the road in their endeavour to get across the traffic. As a result, Mr. W P Robinson, the County Surveyor, said that the entrance would be widened and the work would commence in a few days and that, when the work was completed, there would be a wide sweep into the by-pass and because this was going to take about three months in construction, "motorists must be patient, as it is a £6,000 job and cannot be completed in a day".

On the following Sunday, the Surrey Comet was able to report that: "The congestion of traffic which caused so much annoyance to motorists at Kingston Vale during the week-end following the opening of the Kingston by-pass was not repeated to such an extent last week-end. Two policemen were on point duty at the entrance to the road, with a sergeant standing by, and they were quite equal to dealing with the large volume of traffic that was passing in the four directions. In the evening when the traffic was mostly going in the direction of Putney the pressure became increasingly great, and unavoidable delay occasionally arose, but that is inevitable when almost all the motorists want to take the same road home."

It was inevitable and, together with death and injury, it characterised the road for decades!

The Esher by-pass

As the new Kingston by-pass was being built, Esher Council was grappling with the impact of its opening on traffic in Esher. It is well understood now, but in the 1920s it had not been realised, that new roads create traffic: new journeys are made which previously were either made less frequently or just not contemplated. That a new arterial road was going to feed new traffic into Esher, the new bottleneck, was inevitable. In due course, the new (and easier) river crossing at Hampton Court increased these traffic levels yet further.

At its meeting in November 1927, just days after the Kingston by-pass opening, Esher Council grappled with the issue. The question for consideration was not which route should be taken for an Esher by-pass, but whether, instead, the Portsmouth Road should be widened. The Council chose the latter and the Surveyor was instructed to prepare a scheme for the widening and improvement of the Portsmouth Road.

Col. W. Butler was one member who championed the cause of an Esher by-pass. He submitted (and this was 1927, remember) that before going forward with a costly scheme for widening, they should ascertain whether the Ministry of Transport would be willing to make an alternative to the present road. He believed there was unanimous agreement that the new by-pass road was being

The Marquis of Granby, just before the new Kingston by-pass opened.

Photo: Surrey Comet

All in one shot: a pony and trap and a motor car on the Kingston by-pass, and bi-plane from Ditton Hill, c1934.   Photo: Surrey Comet

brought in to the main Portsmouth Road at a point where no-one, if the scheme could be begun again, would have it brought in. This was a big statement; it is as true today as it was when Col. Butler made it. But at that time there was formidable opposition from business people to the suggestion of by-passing Esher, and also from people in that residential part through which a suggested by-pass road would go. This would be echoed (and amplified by concern about the Commons) in the 1930s and then again in the 1960s and 1970s.

CHAPTER 3:
BACKGROUND TO THE 1930s HOUSING BOOM

On 12 July 1925 Southern Railway expanded their electric train network, including the route to Guildford via Cobham.

Source: Surrey Comet

By way of background, we have seen how the Kingston by-pass and the railway came into the reckoning of the origins of Hinchley Wood, but we must cast the net wider. What happened in Hinchley Wood in the 1930s was not in isolation of what was going on elsewhere in and around London's suburbs: there was a huge housing boom going on and it is necessary to give a brief explanation of this to understand better the phenomenon of Hinchley Wood which, although of a generally much higher standard than its 1930s peers, was just a part of a widespread expansion.

The 1930s, a decade of contradiction and paradox

The 1930s was an extraordinary decade of contradiction and paradox. There had never been anything like it before and ordinary people were perplexed by it. For example, there was the paradox of a boom in housing and consumer goods coinciding with desperate levels of unemployment in the north of England leading to the famous hunger marches. Policy contradictions at home polarised on whether government should spend its way out of the economic depression and run a budget deficit, or economise and keep the budget balanced. Abroad, there was trouble for Britain caused by conflict between Arabs and Jews in Palestine; India agitated for independence; Egypt too but the Suez Canal couldn't be given up and the Irish question, as ever, rumbled on. Communism was the great bogey: fascism was emerging to oppose it; Italy was in the grip of a dictatorship; Spain had a civil war, followed by a dictatorship. The King died and his son abdicated. The nazi tyrant, having been barely noticed when he first came to power in January 1933, induced the greatest contradiction: when it became clear, about mid way through the decade that there was something darkly ominous about where his posturing might lead, it was several years, and nearly too late, before the appeasers were routed by the re-armers.

All this, and more, took place in a decade in which the development of Hinchley Wood went ahead at a dizzy pace and which was never deranged until war became inevitable in 1939. It seems extraordinary, but it happened all over suburban London. The war stopped the continuous development of the suburbs of London in its tracks, but Hinchley Wood was almost finished, with the notable exception of its church and its primary school. What needs some explanation is how the new settlement of Hinchley Wood could achieve such rapid success in this perplexing decade.

In 1929 Britain was at a high tide of prosperity even though over one million were unemployed, but a bubble burst. In October 1929 the great economic Depression broke over the world: British exporters saw their markets disappear. By the end of 1930 unemployment had reached two and a half million. Such was the economic background when the building of the new settlement started.

September 1931 marked the watershed of English history between the wars. In a new crisis which rocked the government with confounding speed, Britain was forced to break the link between the value of sterling and gold. In a dramatic announcement, the government said that the move had been forced to prevent further withdrawals of gold and to stop speculation against the pound. There had never been anything quite like this. The anti-climax after the break with gold took everyone by surprise, as indeed had the crisis in the first place. Ramsey MacDonald eased from being Prime Minister of a minority Labour government to being Prime Minister of a National government. This was confirmed by the general election which was held in the month following the crisis, October 1931. The National government proposed a programme of severe austerity and sacrifice: the unemployed could get no succour from such parsimony. The pound was devalued by about a quarter but people carried on spending the "pounds in your pocket" and, more due to cyclical influences than government action, the economy began its upturn in 1933.

The start of Hinchley Wood coincided with grim economic news, but war seemed utterly remote. In the course of the decade, the economy slowly recovered, but from mid way through the decade, gradually, the people came to realise that war was inevitable.

Economic imbalances

One of the 1930s paradoxes was the unbalanced way in which the Depression impacted on different parts of the country. This was supported by anecdotal evidence of my own family history. During my childhood there was frequent family reference to the 1930s: my grandfather was in and out of work, mostly out, in a Lancashire cotton town whereas my father, an insurance official and now in the south east, was never out of work; always had a motor car and took an annual holiday. Although I didn't realise it at the time, the two different circumstances of my family history of the 1930s was the whole country's in microcosm: despair and sufficiency side by side!

The price of imports tumbled during the first year of the Depression while the price of exports stayed much the same. The result was that we were able to import as much as before but at much reduced cost. Wages remained more or less stable but because prices went down, the same wages could buy more goods. Those people who were in work discovered that the economic imbalances meant they had never been better off.

The staple industries of the north contracted; these were remote from London whose light industries actually started to prosper. Alongside this, there had already been a shift in the pattern of new jobs towards clerical and administration work: in local government, the civil service, insurance and the like; just the sort of activity that London was good at supporting. Its workers spent their money on domestic comforts; when hire purchase was invented, they spent other people's money as well as their own on electric irons, vacuum cleaners and, invariably, radio sets.

Broadly, it was the new middle class that was in work; aspiring, creatures of the 20th century, attracted by home ownership, moving away from the centres of towns and attracted to the suburbs. Through a fluke in international markets, this group found they had stable wages, falling prices and cheap money all at a time when the suburbs beckoned. This is the extraordinary paradox of the 1930s: mass unemployment on the one hand, while large parts of the population were enjoying a richer life than they had ever known. It didn't make sense; it couldn't last: it didn't! The Nazis brought the decade to its end and with it unemployment and then, hardship for everyone. Perversely, the war saw to it that the paradoxical imbalance of massive and endemic unemployment in the industrial towns of the north, alongside the great housing boom in the south, righted itself. The pool of unemployed labour became a resource which was soon put back to work; the housing boom came to a full stop.

Southern Electric

When speaking of the extraordinary pre-war growth of London's suburbs, the role of Southern Electric, the brand name of Southern Railway for their electric services, cannot be over-stated. We have already seen in Chapter 1 how in 1925 the Southern Railway vastly expanded its coverage over its routes into London. Similar things were happening on the Underground. Although we are not concerned with these for our story, it is important to appreciate that the improvement in transport systems was going on all over London's suburbs, both existing and those yet to be built.

The increase in frequency of service and the speed which electrification allowed was astonishing. The passengers loved the cleaner travelling too. Southern Railway knew all this and they exploited their new service for all it was worth, actively promoting the pleasures for London workers of moving further out "into the country": but for most it was to be further out into the new suburbs. What they were doing, and they were very successful at it, was encouraging a trend which had already started. People did not want to live in the centre of towns any more. When they were given the chance to move out, they jumped at it.

Southern Railway promoted commuting to work in London from the country.
Source: Southern Railway

As a broad measure of this 1930s trend, the population of London fell by over 30% in the years 1931 to 1939;* Wimbledon's population fell by 19%; Richmond's by 13% and Kingston's by 5%. In the same eight years, the population of Esher rose by 37%.

Southern Electric published a handbook called *Country Homes at London's Door*, giving details of over 100 settlements in Surrey, Kent and Middlesex, which had a convenient station. They were selling the idea of commuting to work by rail. The recent expansion had, they trumpeted: "opened up virgin country for the busy city worker" by bringing within easy daily reach of London "many places in and surrounded by the real, beautiful country, to be found everywhere south of the Metropolis". They said: "London's daily workers can spend their leisure and sleep in pure air and in a beautiful country which before was more or less inaccessible because of the time taken, the infrequency of trains and the greater comparative cost". The handbook gave details of each of the places promoted with helpful information on housing conditions and costs and particulars as to the surrounding country; population; subsoil; altitude; provision for sports and recreation; utilities; the character of shops and schools; as well, of course, as rail fares.

After electrification, cheap tickets to London were promoted.

Source: Surrey Comet

Places familiar to us which were given their own vignette were Surbiton, Thames Ditton, Claygate, Oxshott and all the settlements on the new Guildford line. There was no mention of Hinchley Wood: this was

before Hinchley Wood station existed; had it been later they would have been proclaiming the merits of the new settlement in the country. In fact, the entry for Thames Ditton says: "… pleasant houses are being built both in Manor Road and Sugden Road and these are on the edge of pure country". The entry for Claygate tells us that the trains, after passing Surbiton "cross the level pasture land that lies between the commons and greens of Ditton and Telegraph Hill …". This "pure country" is where Hinchley Wood was to be placed, very soon!

Southern Electric caught the mood of the times and prospered from the increased traffic. In the light of the conditions and impulses of the 1930s described above, with affordability reaching out to the middle classes, the suburban expansion was assured. When Hinchley Wood station came to be built, high quality housing quickly followed it; its success was assured in spite of the economic circumstances in the beginning.

The planning scenario

Hinchley Wood, in a move by Esher Council, was "town planned"; this was in an era before the concept of town and country planning was endemic, for it had very little statutory backing, and until the 1947 Act, operated alongside the presumption that if a land owner was prevented from doing what he wished by a local authority, he had a right to compensation. Most readers will be broadly familiar with the town and country planning regime that applies today. The present position, put simply, is that landowners have a right to use their land only for its existing use, or in accordance with the local development plan: this will have been adopted, probably with several iterations, and after extensive public consultation over many years and careful professional input by the local planning authority. There is also a major role for central government.

Nothing recognisably like this existed in the 1930s where there was no role for central government: thoughts at the regional level were no-one's responsibility: cooperation between neighbouring local authorities was rare and in any event, they were much smaller and weaker bodies than we know today: and unless an authority took the initiative, which Esher did, builders could exercise a right to build paying heed to matters of public health but not to the long term impact of what they were doing. In these circumstances, much of what happened in the 1930s has been roundly criticised.*

Such planning legislation that did exist in the 1930s owed its origin to the need for control over public health rather than to planning. The basic presumption had been that landowners could profit from the exploitation of their land as they chose. Local authorities were, however, able to zone land and Esher Council zoned what was to become Hinchley Wood as "housing". Other choices that were available were, say, light industry or "private open space". In practice, by zoning Hinchley Wood for housing with its associated shopping area, Esher Council

---

* The normal census would have been in 1941. The week that war was declared the government's emergency plans for a quick population count were approved by Parliament

---

* Semi-detached London, Alan A Jackson, 1973

could effectively control development: it made the key decision to set the density of development (houses per acre) at a level which gave a plot size which was more generous than, generally, elsewhere; and determined the road widths and layouts. In other districts, where the local authorities were less proactive, building went on more or less unhindered according to what developers thought the market wanted.

How was it all financed?

Like any other boom the housing boom of the 1930s couldn't have happened without an engine of finance. Housing became somewhat artificially, and perhaps for the first time in history, very affordable for the middle class. Money was made deliberately cheap and world conditions in the great Depression made general prices fall in real terms. The building society movement awakened to the conditions of the time, i.e. a plentiful supply of affordable housing to meet the demand from those people in the stable white collar employment which was available, and even growing, in London's economy.

Many of the first time buyers in the 1930s were not newly formed family units but people who had hitherto rented their homes, which was quite normal. No data is available to give us a profile of the first owners of Hinchley Wood homes. From my own knowledge I know that many first owners in the 1930s were newly-weds but many, I suggest, had previously lived elsewhere in rented homes. The building societies even went as far as placing adverts to extol the virtues of buying a property on a mortgage; these adverts often sat on the same page as the adverts of the builders selling their product. The Westbourne Park Building Society placed many adverts in the Surrey Comet in 1933, a year of huge building activity in Hinchley Wood, explaining that: "The Society advances a large portion of the purchase price of the property which you select. This advance is then returned by low monthly repayments which are inclusive of principal and interest. These payments are little in excess of the amount otherwise required for rent, but whilst rent paid makes no provision for the future, every repayment made to a Building Society brings nearer the day when the deeds of the property are freed and no more payments incurred."

This may be commonplace now but in the 1930s it was novel. As the advert went on the say: " … Conditions for house purchase have not been so favourable for many years". This was an under-statement. In explanation the advert said: "This is mainly due to two distinct causes: (1) Houses are cheaper because the cost of materials has reached a lower level and, (2) the Building Societies recently [in 1932] reduced mortgage rates which are now lower than at any period since the war."

There was a rush to invest money in the building societies because their security and interest rates were favourably regarded in the prevailing conditions of cheap money and perplexing international markets. This led to an embarrassingly high level of deposits. The building societies had to do something with the money flowing in; although cautious at first, they decided to finance the boom. Their market was those borrowers who had stable jobs; just the sort of people who wanted to move to Hinchley Wood! They moved in throughout the decade.

Nationally, the societies lent £32m in 1923 but by 1932 this grew to £103m while in 1936, the peak year of the period, they lent £140m. According to Jackson*, the predecessor of Abbey National Building Society grew its number of borrowers from 9,300 in 1926 to 82,000 by 1936. This source of finance provided the engine for the 1930s housing boom in which huge swathes of land around London were developed for housing. The development of Hinchley Wood was just part of that process.

---

* Semi-detached London, Alan A Jackson, 1973

CHAPTER 4:
A NEW SETTLEMENT IS PLANNED

Hinchley Wood station, c1931.

Photo: Source unknown, courtesy of Anita Witten, Peter Hanna

In this chapter I develop the argument that while the Kingston by-pass was the key ingredient in its conception, it was its railway station which gave Hinchley Wood its coherence, and which created a market which produced the rapid development of the new settlement. But we must consider how these two factors worked together, and the roles played by various parties in bringing the threads together, so that building could start, and proceed very quickly, from 1930.

The impact of the Kingston by-pass

The Kingston by-pass opened up huge tracts of land for development. Royston Pike (a key figure in our story and one of the men to whose memory this book is dedicated) claimed that even before the first sod was cut, the speculative possibilities which might be thrown up by the new road were being considered. There was intense activity in the 1920s at the County Council offices in Kingston, the District Councils along its route, including Esher of course, as well as the offices of Southern Railway in Waterloo. Royston Pike, a professional historian, described the impact of the Kingston by-pass as "revolutionary"! In the 1920s, Drivers Jonas & Co.*, a surveying partnership, was active on behalf of its client, the Speer Estate, whose land was opened up for development by the by-pass. As an example of what Royston Pike was referring to, they put forward a proposal in 1926 to have a sewer laid under the by-pass at Manor Road to facilitate development.

The evidence of what took place along the other stretches of the Kingston by-pass is plain to see: on both sides of the road (except at Wimbledon Common) housing and light industrial development took place; there

can't be much doubt that the land on which Hinchley Wood was built would have been developed: the pressures would have been irresistible. The modern development of Manor Road, which had already started in the early 1920s, would have continued, ribbon style, until Thames Ditton was connected to Claygate. At the time, according to Royston Pike, Manor Road was for the most part nothing more than a farm track, rutted and full of holes and on either side grew thickets, brambles and trees: but it is inconceivable that a road, however quaint, that had a connection to the new arterial road would be left undisturbed. It was bound to be a stimulus to development, but would it be factories or houses built in fields, randomly, or would it be a planned settlement?

From my research I have been persuaded by the evidence that the by-pass alone was sufficient to ensure that the land which comprises Hinchley Wood would have been developed. However, if we ask the question: What brought about the rapid emergence of Hinchley Wood as a coherent, identifiable settlement, with a housing stock so plainly superior to its contemporary peers? then the answer is not the Kingston by-pass alone. It was the combination of the superior road communications which that road brought, together with an excellent train service from a brand new station: and some far-seeing personalities.

Crouch develops a plan for a new settlement

Anita Witten studied the emergence of Hinchley Wood for her Master's dissertation*: she tells us that when Hinchley Wood was countryside the landowners were the Banks Estate, which included Couchmore Farm and Upper Couchmore Farm: the Speer Estate, which included Manor Farm and land on each side of Claygate Lane:

* A surveying partnership which survives to this day in independent ownership in Mayfair

* "The development of an outer London suburban village, Hinchley Wood, near Esher, Surrey": an unpublished Master's dissertation, Anita Witten

Map of Hinchley Wood area : 1930 (when the station came)

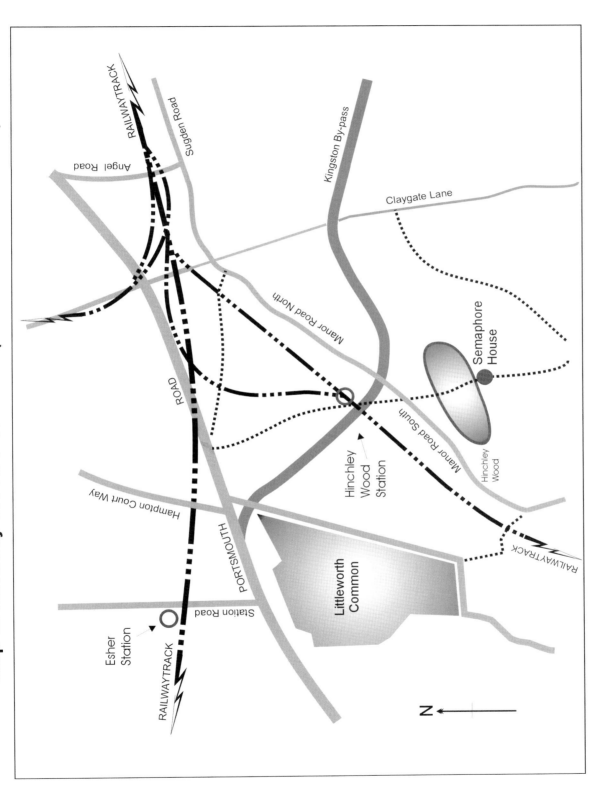

and the Lovelace Estate which owned the land to the east of this, including Surbiton golf course. (For the present we must leave aside the Lovelace Estate land because it is not part of the story at this point.)

No-one seems to know the exact circumstances of when the land belonging to the Banks and Speer Estates was bought for development. We know from the compulsory purchase notice that the Banks Estate sold land in 1923 for the by-pass. The first mention at Esher Council of the development of the 'Couchmore Estate' is in December 1926 (when the by-pass was nearing completion) but the minutes don't tell us by whom the plans were presented; it would be either an agent on behalf of the landowner: or was it a Mr G T Crouch, a property developer/builder who operated in the surrounding area? The Banks and Speer land was somehow brought under control by Crouch, probably in the mid 1920s.

Crouch was clearly a man of great vision. He it was who seems to have conceived the development plan; he had in mind the good road communications offered by the by-pass and, he could see how readily the railway's potential could be exploited simply by building a station. He presented several iterations of his plan to Esher Council who had zoned the whole area as a superior new settlement. At its meeting in September 1929, Esher Council considered a "revised preliminary layout" of what was proposed to be called "Hinchley Wood": the plans showed plots for 1,017 houses on 147 acres at 6.9 houses per acre.

Hinchley Wood works well in terms of how the street scenes and road layouts look and feel; much of the credit for this belongs to Esher Council and Horace Fread, their long serving Surveyor; this is the point at which the Council's decision to take control (by zoning the land for housing development), ensured that Hinchley Wood was to be a superior place of some character. The Council took absolute control of the density of development, and was careful to induce developers to build to a quality that would set the tone of the district. The Council also had some considerable influence on road layouts and widths: the absence of clinical, street grid layouts in Hinchley Wood is probably also due to the Council's influence.

Hinchley Wood railway station

Esher Council settled the "town plan" for the new district and permission was given to Crouch to build in September 1929; but first he had to have the station built: he lost no time. In the following month, October, he struck the deal with Southern Railway for the construction of Hinchley Wood railway station: but the story started earlier.

When the New Line to Guildford was laid down in 1885, there was no purpose in considering any stop between Surbiton and Claygate, but in the early 1920s, by which time some development had taken place in Long Ditton, the notion of a halt was promulgated by Esher Council, somewhere in the Angel Road area. The Southern Railway was no more interested in such a proposition than they were a little later when the Council aired the new idea of building a station "where the

Kingston by-pass was going to cross the New Line". Stations cost money and the railway company would only pay for stations if it judged that they would bring incremental traffic.

DISTRICT COUNCIL.

Railway facilities Again Under Discussion.

HALT BETWEEN CLAYGATE AND DITTON OPPOSED.

Surrey Comet: 12 December 1925

At a meeting in December 1925, Esher Council considered a petition from residents of Manor Road for the provision of a station. The Council could not make up its mind on the issue: it was a suggestion that wasn't coming at the issue from the right direction. The Southern Railway had a financial game to play: and they could wait! In the meanwhile the small number of travelling residents from Manor Road would doubtless have had to continue walking either to Esher or Thames Ditton stations. When the station was built, it was not through their petition: they were just the beneficiaries of a grand plan which, had they but known it, was to rob their road of its rustic charm. The case for a station at Hinchley Wood had to be smoothed with a subsidy by Crouch.

Hinchley Wood station under construction, 1930.

Photo: Surrey Comet

Like the landowners who profited from the building of the New Line in the first place, residential developers were quick to spot how a station would create demand for houses. Hinchley Wood station was subsidised for only one reason: it was to create a new demand for houses. The Southern Railway was not itself insensible to the impact of new railway infrastructure on land values. In his book*, Jackson tells us that at its annual general meeting

* Semi-detached London: Alan A Jackson, 1973

18

Early shot of the down platform.
Photo: J L Smith, the Lens of Sutton Collection

Early shot of the up platform.
Photo: J L Smith, the Lens of Sutton Collection

in 1927, its chairman called attention to the "great increment in the value of the land, which goes into the pockets of vigilant people at our expense". Although they were alive to the phenomenon they wearied in their pique at not being able to exploit it for themselves. The reason for this lay with Parliament: railway companies were privileged in that they were given statutory power to acquire land for the purposes of their undertakings; the corollary of this was that they were obliged to sell surplus land. They were unable, therefore, to participate in the increase in land values, which their facilities might create*. The most they could do to reflect their bargaining position was to trade a new station at Hinchley Wood for a subsidy from the party which most required it: our Mr Crouch.

In October 1929 it is recorded in the minutes of the Southern Railway that Crouch would contribute £2,500 towards the cost (about one-third) of the building of the station and convey at no cost to Southern Railway, the necessary land: this was not unduly onerous for Crouch because the station was to be built at the point where the tracks divided on land which had been acquired by the railway company when the fly-under was built in 1908. The only additional land required, which Crouch gave, was for the footpaths leading from the public highways (from Station Approach and Hillmont Road neither of which were yet built) to the footbridge over the tracks. (There had been a footbridge over the tracks at this point ever since the railway was built: it carried an old footpath from Telegraph Hill to Thames Ditton.)

In all the circumstances, this seemed a very good deal for Crouch. The following month the minutes record that in addition the Railway would buy some more land from Crouch at £420 per acre on which to build a goods yard! This was the 1920s and a huge proportion of the movement of goods was still done by rail: Claygate's goods yard didn't close until 1963. In the event, the goods yard at Hinchley Wood was never built but the land was retained, ultimately to allow a car park. Reflecting the

Southern Railway's interest, namely an increase in traffic revenue, a guarantee was introduced into the deal: Crouch had to deposit £500, which would be forfeited if 150 houses weren't built within three years. This threshold was safely met a year after the station opened, such was the speed at which building took place.

The deal seems to have been contracted in March 1930. In the intervening period the minutes tell us that Crouch was in fact fronting the deal for a Mr. Percy Fisher; nothing seems to be known of this character. In the absence of any information about the business relationship between these two parties (Mr. Fisher kept a very low profile and has not appeared in any other primary sources which I have researched) I have attributed to Crouch the rest of the Hinchley Wood story insofar as he was involved. His is the name which keeps appearing and reappearing in the primary sources so I can do no other.

The deal having been settled, the Southern Railway lost no time in going out to tender. The civil engineering department of the Railway handled the construction, it being a very straightforward job with no architectural demand. Just five months after the first tender was accepted, the construction was finished in time to allow the station to open, only seven months after the deal was done. The Surrey Comet was able to announce that the new railway station, to be known as Hinchley Wood, was to open on Monday 20 October 1930 for passengers and parcels! There was no ceremony: no photographs to record the event and almost certainly, hardly any passengers either; they were to come a little later, at first just a few; then dozens, scores and finally, by the hundreds.

Hinchley Wood is on the map!

Hinchley Wood was, strictly, already on the map (it was the name of the wooded area on the northern slopes of Telegraph Hill): but when the station name appeared on the platforms announcing to the world the name "Hinchley Wood", this was the point when, truly, the name was on the map! Apart from the station, freshly opened and giving its name to the new settlement, all that was there before was Esher Filling Station (built in 1928,

---

* The modern Hong Kong Mass Transit system was in large measure financed by the increment in land values over and near its new stations.

Spring in "Hinchley Wood", 2002.

Passage to "Hinchley Wood" from Hillcrest Gardens, 2002.

In "Hinchley Wood": steps leading to Telegraph Hill, 2002.

Passage from Manor Road South to "Hinchley Wood", 2002.

otherwise it might have been called Hinchley Wood Filling Station!) and a few houses at the Thames Ditton end of Manor Road. But Hinchley Wood was destined to become a settlement a cut above its 1930s peers. No-one knows how the name for the settlement and its station arose. Was it Esher Council, Southern Railway or Crouch who first alighted upon the name? I expect that whoever it was that was trying to think of a name, looked at the Ordnance Survey map and found "Hinchley Wood" on Telegraph Hill. The first reference I have found to the suggested name was in 1929 when the development plan was presented to Esher Council. Anyway, when the station opened, there was the name, a comfortable name: a name which was readily adopted by everyone who came and which has served well. It is a very pleasant name.

In October 1929, just as Crouch was committing to Southern Railway, the world changed; the stock market, which had been driven up by a speculative frenzy on Wall Street reached an unsustainable peak; when all investors rushed to sell at once, the market crashed. No-one knew what was going to happen: fortunes were lost: the great Depression began.

Crouch and his backers had bought all this land, and he had contracted with Southern Railway to build 150 houses in the first three years after the station opened. It wasn't an option for him to see how the wind was blowing from the USA before committing himself to building houses; he was on the hook! It must have been a very uncomfortable time for him as the gloomy events in the USA unfolded.

CHAPTER 5:
HINCHLEY WOOD: THE DEVELOPMENT TAKES OFF

An aerial view c1933: the Hinchley Wood Hotel is up: the north side of station Approach is incomplete; the roads are laid out on the second Berg estate: Cumberland Drive has not started construction. Photo: Ariel Photos, courtesy, Elmbridge Museum

All the components were now in place: the Kingston by-pass; a new railway station; a town plan and Crouch, the entrepreneur, in charge. The year 1930 was the year in which Hinchley Wood began, but as we have seen, this period brought some very harsh economic conditions too. Although it could not have felt like it at the time, we were, in fact, standing on the threshold of an astonishing housing boom: a coincidence which, naturally, had its own major impact in Hinchley Wood, of multiplying the effect of the stimuli of infrastructure improvements which were already in place.

The boom did not create Hinchley Wood; but when it came it contributed to the speed with which everything happened: from a standing start in 1930, Hinchley Wood had its first shops and its residents' association by 1931; its first councillor by 1933; its recognition as a separate ward with its own polling station in 1935. It celebrated its first Christian service in 1933 and by 1935 it had built its Hall Church (which was to serve until the proper church was built in 1953); and by 1939 there were over 2000 new adult residents. The station was the magnet drawing London's workers to *"a place in the country"* which the Southern Railway had been promoting.

Crouch new this, and even before the boom had any impact, development was fast. In this chapter we will consider how it all happened.

Crouch brings in three other developers

In modern times it is not at all the exception for a developer who has achieved planning permission for 1000 houses to parcel it up and lay off some of the land to his friends in the industry. This practice certainly has the effect of sharing risks but the motivation, on a big development such as Hinchley Wood, is also to achieve a diversity of product: different house types and styles so that as broad a spectrum as possible of the house buying public is attracted to look at all the offerings. Whether for this reason, or not, Crouch sold the greater part of the land to three other house builders.

Crouch divided the land into four parcels. Retaining one for himself, he sold the other three to local builders, Montgomery, Bergs and Stokes (who sold some of his land to Rose). As soon as Bergs had bought their land they got off to a flying start and had built some of Hinchley Drive, where about a dozen people were already living even

TELLS OF A STRANGE ENCOUNTER WITH A STAGE COACH.

And How It Led to Comparison of New and Old in Esher and Dittons.

GHOSTLY DRIVER AMAZED BY RAPID BUILDING.

"Landed Gentry" of Hinchley Wood at Six Houses to the Acre.

"Well I'm blessed!" exclaimed that ghost of old Tom as he sat on the box of the phantom coach that sped along the Portsmouth Road, in the direction of Esher.

"It breaks my very heart, it does, to see the woodland shattered so, and these new houses built, I see, to house the new landed gentry."

Very few people in Esher know about this phantom coach that is drawn along the Portsmouth Road by four bays once every year. It moves silently over the snow, disturbing nobody, so that, unless one knows just where to look, and the time to be at a certain point, there is no chance of seeing the phantom coach of the great Portsmouth Road. It was on Monday night that I saw the coach, and met old Tom whipping his horses along over the driven snow.

Estate of a Thousand Houses.

Tom told me that he had lost time at the last change of horse and was in a hurry but he would be very glad if I would tell him all about the changes in Esher and the Dittons.

And so I started straight away. "Well," I began, "that's the Hinchley Wood estate that we've just passed, and it's going to be a really fine place when it's finished."

Tom wiped his mouth with the back of his hand and wanted to know what I meant by a "fine place."

And so I tried to tell him what an excellent residential quarter of Esher this spot is going to be.

"But are they the kind o' folk who'll use my coach? That's what I wants t' know?" he persisted.

I told him that people did not travel by coach and horses these days, and that Hinchley Wood had its own railway station and was soon to have its own shopping centre. But that didn't appeal to Tom, and so I tried to tell him that there would be about 1,000 houses at Hinchley Wood eventually, and that it would have a density of about six houses to the acre.

Retaining Countryside Charm.

"Six to an acre. T'is a mighty waste o' land they're allowing!"

"No, Tom!" I said gently. "It is not a waste of land, really. You see today we have what are known as town planning schemes.

"An' what are they?"

"Well," I said, "a town planning scheme is made by the Esher District Council—"

"What's that do?"

"The land is set out so that the Council says which shall be used for houses and which shall be used for other buildings and such like. And that results in fine houses being built and laid out in the best possible way, and the charm of the countryside being retained as far as possible, as you saw for yourself at Hinchley Wood."

"Do people say what ye shall do with ye own land?"

"Yes Tom, they do! You see, these kinds of things have to be done, otherwise there would be a terrible state of affairs and people would be building anyhow, and anywhere, with ugly houses next to nice houses and that sort of thing.

There'll be a lot of development on this Hinchley Wood estate; they're going to build a school here, as well as a church. Already the Bishop of Guildford has been down here to give his opinion on the site and-"

A £14,000 "Hint."

"All along that road we've just passed, houses will be built," I went on. "That road is called the Kingston by-pass and was built to relieve traffic from the main road you've travelled on so often."   I saw him fumbling about in his pocket, and I guessed it was for his flask. He took a wee nip, and put it back again.

"Of course, Tom, with all this development going on, it was only natural they'd build a sort of hostel in these parts. We call them hotels, now. Well, they're building one at the junction of Manor Road and that Kingston by-pass at a cost of £14,000! Just think of that, £14,000!" But there was no response to the hint.

"Not 'arf so many trees about as there used to be", observed Tom. "An' these ice bound roads don't suit me horses. Gerrup can't ye!" he yelled as one of the horses slipped. "What ye a playing at I should like to know!"

And so after we jogged along quietly for quite a time.

400 More Houses This Year.

"Of course, Tom," I ventured to say, "building today is far different to what it used to be. Just think, during the last four years 458 houses were built in the Esher district and during this year 400 more will be built. What do you think of that?"

"Can't be done!" he argued. "Not enough bricklayers and mates in these parts to do it. Only t'other day when I stopped at the cross-roads to water me horses, Master Pegg told me t'was himself that was looking for more men – besides the brickyard couldn't make 'nuff bricks in the time."

But what was the use of arguing with Tom?

The Enchanting Commons.

He told me quite a long story of how he used to travel through Esher with his coach and the buxom wenches who lived there then; and the beauty of trees and the joys of the common lands, whereon the cattle used to browse and doze in the summer heat. Of the lake set amidst the common, just off the Portsmouth Road, and of its enchantment during May time. He said that there was some talk of this place being an enchanted lake on Mid-Summer's Day and that some folk had taken their oath they had seen fairy revels amidst the sylvan glades.

"But Tom, you don't mean to tell me that there are fairies on Esher Common or Giggs Hill Green do you?" I asked in amazement.

"There are," he replied. "Haven't ye seen the rings on the green that the elfs' feet make as they dance in a ring, and besides . . . . .

And then, as the lights of a motor car swept along the road, old Tom vanished.

H.A.B.

Source: Surrey Comet, 14 March 1931

J T Crouch advertisement, 1933.   Photo: Surrey Comet

advert displaying his offerings at Hinchley Wood. What it said about Hinchley Wood and Crouch's houses is shown on page 24. It is worthy of being read without comment for it gives an excellent description of what the market was being offered.

That Crouch was a successful house builder and developer there can be no doubt. He worked over a wide area in the 1930s on different housing ventures and allied shopping facilities: the most notable was the Tudor Estate in north Kingston. The fact that he kept for himself the core of the Hinchley Wood settlement, the shops, Manor Road (North and South) near the shops and later Manor Drive (western end), shows, I think, his effort at obtaining a critical mass quickly.

before the station opened. Speed was probably part of Crouch's plan because he had to be mindful of his commitment to Southern Railway to build 150 houses in the first three years.

The Surrey Comet notices Hinchley Wood

Just a few months after the station opened, the Surrey Comet noticed what was going on and decided to tell its readers about it. Esher Filling Station, which only a few months earlier was standing in isolation, was beginning to be enveloped by the building work, specially by Bergs who were now working in Hillcrest Gardens and Hinchley Drive. The semi-detached houses at the south end of Manor Road North, being built by Crouch, were almost finished and Couchmore Avenue had started its westerly extension. The scene from the by-pass was changing and the Surrey Comet felt some explanation was in order. In March 1931 the newspaper ran an article, written in a parody style, of an imaginary conversation between a stagecoach driver ghost and his present day passenger who explains to his driver what is going on. An edited version is shown on page 22.

The article brings out some interesting features. It tells us of the future development of the Hinchley Wood Hotel (see Chapter 6) and, somewhat prematurely, the church (see Chapter 14), and schools (see Chapter 11). It makes reference to the town planning scheme and Esher Council's role in it: "Hinchley Wood is going to be a really fine place when it is finished" says the article; "an excellent residential quarter". It talks, intriguingly, of the new "landed gentry living in housing densities of six to the acre". Compared with other new suburbs, the density was generous.

Publicity for Hinchley Wood, and for Crouch

We are not told who was the informant for the 1931 stage coach article but we can speculate that it was Crouch: we can be more certain that he was behind what appeared in December 1933 when the Surrey Comet devoted a whole page to editorial material on Crouch and a half page

How the numbers accumulated

For the purposes of observing the rapid growth of Hinchley Wood's population, I have used the electoral rolls from 1929 to 1939 as a measure of occupancy. These rolls are homogenous as a basis, e.g. all adults over 21. No electoral rolls exist for 1940 to 1944. (Exceptionally, because of the wartime national government, no general election was held after the one in 1935 until 1945: but all building stopped in 1939 or early 1940 anyway.)

Manor Road, looking south c1930.   Photo: Surrey Comet

Manor Road, looking north 1931.   Photo: Surrey Comet

HOW A BUILDER ANSWERED A MODERN NEED

MR. CROUCH'S WORK AT HINCHLEY WOOD

A great deal of pleased surprise has been expressed by those whose ways have taken them recently to the Hinchley Wood district near Esher. Amongst the lovely heaths of this part of Surrey, and running up the gentle slopes, they have discovered a township of beautiful houses worthy even of this setting. This is the estate developed on unusual lines by Messrs. G. T. Crouch, and it is of interest to note some of the leading features of the development—particularly

The choice of an easily accessible site
The variety of designs and
Facilities offered for individual ownership

Very quickly after the war, intense building activity took place, and any number of estates were opened up. But these were on the fringe of London, reached by the accustomed routes. It required a man of shrewd foresight to appreciate that modern improvements in transport could be utilised to enable people to live in a recognised beauty-spot like the Esher district, and yet be within easy reach of town. Such a man is Mr. Crouch, the principal of the well-known building firm that bears his name.

A Land of Interest—A Land of Ease.

Esher itself has for long had an interest all its own. The little town, with its pleasant, busy old shops, its Green breaking the main street, its ivy-clustered, self-composed houses, speaks of the leisured refinement of Georgian days. Sandown Park, at the entrance to Esher, is an old centre of attraction to the sporting world. And yet, not far away are Kingston, a still more ancient town, but full of modern shops and recreations, and Surbiton, that thriving up-to-date community. An estate between these places would take advantage of all their amenities and conveniences.

Ease of Access.

The Kingston By-pass road was planned debouching into the old Portsmouth Road this side of Esher, and Mr. Crouch realised at once the facilities this offered. Just short of the Esher end, his estate is now developing off each side of the road. But that is by no means all. An arrangement was quickly come to with the Southern Railway, for a station to be built adjoining the estate. The result is, that Hinchley Wood is almost incomparable in its ease of access. Actually, it only takes twenty minutes to travel from the estate to Waterloo, while by road, the journey along the By-pass is of course as easy as it is charming—for this is an arterial road distinguished by the beauty of its outlook.

In keeping with the Locality.

These being the conditions of the district, it seemed proper that the houses to be erected there should conform to a definite high standard; and such they admittedly are. The interesting fact that quite a number of architects reside there is evidence—were any needed—of their constructional merit. There are semi-detached and detached houses, at prices from £995 upwards, but there are two characteristics common to them all—solid building and splendid interior finish. Add the spacious roads, with their trees and grass borders, and the beautiful, healthy setting of common and hillside, and it is no wonder that there is an air of happiness and prosperity over the whole estate.

Unique Designs.

To erect, in the old style, streets of standardised houses here would have been entirely blameworthy, and in fact the designs are so many that to select some for mention presents a difficulty. But those who saw at a recent Ideal Home Exhibition the famous "Tudor" house will be glad to know that this interesting design is reproduced here, with its massive beams, long sloping roof and latticed windows. Many, again, will want to make their own the detached Chalet, with its great deep embrasured window and its lesser oriel set in a front reminiscent of a baronial hall. Another design which is constantly admired is the £1,495 type; entering by a tiled, half-timbered porch, one finds oneself in a spacious panelled hall, from which double doors admit into an imposing dining room.

Interior Delights.

But though visitors appreciate one after another of these designs, they still confess to amazement at the sumptuousness of the interiors. The oak panelled hall and enclosed staircase give a noticeable dignity to each house — the beautiful latticed windows give an atmosphere of brightness. Each kitchen is large, each is beautifully tiled and fitted with that most convenient of cabinets—many compartmented, for crockery, brushes, ironing-table and the like, so that orderliness may reign supreme. And as for the bathroom, the effect is a lustrous one from the gleam of chromium-plated fittings and the beautifully patterned white and black or tinted tiling of the walls. To move to one of these houses is very often to change the whole atmosphere of daily life from drabness to brightness and gaiety.

Financial Arrangements.

It used generally to be the case that buying a house meant either putting all the money down at once or going to a great deal of trouble to arrange a mortgage. A good many houses at Hinchley Wood are, in fact, bought in full at once, but on very many, only a deposit is made, the balance being repaid on a weekly basis over a term of years.

Generally, a deposit of 10 per cent, is acceptable, but as illustrating the particularly favourable terms, Messrs. Crouch, with their vast organisation, are able to arrange, it may be mentioned that on various types, a deposit of as little as £50 is accepted, or alternatively a weekly repayment as low as 27s. 11d.

A Very Great Opportunity.

These are not days when decisions are to be delayed. The exacting conditions of modern life require that the advantages of modern life should be enjoyed to the full—particularly in regard to the house in which one lives. It is for this reason that attention is directed to this delightful opportunity for a healthful life, yet on an economical basis, at Hinchley Wood.

Source: Surrey Comet, 9 December 1933

The 1929 roll showed 122 people already living in the roads which were part of the Hinchley Wood town plan: in Couchmore Avenue and Manor Road. By 1939 the adult population in the new areas was 2,404, an increase in the decade of 2,282. The increase shown by the 1934 roll, halfway through the decade, was 1,083 adults, or very nearly one half: but when you consider that Crouch did not fire the starting gun until 1930: and the station didn't open until October 1930: and when you consider the lead times involved in building the houses and selling them, then the fact that the Hinchley Wood town plan was about half-way finished in 1934 gives ample testimony to the speed at which everything happened.

If Crouch had ever lost sleep over the Depression coinciding with his commitment to Southern Railway to build 150 houses in three years, it could only have been months before he knew he was safe. The speed of development achieved the blessing that when new building stopped in 1939, Hinchley Wood was a viable community large enough to sustain itself; in what town planners call a 'nuclear village'. Even employment opportunities had arrived (by accident and unplanned) in the shape of the Milk Marketing Board in 1939 (see Chapter 6). More unplanned employment opportunity was to arrive in the form of the Ordnance Survey office, during the war, and the Surtax Office after the war.

To assist with understanding of how Hinchley Wood was developed in the 1930s, there is a bar chart on page 27. Some licence has been taken in order to avoid too much information spoiling the message. The bars represent years in which new occupants took up residence. Within each bar there will be, of course, a start, a peak and a tail: these are not shown for individual roads but this picture is best given in the aggregate. On page 28 there is a histogram which shows the same data organised in adjacent pairs of years to give a smoothing effect. Again, we are dealing with numbers of first occupants as shown by the electoral roll; division by two will convert to the number of houses with only a small risk of overstatement.

The histogram shows the fast build up of newcomers to Hinchley Wood. Because the house builders were on

site simultaneously, and because they were producing a product for which there was a strong demand, the activity in the years 1932 to 1937 was, more or less, on a high plateau. The peak year for newcomers was 1933 with just under 400, but in each of the years 1934 to 1936 there were about 300 newcomers. Even though the available data from electoral rolls stops, suddenly, in 1939 it does not matter. By that year practically everyone knew that war was coming and building work wound down. Even so, in a rush as it were to get everything all wrapped up, there were over 200 newcomers in 1939. There were also some in 1940 when the final tidying up took place before everything stopped for the duration. The unfinished areas were the Medina Avenue and Heathside estate, a part of Greenways and the land between the railway lines (see Chapter 10).

More on the builders

None of the big names in the building industry was involved in Hinchley Wood. All the builders in Hinchley Wood, including of course the few smaller ones, were small to medium, proprietorially run more or less local affairs. When the war came, they were able to make a painless transition from the boom conditions to repairing bomb damage and other military work. They all continued in business locally after the war (I am not sure about Rose) and Crouch, Montgomery and Bergs were all active in the 1950s. Crouch's head office was in Morden in the 1930s, but all the others were in Hinchley Wood, on site, or in Thames Ditton: Montgomery's sales pitch was that he actually lived on his estate.

A characteristic of all the Hinchley Wood builders was the closeness of their proprietors to the market; physically in the location of their offices and their own local presence on a day-to-day basis. They were all selling directly to the public without the use of agents. Although they were all operating at the same time, there was a sufficient differentiation between their products to appeal to a wide market. At a higher level, it seems to me, they all had self-confidence in the new settlement which, in the aggregate of their efforts, they were producing. As to the quality of the location, they all sang off the same hymn sheet; they had a common interest in getting buyers to visit Hinchley Wood, and then letting them discriminate among the range of offerings, by price, semi-detached or detached, standard or custom built.

Bergs

Of all the builders it is Bergs which created the strongest brand. Its association with quality houses lasted well into the 1950s, but in the post-war era they were handicapped by not being able to use as high a quality of materials. Nevertheless, the Berg brand endured and it is was not until the company was taken over in the 1960s that the brand faded away. Anita Witten tells us that the two brothers, Ellis and Lawrence Berg had started building on spare land at the family home, Penton Hall, Staines in 1924 and, by progression, they were by 1934, to quote

A 1931 shot of the Manor Road crossing of the by-pass.
Photo: Surrey Comet

Early post-war photo of Manor Drive, looking towards Manor Road.   Photo: Gerry and Janet Hall

Early post-war photo of Manor Drive, looking east: note pig bin near lamp post.   Photo: Gerry and Janet Hall

Hinchley Wood - Years of occupation of first residents

	1930	1931	1932	1933	1934	1935	1936	1937	1938	1939
First Berg Estate										
Hinchley Drive	■	■	■	■	■					
Hillcrest Gardens		■	■	■	■					
Hinchley Close		■	■	■						
Montgomery Estate										
Couchmore Avenue (extension)	■	■	■	■			■			
Westmont Road			■	■	■					
Montgomery Avenue			■	■	■	■				
Eastmont Road				■	■	■				
Hillmont Road						■	■	■	■	■
Southmont Road							■	■	■	■
Crouch Estate										
Manor Roads South and North (part)			■	■	■	■		■	■	■
Manor Drive (part)				■	■	■	■			
Meadow Close						■	■	■	■	■
Station Approach		■	■	■	■	■	■			
Rose Estate										
Claygate Lane (near school)			■						■	■
Manor Drive (part)				■	■	■	■			
Cumberland Drive					■	■	■	■		
Hinchley Way				■	■				■	■
Chesterfield Drive						■	■	■		
Second Berg Estate										
Old Claygate Lane (south of by-pass)					■	■	■	■		
Avondale Avenue					■	■	■	■	■	■
Southwood Gardens						■	■	■	■	■
Others										
Greenways					■	■	■	■	■	
Greenwood Road					■	■	■	■	■	■
Orchard Avenue						■	■	■	■	■
Brooklands Road					■					
Heathside and Medina Avenue (1st phase)									■	■

their own slogan, building on six estates at 12 different prices to 24 different designs.

The two Berg estates in Hinchley Wood had several features distinguishing them from the offerings of their competitors: every house was detached. (This is true of Manor Road South and Greenways too, but those roads do not have the same one-builder stamp as do the Berg estates.) In location terms, all their houses were on the south side of the by-pass and all the perimeter roads followed the outlines of the fields which had originally been sold for development. Consequently, all the southern limits of the Berg estates (parts of Hillcrest Gardens, Hinchley Close, parts of Avondale Avenue and Claygate Lane) had a contiguous boundary with either Telegraph Hill, farmland or Surbiton golf course, all of which could be accessed by footpaths somewhere on the estates. In contrast to the southern boundary, which was designated 'Green Belt' after the war, the northern boundary was contiguous with the by-pass, betwixt heaven and hell, it could be said.

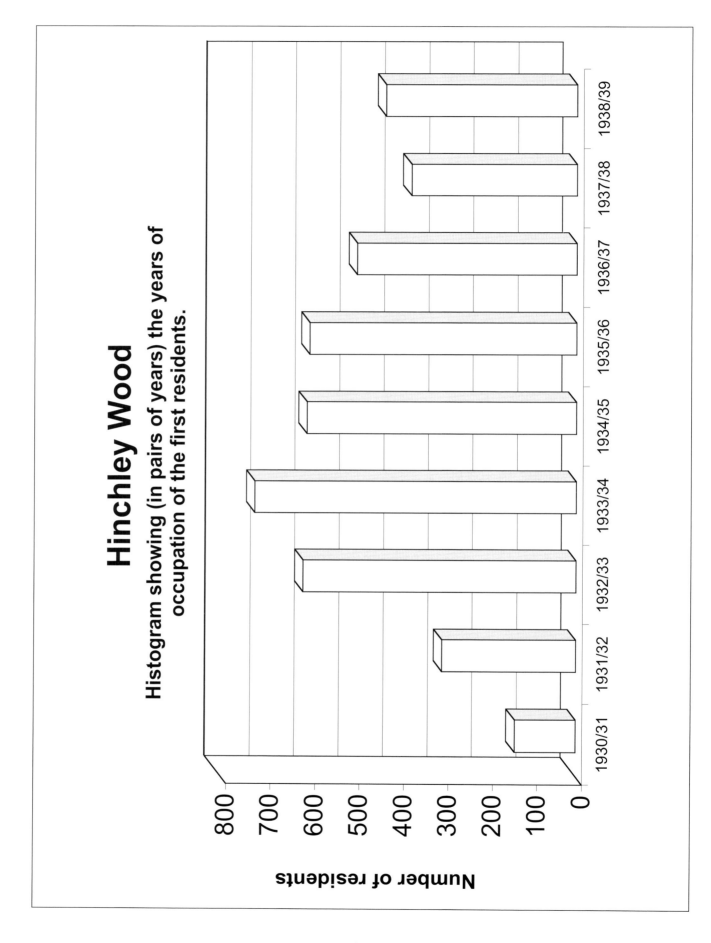

Hinchley Wood

Histogram showing (in pairs of years) the years of occupation of the first residents.

E & L BERGS NEAR TO TOWN
SURREY ESTATES

HINCHLEY WOOD, ESHER
Estate Office on Kingston By-pass. Hinchley Wood Station 8 minutes. Fast electric trains from Waterloo every 20 minutes to Hinchley Wood Station in 21 minutes. Green Line Coaches every 15 minutes from Oxford Circus via Hammersmith to Hinchley Wood.
Detached Houses £1,095 to £1,800

ASHTEAD WOODS ESTATE
ASHTEAD STATION IS ON THE ESTATE. Fast electric trains from Ashtead to Waterloo, Victoria and London Bridge every few minutes.
Semi-detached Houses £750 to £1,095
Detached Houses £1,095 to £1,800

WENTWORTH ESTATE
DITTON ROAD, SURBITON. THE FINEST POSITION IN THE DISTRICT. Houses 3-6 Bedrooms. Office at Hinchley Wood, a few minutes from the Estate.
Detached Houses £1,500 to £3,000

A GOOD SELECTION OF FURNISHED AND UNFURNISHED SHOWHOUSES ALWAYS READY FOR YOUR INSPECTION

E. & L. BERG, LTD.
Head Office: HINCHLEY WOOD ESTATE KINGSTON BY-PASS, ESHER
Telephone: EMBERBROOK 2555 6 7

Source: Elmbridge Museum

Berg advertisement for their second estate, 1934. Source: Surrey Comet

full exploitation of the grades on the northern slopes of Telegraph Hill, and by exploiting the curves in the streets, has created a street scene of enduring quality. Because Bergs had complete control over the detailed presentation of the estates, they were able to adopt a consistent front boundary style: the whole estate was originally built with low brick walls to the front gardens which added to the feeling of coherence. A change in fashion has led to many of them having been pulled down, reflecting the

ESHER
SURREY

AN ILLUSTRATED GUIDE
AND MAP TO THE
RESIDENTIAL AMENITIES
AND SHOPPING FACILITIES
OFFERED ON THE
HINCHLEY WOOD ESTATE
ESHER

Presented with the Compliments of
E. & L. BERG
ESTATE DEVELOPERS AND BUILDING CONTRACTORS.

ESTATE OFFICE,
HINCHLEY WOOD ESTATE,
ESHER, SURREY.

Telephone - - - Emberbrook 1817

Source: Elmbridge Museum

The existence of these inviolate boundaries to the two estates, created the opportunity for producing what is without doubt, both the most harmonious and pleasing quadrant of the whole settlement. A single architect designed the whole of the two estates to five basic designs but with individual variations to justify the claim 'all different'. (This was the point of Rose's jibe: his houses in Cumberland Drive really were all different.) The houses had either three, four or occasionally, five bedrooms and were priced between £1150 and £2,000. To reinforce the feeling of difference, each house was built with different colour facing bricks and roofing tiles. Maybe the houses are all from five basic designs; but the architect, making

contemporary preference for more open front gardens.

Another feature of Berg houses, was the glazed double internal doors. These would interconnect either between two reception rooms or one of them and the hall. All the external windows were leaded lights fitted to Crittall window casements. A delightful feature was that all the

29

Berg advertisement, 1933.   Source: Surrey Comet

Postcard from 1930s, "Old" Claygate Lane, looking south.
Photo: courtesy Elmbridge Museum

halls were oak panelled. Most of the houses had the trademark inglenook fireplace by Claygate Fireplaces (this may have been standard only on the second estate) who were making them locally at the time. Growing up as my wife and I did in the 1950s and 1960s, we failed to notice at the time that the 1930s houses had any charm. How imperceptive we were in our immaturity; we have to confess to an act of vandalism that we allowed ourselves by removing the Claygate fireplace from 105 Claygate Lane in the 1970s. Sorry! In mitigation, we spent a large part of our leisure time restoring the hall panelling to a limed oak finish.

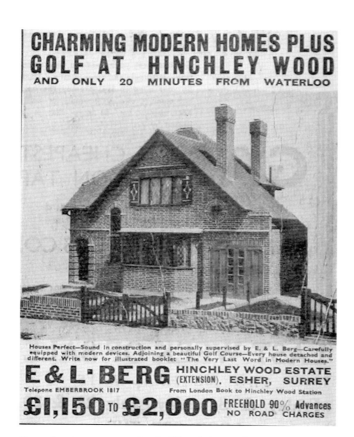

Berg advertisement promoting "golf" at their second estate.
Source: Surrey Comet

A 1937 photo in the back garden of a house in Manor Drive; with no trees yet to block the view, across the by-pass can be seen a house in Hillcrest Gardens; to the left are houses in Avondale Avenue.
Photo: Gerry and Janet Hall

Rose

Rose developed part of Manor Drive, Hinchley Way, parts of Claygate Lane (where the schools are), Chesterfield Drive and Cumberland Drive where he built some but not all of the houses. The distinctive feature of the last two named roads is their shrub planters (otherwise known as coffins) between the footpaths and the roads. In fact, Rose also wanted to put these in Claygate Lane but this was frustrated by a long running dispute about responsibility to make up the road (this part of Claygate Lane was not made up until the mid 1950s).

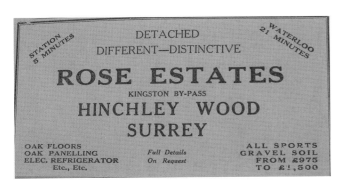

DETACHED
DIFFERENT—DISTINCTIVE
ROSE ESTATES
KINGSTON BY-PASS
**HINCHLEY WOOD
SURREY**

STATION 5 MINUTES | WATERLOO 21 MINUTES

OAK FLOORS
OAK PANELLING
ELEC. REFRIGERATOR
Etc., Etc.

*Full Details
On Request*

ALL SPORTS
GRAVEL SOIL
FROM £975
TO £1,500

Rose Estates advertisement, 1933.   Source: Surrey Comet

Rose was particularly pleased with Cumberland Drive, noting the unusually attractive layout of the road which "is just slightly winding, which is so much more interesting than dead straight". Rose claimed a design which was decidedly charming emphasising the 'class' appearance of every house in the road, all of which are different. Actually he said "distinctly" different; this was just a little swipe at Bergs, whose offering was all of a theme around five basic designs. Although Rose was offering designs of which "everyone is different" he was actually operating with a stock of 15 to 20 designs. Others were built to customer's own design. The price range he was offering was from £1,050 to £1,600.

Although Rose's claims for Cumberland Drive are supportable, even today, he is not entitled to all the credit for the quality of the houses nor for the way they give a pleasant street scene of coherent character. When the Speer Estate sold the land on which Cumberland Drive was built, they reserved important powers. For each plot there was to be one house only of not less than 15,000 cubic feet. Moreover, to control this, all purchasers had to submit their plans to Drivers Jonas & Co., who were agents to the Speer Estate and who, for a fee of one guinea, would opine on whether the elevations and dimensions fell within the high standard required by the Speer Estate. The quality of the street scene of Cumberland Drive is a testimony to the rigorous control which was applied.

Rose's sales copy regarded the location as very superior; it comes straight from the Southern Railway's theme: "A country home at London's door" by claiming that:

> "*A most important factor for consideration is that the whole of the district is town planned at six houses to the acre; on the Rose estates the density is only five; this ensures that the purchase of a house on the Rose estate is truly an investment. Hinchley Wood is purely a high-class residential area; the district is one which will always attract buyers ...*" At this point the copy descends into "*buy now while stocks last*". More relevant is:
>
> "*When visiting the site, we would ask you to particularly notice the delightful district, the distinctive layout of the roads, the completely varied and pleasing designs of the houses* [Rose's houses], *the unquestionably first class construction and the many details of interior finish...*"
>
> "*Accessibility from town is remarkably good (Waterloo*

21 minutes) and by road, Hyde Park Corner can be reached in 35 minutes." (This has been confirmed to me by an Esher resident who told me that in 1947 he used to leave his home in Esher at 8.15, drive to London and, having parked his car outside his office in Piccadilly, was at his desk before 9.00am.)

> "*To the City from Waterloo by tube is a very short journey indeed. Any part of the Rose estate is under 10 minutes walk from Hinchley Wood Station, and Green Line coaches from Oxford Circus pass the estate.*"

Stokes

For all Rose's trumpeting about Cumberland Drive he had actually bought the land off a local builder, George Stokes, who operated from Thames Ditton, and who retained a few of the plots at the Manor Road end. In 1934, Stokes offered one to Mr J Limpus, another builder from Surbiton who bought it. Stokes was content to allow Limpus to build his own house. This he duly did and the house became No 10; it remained the family home at least until the 1980s, when all the papers concerning the purchase and ownership of the property were given to Elmbridge Museum.

Mr Limpus paid Stokes £230 for the plot at the rate of £5 per foot for the 46 feet of frontage (and a depth of 152 feet). Everything was measured in frontage in those days (it is area today) probably because the cost of unmade-up roads was a big item for the future: the cost of making-up would be levied by the length of frontage.

In fact, the whole business of sorting out responsibility for footpaths and some roads was a major muddle over several parts of Hinchley Wood which, in many cases, was not resolved until well after the war. In the case of Mr Limpus' plot and others nearby, it wasn't sorted out until the 1960s, when because of an unresolved dispute in Rose's day, the road was still unadopted, and so the Council did not sweep the road or tidy the verges. Moreover, there was a 185 foot stretch of footpath at the northwest end, including outside No. 10, which had remained unmade-up for 30 years. At this time the residents got together: a solution was needed which would include the Council adopting the road. The question of what to do with the coffins also had to be settled. As one of the residents wrote at the time: "Cumberland Drive as originally laid out has a unique charm. I agree the height of the bushes should be kept to a minimum and the trees trimmed for the benefit of motorists. To remove [the coffins] entirely would spoil the whole feature of the road." The coffins stayed.

When Mr Limpus bought his plot from Stokes, it is interesting to note that Stokes offered him three other plots. These were:

Sugden Road: £330 for 55 feet of frontage @ £6 per foot and a depth of 272 feet.
Manor Road: £227.10s for 35 feet of frontage @ £6.10s per foot and a depth of 265 feet.
Portsmouth Avenue: £408 for 48 feet of frontage @ £8.10s a foot and a depth of 160 feet.

The prices of these plots are only vaguely comparable because there were varying future liabilities for road charges: the plots in Manor Road and Portsmouth Avenue (in Thames Ditton) were offered with no road charges. The Cumberland drive plot at £5 per foot appears to be much the cheapest.

Stokes built piecemeal in other parts of Hinchley Wood. As well as a few houses in Manor Road and Cumberland Drive, he contributed some houses to the eclectic collection in Manor Drive.

Stroud

Not much seems to be known about the builder R J Stroud except that he lived in a house called Ridge House in Manor Road South. He built Greenways, except for four houses near the by-pass which Crouch built (from Anita Witten), some houses in Manor Road South and Greenwood Road. His work in Manor Road South was from the access to Telegraph Hill south to Oaken Lane. About 90 houses were planned, going through in ones or twos as individual buyers were found for them. The offering was for "detached residences of charm and character" priced between £995 and £1,500.

His work in Greenwood Road was of a completely different character. The minutes of Esher Council in the 1930s are littered with references to the land on which it was built; it seems that it was quite a continuing problem and probably one of Esher Council's mistakes. The land had formed part of Greenwood Lodge, an old probably grand Victorian house and estate where Greenwood Road is now, off Manor Road North.

The story seems to be as follows: the legislative response to Lloyd George's famous 'houses fit for heroes' slogan placed responsibility for supplying low-rent housing firmly on the shoulders of local authorities. They leapt at the chance of joining the scheme because it was subsidised, rents being set at levels which were nowhere near economic. The government became in danger of running out of money, and had to stop the scheme. Esher Council, it seems had said: "We'll have a bit of that; let's buy Greenwood Lodge": which they did but it would appear that they were then stuck with it when the government scheme was withdrawn. When they attempted to sell it, at auction on several occasions, it failed to reach its reserve price as set by the Ministry. Ultimately, Stroud got the Council off the hook after they had, very sensibly, prepared a development scheme.

Stroud offered "the maximum of accommodation for a minimum of cost" in their development of chalet bungalows. They claimed that: "These new style residences have the largest sized rooms of many similar priced houses in the outer London area" and that: "… many more expensive houses have considerably smaller rooms." These were the positive features which were needed to overcome other factors not in their favour. It was a bit of a remote location: "just off the beaten track". Although handy for the Angel pub, these houses were some distance from the station and shops, being nearer in fact to the Sugden Road shops.

Source: Hinchley Wood Times, April 1939
(Elmbridge Museum)

Montgomery

Frank Montgomery, who with his brother and father comprised the building firm of their name, ignored the 1930s fashion of preferring road names which avoided any hint of suburban connotations: the Acacia Avenue syndrome when 'Drive', 'Gardens', 'Avenue', 'Way', 'Lane', 'Close', were usually preferred in the rest of Hinchley Wood, rather than 'Road'. He was content to name four of the six roads he developed 'Road' but to reinforce the coherence of the estate, he added the prefix of his name to the road names. Thus we have Eastmont, Westmont and Southmont Roads (which have some relationship with the compass) but Hillmont Road has no hill!. Just to make sure there was no mistaking his work he had the fifth named 'Montgomery Avenue'.

Aerial view of the Montgomery Estate c1937.
Photo: Ariel Photos, courtesy, Elmbridge Museum

The offerings on the estate, on which Montgomery was working from the beginning in 1930 to 1939, were of three bedroom semi-detached houses from £995 and four bedroom detached from £1,425, and all with cavity walls and solid wood block floors; theirs were the only houses in Hinchley Wood to have cavity wall construction as standard. Some of the houses built to order were fitted with Claygate fireplaces.

Unusually in Hinchley Wood, the roads for the Montgomery estate were built before the houses; they had been the early builders of concrete roads in Middlesex, where they started business. Evidently the construction technique was adopted by Rose in his estates, while Berg and Crouch only put the foundations in and, much to the irritation of early residents, the unmade roads rapidly became potholed.

As far as location is concerned, Montgomery could justly make claim that his houses were near to the station. Originally, there had been a plan to straddle the railway with shops but this was changed so that they were all in Station Approach. This meant that, for many a housewife (most of whom had no access to a car, even if there was one in the family) there was a weary trudge back from the shops and over the railway footbridge.

One of the truly justified, and probably very persuasive, lines in the sales pitch was that Frank Montgomery lived on the estate (in Couchmore Avenue). This was an unusual personal touch reflecting the Hinchley Wood theme but which carried it to its limit.

Frank Montgomery's site office.
Photo: courtesy, Anita Witten and Peter Hanna

Source: Elmbridge Museum

CHAPTER 6:
NON-HOUSING DEVELOPMENT

Esher Filling Station, c1929: note the cows to the left.

Photo: courtesy Elmbridge Museum

In this chapter is gathered together a review of the non-housing development which took place in Hinchley Wood. The story of Esher Filling Station actually started before Hinchley Wood existed; it is an interesting story but because it has nothing to do with how Hinchley Wood emerged, chronology has been overlooked, so that it can take its place here with other commercial development

Esher Filling Station

Esher Filling Station (or EFS as it was more affectionately known by all who knew it) was the first building in what was to become Hinchley Wood: but that lay in the future: "At last the great day arrived and on 28 November 1928 we were ready to open and I ... stood trembling at the entrance to the archway where our five hand held pumps were quivering to be used." So wrote Marion Barker, the proprietress of Esher Filling Station, over 40 years later in her short account of her eventful life*. If you had been there on that November day in 1928 you would have found, freshly opened for business, the Esher Filling Station: not it should be noted, Hinchley Wood Filling Station, for there was no such place. On that morning you would have found nothing but the single tracked 30 foot concrete carriageway that was the Kingston by-pass and its intersection with a gated Manor Road; an intersection which made no concession to traffic management such as traffic lights (the cycle of traffic

lights we are familiar with was not set as a standard until the following year) or central reservations. In fact there was nothing there except the by-pass, the bridge over the railway and a country road called Manor Road: around the site were farm fields on all sides of the intersection with slopes behind the filling station gently climbing to Telegraph Hill.

Picture the scene on that November morning! Miss Barker's account tells the story of waiting for the first customer; a moment surely to be savoured. Up sweeps a handsome Ford, a lady at the wheel. You can feel the tension even though it is over 70 years ago. A nervous twitch accompanied by the thought: would the first sale be premium or regular? Four gallons or five? Resisting the temptation to move too quickly to a pump, the owners gaped as the car swept by only to turn and go off in a different direction; just like some readers who may have used the site, guiltily, as a convenient turning point!

As Miss Barker continues in her account: "The building was on a site in a field many miles from electricity, water and houses. I had to get a second hand Austin 7 car" [to power a generator] "for the electricity and light". The remoteness of the site was such that some eyebrows had been raised, she says, about the wisdom of the venture: surely none would be raised by any of those far-seeing people who could see what was coming in relation to the growth of car ownership. In 1920 the number of private cars registered was 200,000; in 1930 it was one million and by the outbreak of war in 1939 it had nearly doubled.

In the late 1920s perhaps the remoteness of the site

* Esher Memoirs, Marion Barker, 1972.

34

Miss Barker, undated.   Photo: courtesy Surrey History Centre

Esher Filling Station, c1948 (the ballroom is now a showroom).
Photo: courtesy Elmbridge Museum

may have given a feeling of riskiness. Certainly, there were problems with carriageway repairs to the by-pass which Miss Barker refers to as a nuisance. Even if business was slow at first, the site was excellent; according to Anita Witten, the Road Board published traffic flow levels in 1930/31 of some 7000 vehicles a day using the by-pass. To build a freehold filling station on that site at that time was an amazingly shrewd investment. That the investment was made, not by a rich oil company but, by Miss Barker and her sick cousin, neither of whom had either training for business or experience of it, makes it a very interesting story.

Miss Barker's memoir contains several vignettes which are very illuminating to our story:

"Bit by bit we engaged a mechanic and another petrol hand... and we succeeded better and better, especially with petrol sales which were really assuming very large quantities, especially at the week-ends when we were selling in thousands of gallons.

Then the railway was built [she meant the station] *which was most fortunate and a great surprise to us as some builders got a permit for developing the land, which consisted of vast fields around us. This was of course a gold mine for us of the most unexpected and very welcome type.*

Presently we felt that we should prepare for the 2000 or more inhabitants who would be coming to the new village called Hinchley Wood within the next two or three years.

Up went the houses and in came the people – our new customers, they were all most decent folk; journalists, heads of banks, and head clerks ..."

Miss Barker, it seems to me, was the sort of woman who was going to succeed whatever she put her mind to. She had had an extremely long and unusual exposure to

bright and successful people and her story shows signs of natural instincts. The story of the arches illustrates the point. Everyone remembers the arches of EFS if they saw them before they were demolished. In submitting the plans to Esher Council for the new filling station, Miss Barker's architects had asserted that they wished to demonstrate their client's desire to prove that it was possible to erect such a building which would be attractive.

But it didn't happen without an intervention from Miss Barker. According to her, the first design by her architect was rejected because: "They looked like railway arches." Miss Barker must have liked the concept, however, because she had them redesigned, she says, making them a little taller and giving them a hint of the orient. The result was the distinctive architectural feature (quite the best of a filling station) whose image impressed itself on the growing number of motorists travelling up and down the by-pass, as well as the new residents of Hinchley Wood.

Esher Filling Station, c1965, now re-branded "Henlys".
Photo: courtesy Elmbridge Museum

During the 1930s, and into the post-war period, until EFS closed (except during the war when war-work was conducted) the filling station became a successful retailer of new and second-hand cars. All this came to an end when changes in the market-place meant that the site was no longer big enough.

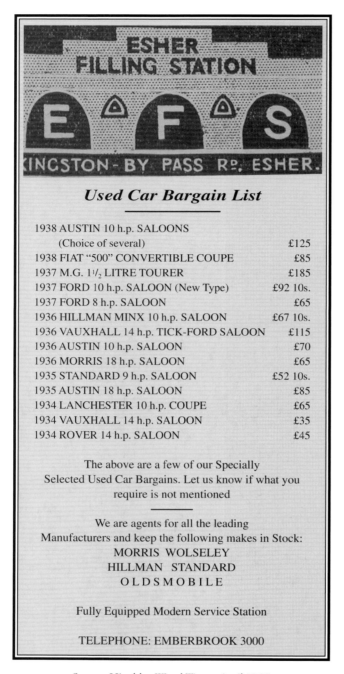

ESHER FILLING STATION

EFS

KINGSTON - BY PASS Rᴰ. ESHER.

Used Car Bargain List

1938 AUSTIN 10 h.p. SALOONS	
(Choice of several)	£125
1938 FIAT "500" CONVERTIBLE COUPE	£85
1937 M.G. 1½ LITRE TOURER	£185
1937 FORD 10 h.p. SALOON (New Type)	£92 10s.
1937 FORD 8 h.p. SALOON	£65
1936 HILLMAN MINX 10 h.p. SALOON	£67 10s.
1936 VAUXHALL 14 h.p. TICK-FORD SALOON	£115
1936 AUSTIN 10 h.p. SALOON	£70
1936 MORRIS 18 h.p. SALOON	£65
1935 STANDARD 9 h.p. SALOON	£52 10s.
1935 AUSTIN 18 h.p. SALOON	£85
1934 LANCHESTER 10 h.p. COUPE	£65
1934 VAUXHALL 14 h.p. SALOON	£35
1934 ROVER 14 h.p. SALOON	£45

The above are a few of our Specially
Selected Used Car Bargains. Let us know if what you
require is not mentioned

We are agents for all the leading
Manufacturers and keep the following makes in Stock:
MORRIS   WOLSELEY
HILLMAN   STANDARD
O L D S M O B I L E

Fully Equipped Modern Service Station

TELEPHONE: EMBERBROOK 3000

Source: Hinchley Wood Times, April 1939
(Elmbridge Museum)

The modern filling station on the EFS site.

The Hinchley Wood Hotel

The Hinchley Wood Hotel opened for business on 2 June 1932. The event was marked by an inaugural lunch hosted by the owners, Watney, Coombe and Reid: a name which has disappeared into history, as has indeed the hotel. The site became locally infamous in 1998 when McDonald's plans to turn it into a drive-to restaurant was stoutly resisted and famously defeated by the residents of Hinchley Wood.

Hinchley Wood Hotel, c1950s.   Photo: courtesy Elmbridge Museum

Originally, the Hotel was a splendid affair. It was built at a reported cost of £14,000, a figure which, even though it probably included the cost of a high grade fit-out, was a handsome sum: the equivalent of nearly 10 detached houses in, say, Hillcrest Gardens. It was a response to the new market created by the motorist: it was a creation of its age known in the 1930s as a "road house". It was not designed as a village pub; although it was one, and served this purpose for 50 years, the site it occupied was just too big to avoid it being swallowed by big business: ultimately it became just a piece of real estate, to be re-developed as flats.

HINCHLEY WOOD

◆

THE PERFECT HOTEL.

◆

Luncheon to Mark Opening at
Hinchley Wood.

Surrey Comet: 4 June 1932

In 1932 it was quite different. It was described by the Surrey Comet, in their report on the opening day as: "a splendidly constructed building of red brick." It occupied a fine site opposite EFS (now the Shell filling station). There were good lines of sight of the building from both directions from the by-pass giving it an imposing position which was attractive to passing trade. Vehicular access was always from Manor Road North, even though there was a pedestrian access from the by-pass.

Hinchley Wood Hotel, c1960s.   Photo: courtesy Elmbridge Museum

The licence for the premises, in some quirk of the day, was transferred from the White Lion in Esher. The significance of this is lost, unlike the mild euphoria displayed by the magistrate who granted the licence: "The combined efforts of all concerned have produced what might be called a perfect hotel." It was said to be among the finest of its kind in Surrey; in its day it almost certainly was. The hotel was described as having: "A well equipped dining room, a public bar as fine and spacious as the average saloon bar, and the saloon bar itself is comfortably and luxuriously fitted, with armchairs uphol-

The last pub sign of the former Hinchley Wood Hotel, 2002.

stered in crimson leather." These chairs survived at least into the 1960s when I was drinking there.

According to research done by Anita Witten (sourced from the AA Handbook of 1933) breakfast at the hotel cost from 2/- to 2/6d; cold lunch 2/-, hot lunch 2/6d; tea from 1/- to 1/6d and high tea, 2/6d; dinner was 3/6d. Until I was researching this book, I had never been able to find anyone who could confirm the use of the hotel by guests for overnight accommodation: Roger Allen, a former resident of Hinchley Way, tells me that before he moved into the district, when he worked for the Milk Marketing Board in the Midlands, he lodged at the hotel in 1958 when he was visiting Thames Ditton.

In the 1960s, from my own knowledge, and quite likely well before that too, the restaurant had a fabulous reputation; for reasons which were never clear at the time, it closed down in the late 1960s or early 1970s and the head waiter, Charles, took many of his customers to his own restaurant which he opened in Horsley. The closure of the restaurant was the thin end of the wedge and the long decline of the place can be marked by this event.

In the 1960s, "Let's meet at The Hinch" was the usual cry when all my friends and acquaintances needed a rendezvous so that a review of options and a decision could be made on the array of available entertainments on any particular Saturday evening. The Hinch was regarded with fondness by us youngsters and by older people too. We had done our under-age drinking there and opening time on a Sunday (7.00 pm) was very conveniently timed: after Evensong finished, the public bar beckoned. As we became older, we were allowed on to the snooker table: a pleasurable local amenity like a snooker table was never going to survive when it was taking space away from restaurant meals!

Site of Hinchley Wood Hotel, 2002.

When McDonald's admitted defeat the site was sold to Taywood Homes who achieved planning consent for 60 units of sheltered housing accommodation, but, regrettably, with no community facilities. This will give welcome diversity to the housing stock: at the cost of there now being no village pub or family eating place, the price is heavy. Time and change were the hotel's enemies; being too big as a village pub, the market decided its fate. Once the pub/restauant closed, it couldn't survive the redevelopment option.

Shop Premises in Hinchley Wood : 1962

Station Approach
United Dairies
Anne Shepherd School of Dancing
(opened 12 November 1945)
Langstones (Newsagent)
Papworth (Greengrocer)
Paul's Restaurant (was The Orange Tree Café)
Searle's (Grocers)
Patricia Stevens (Ladies Hairdresser)
Maurice Webb (Estate Agent)
Esher School of Motoring
Westminster Bank
Cooper (Radio, Television & Electrical)
E R & M J Cake Specialists (Baker: otherwise known as Ted Missing)
A.S. Pink & Son (Butcher)
H A Roberts (Baker: shortly to become Floral Nurseries)
Walton, Hassell & Port (Grocer)
EFS Motors (Showroom)

Manor Road North
Hinchley Wood Wine & Spirit Cellars
Martin & Scamell (Auctioneers)
Wallis Jones (Pharmacist)
Platt's Stores Ltd (Confectioner)
Platt's Stores Ltd (Grocer)
Foster (Library and Post Office)
Baldwin Bros (Butcher)
La Boutique (Ladies' Outfitter)
Hinchley Cleaners
C & A Blake (Boot & Shoe)
N L Choules (Greengrocer)
B C Inman (Confectioner)
Coopers Stores (Wool store)
Coopers Stores (Ironmonger)

Manor Drive
Floral Nurseries

Source: Kelly's Directory, 1962

Site of Hinchley Wood Hotel, 2002.

The shops

The shops were developed by Crouch, starting on the north side of Station Approach. They were considered at the time to be "architecturally very satisfactory": they are still. Unsurprisingly, one of the first shops to open was the newsagent which probably opened early in 1931. When a Surrey Comet representative visited Hinchley Wood in July of that year he found a considerable discontent owing to the lack of postal facilities: there was no post office so parcels, registered letters and telegrams could not be dealt with locally; there was no public telephone and the letter box was frequently full. The first of many of Hinchley Wood's petitions was organised by Mr. North, the newsagent, and was signed by 250 people, the population of Hinchley Wood being reckoned at the time to be about 300. By November 1931, Mr. and Mrs. North had been appointed sub-postmasters and part of their shop was converted for the purpose. This, of course, is where the present newsagent is (Langstones after Mr. North) the post office having moved sometime after the war.

Another early occupier* was J. A. Keen, probably in 1932, who operated a dairy business at No. 1 Station Approach (taken over by United Dairies after the war). Mr. Keen operated from Manor Farm and was destined to play a role in the provision of a site for the Church.

The shops were built in phases and were substantially finished by 1937 or 1938, by which time the local population could support a viable local shopping parade. Lloyds Bank came in 1933 and Westminster Bank in 1936. A few other names from the 1930s will be remembered by older residents: Walton Hassell & Port, grocers; The Orange Tree Café, often used by the Residents' Association for their meetings, and still there in the 1950s; Cooper's Stores, the ironmongers: Hinchley Wood had been and continues to be blessed with a good ironmonger, and, of course, Mr. Wallis Jones has left his name on the pharmacy even until today.

Most of the pre-war names have disappeared: even a snapshot in 1962 reveals that the names have all gone except Floral Nurseries and Wallis Jones: the list is shown above.

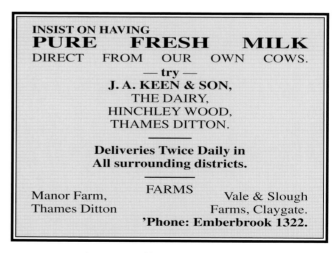

INSIST ON HAVING
PURE   FRESH   MILK
DIRECT   FROM   OUR   OWN   COWS.
— try —
J. A. KEEN & SON,
THE DAIRY,
HINCHLEY WOOD,
THAMES DITTON.

**Deliveries Twice Daily in
All surrounding districts.**

FARMS
Manor Farm,   Vale & Slough
Thames Ditton   Farms, Claygate.
'Phone: Emberbrook 1322.

Source: Hinchley Wood Times, 1939
(Elmbridge Museum)

---

* Much of my information on shops has come from Anita Witten.

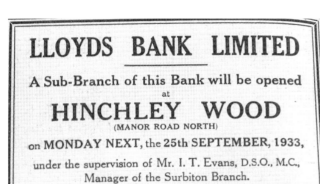

Lloyds Bank opens, 1933.   Source: Surrey Comet

The scale and scope of the shopping offering in Hinchley Wood seems to have been gauged correctly from the beginning and to have remained right, more or less, to the present day, when the wider retail scene is scarcely recognisable (and food shopping not at all) from the 1930s. There has been, over the years, no problem void premises. A cinema, which was included in the town plan in the area of the builders' merchant, was never seriously contemplated for building: conversely, the Church was not town planned, and had much difficulty getting a site.

The Milk Marketing Board

The Milk Marketing Board, which was headquartered in Thames Ditton by Giggs Hill Green from 1939 to 1994, is relevant to our story in the context of the important local employment opportunities it gave to Hinchley Wood people: at all levels from senior management to clerical jobs. Many a Hinchley Wood household has had either a breadwinner employed by the Board or a second income from either full or part time work. The irony is that it was all an accident in planning terms. As we have seen, Hinchley Wood was built for people who earned their livings by travelling to work somewhere else, usually London. In the original plans that were drawn up for Hinchley Wood, no thought was given to local employment: the Board moved to Thames Ditton simply because there was an available site!

**SAVED FROM ESTATE
DEVELOPER**

◆

**Ditton Grange to be
Milk Marketing Board's Headquarters**

◆

**SAVILE HOME FETCHES
£29,500**

Surrey Comet: 2 July 1938

The Board had begun life in 1933 as a producer co-operative backed by statutory authority. The milk marketing plan was to be implemented by the Board, who became the monopoly buyer of milk. The Board, owned by the milk producers, had as its prime function the marketing of milk to the consumer in England and Wales.

In reporting the Board's successful bid at auction of £29,500, to buy the 33 acre Ditton Grange estate, the Surrey Comet offered the news as a deliverance from more housing development. In this stance it was echoing the dismay with which it reported the proposed massive housing development on the Lovelace Estate land, as we shall see in Chapter 12. The auction was keenly fought with many developers in the room, hot to put up nearly 200 or so houses.

On the site were constructed the purpose-built headquarters to where over 1000 staff moved in September 1939. The building was not actually finished until the following year; evidently the materials required to fit out the building could only be procured on the condition that the premises would be available for a reserve hospital site during the war emergency. Over the next 55 years until it closed in 1994 the Board's headquarters graced the Portsmouth Road with its brick façade designed to a high 1930s architectural standard, reminiscent of many RAF stations built in the same period, and of the Hawker offices in Richmond Road, Kingston, which were actually built after the war (now demolished to make way for more housing).

The offices were demolished in 1995. Tesco wanted to put up a hypermarket on the site; this didn't get planning permission so the site was redeveloped for more housing but in addition community facilities were also provided; these included Giggs Hill Surgery where many Hinchley Wood residents attend.

Community hall

As early as 1932 the need for a community hall had become evident: in June of that year, when the difficulties of where to site such a facility and how to fund it, were becoming plain, Miss Barker announced that she was minded to build a hall on her EFS premises. This was welcomed and she built a 30 foot ballroom with a sprung floor for dancing which she hired out to local groups for meetings, dances and, importantly for the later part of our story, church services. Worshippers at St Christopher's know from handed down stories, that EFS was the place where worship took place in the early days but other readers may not know that it was this connection which gave the name of St Christopher to the parish Church: this was in recognition of the patron saint of travellers and EFS's role in supplying some of their needs.

Although the EFS hall served its purpose well, it clearly didn't meet all a growing community's needs: it was too small for some meetings: at the 1934 autumn general meeting of the Residents' Association "latecomers were unable to gain admission". Perhaps also, people felt that a hall in community control, as well as something bigger, was more appropriate than a privately owned facility.

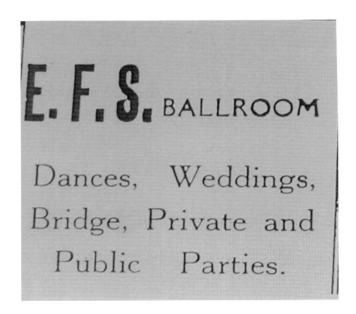

Advertisement in Hinchley Wood Times, c1934.
Source: courtesy Elmbridge Museum

munity hall can be attributed plainly to one omission in the town plan of 1929: no provision was made for a site for a church or parish hall; it was a bad omission. The successful struggle to overcome this void is the subject of later chapters.

Air displays from Ditton Hill, 1934.
Source: Surrey Comet

Although what is now the parish hall was opened in 1935, it was at the time serving as the parish Church and was not generally available at week-ends. In 1938 the Residents' Association decided to publish a letter in the Hinchley Wood Times to establish the degree of support for the construction of a hall as a civic centre. There is no record of the reaction to this letter neither to how such a project would be funded nor to where it would be located, but in any event the war intervened.

The EFS hall was ultimately converted into a car showroom, and the garage itself used for war-work. In 1951 a sub-committee had been working (we don't know for how long) on its brief of ascertaining the extent of the demand for a village hall and the possibilities for bringing a scheme to fruition. This was probably after Hinchley Wood Lawn Tennis Club had closed (to make way for the builders' merchant). In any event, the advice of the sub-committee was plain: "Since [our] appointment, it has been made known that a licence has been granted for the building of a new church. When the new church is built, the church council wishes to make the present church hall available for general use by all organisations and associations of the parish."

So, that was that: and has been ever since. That the people of Hinchley Wood had to wait 20 years for a com-

Ditton Hill Municipal Airport

Kingston Council, and its Chamber of Commerce, perhaps mindful of the town having averted its gaze when the railways came, thought it a splendid idea to have a municipal airport in the district: Surbiton agreed. There was already a minor air strip somewhere on Ditton Hill. In the early 1930s, flying was, of course, novel and air displays were a popular day out. Sir Alan Cobham, an aviation pioneer who gave his name to a leading aerospace company which pioneered in-flight refuelling, organised great air displays from Ditton Hill. Low flying was regarded as a nuisance by the Residents' Association but an airport? Here was something against which to object. A petition was to be organised but before anyone could get worked up about the issue, the proposed site was moved to the other side of Chessington. In May 1934 Hook Residents' Association wrote seeking co-operation in objection. Before substance could be put on Hinchley Wood's willingness to co-operate the subject seems to have died, never to be resurrected. This explains why Harold Everett, in his monograph about the Residents' Association, had to leave the subject, as it were "up in the air".

CHAPTER 7: CIVIC LIFE

Memorial Gardens, 2002 with flag at half mast following the death of HM the Queen Mother.

Hinchley Wood, as a recognised place for civic purposes was, at first, an indistinguishable part of Thames Ditton from which it achieved its own separate being. We have seen how Hinchley Wood distinguished itself with its town plan, and how its location was excellent with the builders promoting its green belt amenity; it further distinguished itself by taking pioneering steps in the collective advancement of community needs.

The origins of Hinchley Wood Residents' Association

In his account of Hinchley Wood Residents' Association*, Harold Everett, a former secretary of the Association, exposes the minor mystery, caused by the records of the early days being lost, of quite when the Association was founded. The fact that the 21st anniversary was celebrated in Coronation Year (1953) gives powerful support to the accepted view that 1932 was the founding year: the facts however do not support this. The evidence shows that Hinchley Wood Residents' Association was founded on 6 November 1931.

It must be remembered that in 1931, Hinchley Wood was not much more than a railway station and a few petrol pumps surrounded by several homes: nevertheless over 70 people turned up to a public meeting which was held on Friday 6 November 1931: to have achieved this attendance at its first public meeting is truly remarkable: and illustrative of how well the Association was to develop. The Surrey Comet gave a large amount of its space to its report on the inaugural meeting of Hinchley Wood Residents' Association on 6 November 1931 under its headline:

COMMUNITY SPIRIT AT HINCHLEY WOOD

◆

Residents' Association formed
with Social and Civic Sides

Surrey Comet: 11 November 1931

---

* A History of the Hinchley Wood Residents' Association – 'Minute by Minute', Harold W Everett, 1985.

The Surrey Comet reported tangible developments in October 1931. A minor reprt told of what was coming:

RESIDENTS' ASSOCIATION FOR HINCHLEY WOOD?

Owing to the rapidly increasing number of houses in Hinchley Wood it is proposed to form a ratepayers' association there. The sponsors of the scheme, Mr. Rosser-James and Mr. Pike, feel that in the future there will be many interests to protect in their district and that an early attempt to form an association will be advisable.

They are, consequently, collecting the names of the local residents and are gradually forming a committee to set the association on foot.

It will be called the Hinchley Wood Residents' Association.

Source: Surrey Comet, 13 October 1931

The report spoke of a unanimous vote on a resolution to form a Residents' Association: Mr. Rosser-James, who presided over the first meeting, was elected the first chairman and Mr. Royston Pike the first secretary.

Aims of the Association

The Association was to be open to all residents of Hinchley Wood: its object was to promote and defend the interests of local citizens. This was to be done on a non-sectarian and non-political basis. Here was the stamp of Royston Pike: he drafted the rules which were adopted. These footings have survived for seventy years; it was here, at this point, that the influence of Royston Pike asserted itself: that party politics and religion should have no place in the Association's affairs.

The sights of the early leaders were, of course, set at modest levels: they could attend to such matters as street lighting, local improvements and the preservation of beauty spots (all of which demanded much attention in the 1930s); and "protect against cemeteries" and other unattractive things being placed in their midst: there was never a suggestion of a cemetery but the Esher by-pass issue emerged in 1935 to derange the pleasant scene.

Mr. Rosser-James suggested the Association should have a social as well as a civic side. Reflecting on the first winter in Hinchley Wood, when those few people who had moved in had found it 'a not very exciting place', it was suggested that the Association should promote social events. A programme of events (dances, lectures, bridge) was started in 1933 and continued, amid great popularity, throughout the 1930s until war broke out.

Of the 10 members attending the committee meeting held in June 1932 (being the earliest surviving record) three are important to our story. Miss Barker (of Esher Filling Station, whom we saw in Chapter 6) was active,

still, in its affairs until early in the 1950s. Dr. Macdonald had a short but key involvement in the affairs of Hinchley Wood as its first member of the Council: we will come back to him: and Royston Pike.

Edgar Royston Pike

To my great regret I never met Royston Pike nor did I attend any of his local history lectures in the 1950s and 1960s, when he was still active in local affairs. No-one else since (there was no-one before) has made a bigger impact on Hinchley Wood affairs; this is not to diminish the efforts of those Residents' Association members or ward councillors in public service since! Not at all: it is simply that Royston Pike's contribution to public life in Hinchley Wood is peerless. It is because he so marked the origins of Hinchley Wood's secular life that I have dedicated this book, in part, to him.

When Royston Pike, with other far-seeing residents, initiated the Residents' Association, no-one could have known the enduring impact it was to have on the evolution of the administration of local affairs: it lives on today with its die still cast with the Royston Pike hallmark: non-party political public service to the community. Save for one exception (where a candidate resigned his party membership in order to qualify) the Hinchley Wood electorate has never voted on to the Council, any candidate who had a party affiliation. Writing, as I am, in a period where the non-party Residents' Association group has control over Elmbridge Borough Council, I can only regret that Royston Pike did not live to see it.

He died in 1980 at the age of 84. He had served on the Council for over 30 years being first elected, unopposed, in 1935 as a ward member for Thames Ditton. He was

Edgar Royston Pike, taken in 1953.
Photo courtesy of Hinchley Wood Residents' Association

chairman of the Council on two occasions and, at the time of his death, president of the Residents' Association.

On the Council, Royston Pike was able to indulge his literary leanings by being prominent in the work of the Library Committee. He started the Esher Library Lectures in King George's Hall and did much to initiate and encourage local history activities, being at the time of his death, president and formerly chairman of Esher District Local History Society. In 1974, as a permanent memorial to his service on the Library Committee, the title of the lecture series was changed to the 'Royston Pike Lectures'; a fine tribute to a man who, although by now retired from public life, had given so much to his fellow members of the community.

The 1933 local elections

1933 was to be a seminal year in the civic development of Hinchley Wood. Although it had been suggested at the December 1932 committee meeting that the Association should put up candidates for the March 1933 local elections, in the end it was a scrambled decision at a meeting on 1 March that six candidates should stand: these were Miss Barker, Dr. Macdonald and Messrs.Wayte, Martin, Singleton and Royston Pike. In went the nominations, which closed on 3 March: off to the printers went the manifesto (settled at a meeting on 9 March and which, sadly, has not been preserved) and then, hot-foot, to the second annual general meeting held the next day.

The Surrey Comet was quick to report on the close of nominations on Friday at noon. The following day it reported:

> ## SCRAMBLE FOR ESHER COUNCIL
> ◆
> ### 55 Nominations Yesterday for 33 Seats
> ◆
> ### 17 CANDIDATES STANDING AT THAMES DITTON
> ◆
> ### Polls in All Eight Wards Except at Stoke d'Abernon
>
> There is a scramble to be on the new Esher Council, which covers the districts of Esher, the Dittons, the Moleseys, Cobham, Claygate and Stoke d'Abernon.
> Yesterday when the time for nominations closed it was found that there were no fewer than 55 candidates for the 33 seats on the newly-constituted body, and only in Stoke is there a lone nomination.
> A fight was expected in the Thames Ditton Ward, but no one, least of all a number of the old candidates, anticipated that as many as 17 people would be put forward for the six seats. This has happened because of a sudden decision on the part of the Hinchley Wood residents' association to put forward a number of candidates.

Source: Surrey Comet, Saturday 4 March 1931

Although the committee minutes do not reveal either the rationale for putting up six candidates (there were six vacancies) or the sharpness of any friction in the debate, there could be no doubt that acrimony crept into the Association's affairs, perhaps for the first time. At the annual general meeting Mr. Riley, the chairman for the evening, conceded that there was 'an acute cleavage of opinion' among committee members on the issue of nominations to the council. One faction considered that because of the unusual situation of there being six vacancies (this was the year that Esher Urban District Council was formed by the absorption of Molesey and Cobham), it represented an opportunity for running a team of candidates and that, as a result, the Association's "prestige would be raised and its activities taken much more seriously by the various authorities". This was the view that prevailed in committee.

It needs to be restated that in 1933, Hinchley Wood had no existence for official purposes separately from Thames Ditton which itself represented a significant part of the Esher Council area with six out of a total of 33 seats. The electorate of Thames Ditton was 3730 voters of whom well under a quarter were from the 'new' Hinchley Wood area. Moreover, the single polling station was in Thames Ditton. In this light some of the committee thought that to put up six candidates was to risk making the Association look insignificant if it gained only a few votes. The Surrey Comet reported on the annual general meeting, at which all the above, and more, had been aired, as revealing a 'split'. It could not resist giving prominence to it in its report of the meeting:

> ## SPLIT IN RATEPAYERS' ASSOCIATION
> ### Over Nomination of Team of Council Candidates
> ◆
> ### MANY PROBLEMS DISCUSSED
>
> "We are lowering the whole tone of the district and of the association by nominating six candidates for the new Esher Council" said Mr. N Strother, a member of Hinchley Wood Residents' Association at their second annual meeting, at Esher Filling Station hall on Friday last week.

Source: Surrey Comet, Wednesday 15 March 1933

Guarding against *"lowering the tone of the district"* was a sentiment given frequent expression by the people of Hinchley Wood: they had come to live in a superior neighbourhood and they wanted to keep it so. Presumably, Mr. Strother was of the opinion that it would lower the tone if the candidates did badly: how else isn't clear.

Both Royston Pike (who had now been elected chairman of the Association) and Mr. Riley, the chairman of the meeting, wrote promptly to the Surrey Comet to smooth over the rumpus:

Sir, - with reference to the report in Wednesday's issue of the SURREY COMET of the recent annual general meeting of the Hinchley Wood Residents' Association there is no "split in the Ratepayers' Association," candidates – Miss Barker, Dr. Macdonald, Messrs. Martin, Singleton, Wayte and the writer – are fighting the election with the full support of the association, and we trust that to-day we shall be favoured with the votes of all ratepayers in Thames Ditton who "want to get a move on" in local affairs. Mr. Booker's advice at the meeting seems to have been given under the misapprehension that voters in the ward had two votes only, whereas they have six apiece.

-Yours, etc.,

E. ROYSTON PIKE,
Chairman, Hinchley Wood Residents'
Association

◆

Mr. T. S. Riley also writes to repudiate any idea of a "split".

"It is true that there was a difference of opinion in committee, but only on the question of the advisability of contesting the election in view of the lack of preparation and inadequate polling facilities. The Committee met the members as a united body and the latter, after full explanations had been given, enthusiastically confirmed the nominations." He adds "that the candidates are putting themselves forward as anxious to represent the interests of the Thames Ditton Ward as a whole".

Surrey Comet, Saturday, 18 March 1933

And so the voters went to the polls. The Surrey Comet reported the results:

THAMES DITTON. SIX SEATS

THOMAS CLAUDE COLLINS	809
LEONARD BUCKINGHAM	723
WILLIAM G. F. THOMPSON	476
WILLIAM JOHN ROBINS	422
SIDNEY HERBERT GALLOP	389
DONALD C. MACDONALD	383
Mary Hilsten Le Grand Jacob	381
Marion Julia Harriet Barker	270
Harold Victor Martin	249
Arthur Edward Wayte	232
Montague Francis Singleton	222
Edgar Royston Pike	211
Albert Joseph Mills	169

Electors, 3,730; voters 1,396; percentage, 37.2

Surrey Comet: Wednesday 22 March 1933

Dr. Macdonald was the only Hinchley Wood candidate to be elected: of the others Miss Barker did the best (she did not try again). Royston Pike, who polled in second to last, experienced his first and only election defeat; he was elected unopposed in 1935 and then never lost an election in his remaining years of public life.

Awakened citizenship

The editor of the Surrey Comet had noticed something different in the air for he announced that: "Hinchley Wood, quite a new residential district, is a bright example of awakened citizenship. Though its solitary polling station was by no means conveniently placed, it is claimed that practically the whole of Hinchley Wood went to the poll."

The election of Dr. Macdonald in March 1933 was a defining moment in the history of the Hinchley Wood Residents' Association: they had only existed for just over a year, since November 1931; building in Hinchley Wood had only started a year before that: and now the new settlement, not even yet recognised officially as having its own separate existence, had its own resident on the Council. Here were the upstarts whose enthusiasm and effectiveness in local affairs was to attract unfavourable (and undignified) jibes from Thames Ditton, as we shall see later. No matter: here was the moment that the Residents' Association announced itself to local government: in every election since, for nearly seventy years now, the Association's candidates have been voted onto the Council, always with the non-party mandate. It is entirely legitimate to claim a direct link between the control which the Residents' Associations group now has on the Council and that first victory in March 1933. The Hinchley Wood Residents' Association was the first to have a member on Esher Council: it was the first because none of the other wards had even formed residents' associations. There was none in Thames Ditton; none in Esher, nor Claygate. Thames Ditton was quick to follow (to counter the perceived influence of Hinchley Wood); Esher followed in the 1930s but Claygate's association was not formed until after the war.

Notice Board erected to mark 70 years of the Hinchley Wood Residents' Association, 2002.

Responding to pressure from the Residents' Association, it was announced in September 1933 that the Surrey County Council had agreed to the splitting of Thames Ditton ward into two: as a result Hinchley Wood was to have its own polling station (at the scout hut in Claygate Lane) within Thames Ditton No. 2 ward. The process of Hinchley Wood's emergence as its own separate ward, which was achieved after the war, had started. In the March 1934 Council election it was claimed by the Residents' Association that 54% of the electorate of Hinchley Wood had voted, but only 23% from Thames Ditton: such was the interest in local politics from the new residents of Hinchley Wood.

Dr. D C Macdonald

Dr. Macdonald was one of the very first residents of Hinchley Wood. He had Bergs build to his specification Brierly House (now No. 2) Hillcrest Gardens into which he moved, and started to practice as a General Practitioner and where he remained in practice until he left the district in 1936. It is convenient to relate here that he was succeeded at the surgery in Hillcrest Gardens by Dr. Clyde in 1936 who stayed there until about 1949 or 1950. In this latter year (at which time the house was unoccupied) Dr. Frederick Fraser (and his wife, Dr. Edith Fraser) moved in. Dr. Frederick practised here until he retired in 1981 and his wife was well known locally as a specialist in children's health.

Dr. D C Macdonald, the first member of Hinchley Wood Residents' Association to be elected to Esher Council, 1933.

Photo: Surrey Comet

According to Anita Witten, Dr. Macdonald had a graduated scale of charges for home visits (the National Health Service did not exist until 1947): a visit to a Montgomery home cost 2/6d, to a Crouch home 5/-, but to a Berg home 7/6d.

Dr. Macdonald was one of the founders of Hinchley Wood Residents' Association, being the vice chairman from its 1931 beginnings. As such, he had been active in its affairs from the very early days. Being the local GP gave him, of course, a prominent profile in the new and growing community. This profile had been enhanced by the lecture series he had commenced (but which in fact did not run for long): the first one being early in 1933 in Miss Burke's school in Manor Road North, on the subject of public health.

Dr. Macdonald was re-elected to the Council in 1934: in a more normal election he came top of the poll in a five way contest for two seats: his re-election in 1934 was also remarkable because he had resigned (unnecessarily) in order to stand again. The second seat was won (by one vote) by Mr. R. A. Moore who had been invited to join the Residents' Association committee only in late 1933.

The evidence suggests that Dr. Macdonald was not entirely comfortable with his membership of the Council. His disenchantment may have arisen from the buffeting he received in relation to his largely unwelcome idea of building a swimming pool and a golf course on Littleworth Common: but at around the same time a spat arose in relations with the newly formed Thames Ditton Residents' Association. One only had to mention the Commons and a chorus of objection would arise if they were to be touched. Dr. Macdonald's innocent suggestion caught the Hinchley Wood Residents' Association on the back foot by association: it would appear that he had not consulted the committee and they were obliged to steer a difficult course between not appearing to disown him but at the same time keeping its distance from his proposals. Difficult times were at hand.

A battle of words was conducted in the Council chamber and this spread to the correspondence columns of the Surrey Comet: some wrote in support, others to object but Mr. Martin, the assistant secretary of the Residents' Association, felt obliged to write in objection of an attack by a member of the Council on Hinchley Wood residents. When putting forward his scheme for Littleworth Common, surely, Mr. Martin wrote, Dr. Macdonald had made plain he was speaking for himself and not for Hinchley Wood Residents' Association. Why then, he pleaded, should a member "suggest that the feeling exists that efforts are being made from Hinchley Wood to 'dominate' the whole district".

Here we have the early signs of the 'upstart' syndrome: Hinchley Wood was just a small part of Thames Ditton but the influence of the young, and very effective, Residents' Association was creating resentment. Thames Ditton reacted by forming its own residents' association.

The spat with Thames Ditton

At its first annual general meeting in February 1935, the chairman of Thames Ditton Residents' Association posed the provocative question: "Will Thames Ditton and Weston Green become a suburb of Hinchley Wood?" That was the question that was worrying Thames Ditton

THE DITTONS

HINCHLEY WOOD A GROWING POWER

Ditton Residents Fear Its Widening Influence

Surrey Comet, 2 September 1935

and the matter was brought to a head by the prospect, at the next election, of Hinchley Wood having four members on the Council and Thames Ditton only two: a result which would be plainly absurd and a further reflection of the perception that Hinchley Wood was getting too big for its boots. Imagine: five years earlier there had been nothing there but Miss Barker's petrol pumps and now it was a cuckoo in Thames Ditton's nest.

It had all started so well, it seemed, when Councillors Macdonald and Moore had reported back to the committee of Hinchley Wood Residents' Association in July 1934 with their 'brief and amusing account' of their attendance at the first meeting of Thames Ditton and Weston Green Residents' Association. The spat developed over a failed deal to fix the candidates' list for the 1935 election. It is scarcely possible to discern from between the lines of the committee minutes just what happened, but it is reasonable to infer, from all the evidence, that Thames Ditton reasserted its influence at the elections and gave Hinchley Wood a bit of a hiding. At the inquest in April 1935 there was a "long and animated discussion" regarding the policy of the Association prior to the election: the secretary had felt obliged to resign because of the issue but the nature of the issue is not revealed.

In November 1935, Dr. Macdonald announced his retirement from the Council, and that he was leaving Hinchley Wood to take up again private practice in Harley Street.

As Dr. Macdonald exits from the Hinchley Wood story, it is the start of Royston Pike's career on the Council for he was elected unopposed to fill the gap left by Dr. Macdonald. He must have targeted a 'peace' with Thames Ditton because in March 1936, at the fifth annual general meeting, he was able to say that agreement had been reached with Thames Ditton Residents' Association that there should be a concordat on representation on Esher Council: Thames Ditton 4 seats; Hinchley Wood 2. Royston Pike had brokered a common sense deal of co-operation between the two associations which has endured to the present day. As the chairman of Thames Ditton Residents' Association remarked: "Perhaps the fact that Hinchley Wood had made an effort to establish itself as an entity – at the cost of absorbing Thames Ditton – had been all to the good as Thames Ditton had now been awakened to its responsibilities."

Good co-operation was quickly re-established when in May 1935 an invitation was received from Thames Ditton Residents' Association inviting co-operation, along with Molesey Residents' Association, in choosing a candidate for the Surrey County Council election. The meeting went further, bending backwards almost to smooth relations with Thames Ditton. A resolution was passed, in the generality, to the effect that Hinchley Wood Residents' Association was keen to co-operate with similar organisations in the area: but, to put flesh on this policy, Thames Ditton Residents' Association was to be invited to a joint meeting of the two general committees. Peace had broken out.

The row had been smoothed over just in time, for in November 1935 Thames Ditton made overtures to Hinchley Wood about joint action in relation to the newly proposed Esher by-pass (see Chapter 9). Now that Hinchley Wood had been shown that other parts of the district could assert themselves too, the rest of the 1930s story shows strong and effective co-operation on shared agendas between the various residents' groups.

"Hinchley Wood Times"

In October 1932 the Manor Press of Ashford wrote to the Association stating that they were about to launch their new monthly local paper "The Hinchley Wood Times" for free house-to-house distribution. Mr. North, the newsagent, arranged the newspaper delivery. This must have been one of the earliest examples of the current vogue for free newspapers. The publisher wanted the Association to affirm its agreement to a statement being made in it to the effect that it was published under the Association's auspices: what this meant wasn't spelled out but clearly it would give the newspaper a perceived respectability.

The risk (of exploitation) was considered but agreement was given on the distinct understanding that no responsibility for the paper, financial or otherwise, was incurred by the Association. Moreover, and in tune with its own doctrine, the Residents' Association made it plain that the consent would be withdrawn if a partisan position were taken by the newspaper on matters of politics or religion.

The benefit was, presumably, that: at no cost to itself, the Association would have available to it an organ of communication to every household whether containing members or potential members. The evidence shows that this facility was amply used, for the proceedings of general meetings of the Association were written up at length in the newspaper and these are preserved as the record of the meetings in the Association's archive.

Sadly, no complete archive of the newspapers has been retained. Some fragments exist at Elmbridge Museum, the most notable of which is the notice appearing in a 1941 edition saying that it would be the last as long as the war conditions prevailed: it did not reappear after the war. The loss of the eight years or so of copy from the key period in the emergence of Hinchley Wood is much regretted; who knows what treasure was within its pages?

The 1930s agenda

Much of the business which was dealt with by the Residents' Association committee in the 1930s can be categorised as housekeeping and discussed here, below: or they are such big issues that they are worthy of their own place in this story. There were four big problems which were the important and protracted issues of Hinchley Wood in the 1930s; they were all tackled by the Association in the 1930s (bar one) and then picked up again as they re-emerged for settlement in the post-war decades. The 'land between the railway lines' was a story which lasted nearly 25 years (and then had a 1990s sequel) and is told in Chapter 10: the Esher by-pass, quite the biggest issue tackled by the Association in the 1930s, is referred to in Chapter 9: the story of the averting of the development of the Lovelace Estate is told in Chapter 12 but the Association's work on this was all post-war: the work of the Association on schools was another 20 year story and this is told in Chapter 11.

Of the domestic matters, there are three which featured continuously in the 1930s: first, "the perennial problem of the Kingston by-pass" and in particular the dangerous junction with Manor Road. It was, throughout the 1930s, a more or less permanent agenda item for the committee and, deservedly so, for death and injury on the by-pass were never far away. Secondly, there was the issue of rating valuations, on which subject Hinchley Wood people were on the horns of a dilemma: a high valuation of property would be the mark of an elevated district, but it brought with it higher rates bills! The third perennial issue was the state of the residential roads and footpaths

Roads and footpaths

The issue of roads and footpaths had not been put to bed by the time the war came: parts of Claygate Lane and Greenways hadn't been made up and we have already heard how the issue of a part of Cumberland Drive's footpath wasn't fixed until the 1960s. Another hangover was the building of a footpath to Medina Avenue from the station which wasn't built until after the war.

All the main four builders came in for complaint on the issue of roads generally. Sometimes (probably very often) there were disputes about liability to pay for making up and future responsibility, and even street lighting. It is all so well regulated today that it is hard to understand the disorder of the 1930s. The new householders wanted everything tidy, naturally enough; the builders didn't want to pay if they co uld shuffle the cost on to the Council, or the frontagers. The Council and the builders were in dispute over the specifications for the roads, footpaths and lighting. The Council would not accept the cost unless the evidence proved their liability and, quite properly, they did their best to make the builders meet their obligations.

The Residents' Association had to note the many complaints and try to find a route out of the muddle. Often the householders ended up contributing, perhaps more than they had expected, particularly on street lighting

---

STATE OF ROADS.

Roads are still a frequent cause of complaint and vituperation on the Berg and Crouch estates. In both cases the builders have ignored requests and protests; apparently their energies and interest are now taken up by other estates. The Rose estate, on the other hand, is much better in this respect; and we whose shoes and tyres are rasped and torn by stones, whose progress is one long stumble from pot-hole to pot-hole, look with envy on our neighbours' solid-surfaced roads. By the way, while on the subject of builders, I may mention that Mr. Rose's care to preserve the "right of way" during his recent operations in Old Claygate Lane aroused favourable comment.

HAVE YOU JOINED THE RESIDENTS' ASSOCIATION?

Source: Hinchley Wood Times (Year unknown)
Elmbridge Museum

---

which, on the evidence, was very inadequate and underspecified. Ultimately, it was all sorted and many estates ended up with very superior street furniture. Some readers will remember the well designed square green lamp standards with lantern lights on top. They are now all gone, replaced with less good looking but probably more effective modern equipment. Hillcrest Gardens and Hinchley Drive still retain their red brick pavements.

Railway services

Although the subject of buses was often on the agenda, it was the train service which was the frequent cause of complaint: overcrowding and timings of trains was of more or less a continuum but which were issues to which Southern Railway responded satisfactorily. In 1933 a success was achieved which today would seem titanic: having already achieved a success in having the last train from Waterloo delayed seven minutes until 11:55pm, the Association wrote to Southern Railway pointing out the need for a second porter during busy periods. Our giggles should turn to gasps when we learn that to this request, Southern Railway said, "Yes".

STATION APPROACH TO BE MADE UP AT LAST

◆

The Esher Urban District Council Surveyor is now preparing plans and specifications for the making up of Station Approach, all the frontagers having agreed to meet the resultant charges.

Having regard to the lapse of time between the preparation of the plans and the actual commencement of the work in the case of other making up jobs in this area, it seems very likely that we shall have to wade our way to the station during one more winter, but, for what it is worth, there will be the satisfaction of knowing that, in all probability, 1936 will see an end to this foot-wearing eyesore.

Source: Hinchley Wood Times, unknown date in 1936

CHAPTER 8: TELEGRAPH HILL

The distant view to Harrow, with St Christopher's Church in the foreground, from the Claygate Lane footpath, 2002.

That we have arrived at Chapter 8, without discussing Telegraph Hill, is not to discount its importance: its charm continues to be an essential component of Hinchley Wood, but in a book which is about the origins of a 1930s settlement, many matters of importance assert their precedence: but now we can give it its due.

As an eleven year old, when my family moved into Avondale Avenue, the blessing of going to live in Hinchley Wood was very much disguised! I left behind what was an idyllic childhood in a simple village near Guildford where the post-war world went round according to the seasons and our childish pleasures revolved mostly round nature. Looking for silver linings, my mother was very quick to identify Telegraph Hill as a plus, even before we moved in; she was right and before long I was to acknowledge and enjoy its pleasures.

In the 1950s, Telegraph Hill was indeed to be a source of much pleasure for a boy. We used catapults at first but later we graduated to airguns. Camps were built; obstacle courses were ridden on bikes and in the autumn there was scrumping to be done in the garden of the then rundown but still inhabited Semaphore House: and we discovered gunpowder! I am amazed to recall what we blew up on Telegraph Hill! Truly was "The Hill" a wonderful place to have on our doorstep.

Claygate Lane, on the Claygate side of The Hill is only a path now, 2002.

Claygate Lane on the Hinchley Wood side of The Hill is an impenetrable medieval track, now replaced with a footpath, 2002.

48

The views

Unhappily, one cannot say Telegraph Hill is unchanged today: yes, the air raid shelter just in the woods above Hillcrest Gardens has gone but one thing is much more noticeably different: the trees around the open space at the top of the hill have grown up too much and the views from The Hill are not nearly as remarkable as they once were. The tree management work in progress as I write is very welcome but the thinning is only aimed at recovering the grassed areas.

While, thankfully, the southern aspect to Claygate remains open, the western and north-western views have been shut out by nature. When the Semaphore Line to Portsmouth opened in 1822, the uninterrupted view to the north-east and south-west was the reason the site was chosen for a telegraph station, giving Telegraph Hill its fame. There never was an eastern view from The Hill in modern times: it can only be seen from Semaphore House; I have been privileged to see it by courtesy of the present owners, Mr. and Mrs. Beverley Abbey. It must be one of the finest easterly views in the south of England. Originally, it was sited for clear line of sight of Coombe Warren; this it still has but it has much more. The whole of London opens up to the gaze, down the Thames

Valley to Canary Wharf: to wake up there on a sunny morning must be as good for lifting the spirits to prepare for the day as any tonic.

It is sad, I think, that no view exists for the public to enjoy of Chatley Heath tower, the next station in the other direction. I have had Eric Bartholomew, who navigated Lancaster bombers during the war, on The Hill with his compass. I think there are only about six or ten trees preventing the line of sight to Chatley Heath. It would be a good idea to open up this view: to erect a little viewing platform and, on Trafalgar Day, have Chatley Heath send the "England expects" message.

Esher Council buys Telegraph Hill

That The Hill is available to the public is attributable to some smart work by Esher Council. In December 1928 the Surrey Comet announced that the Council, knowing that development would soon be taking place, was going to acquire 25 acres of land on Telegraph Hill. The greater part of this formed part of Upper Couchmore Farm, including Semaphore House, then the property of the Banks Estate, and about two acres was acquired from the Speer Estate. The total cost to the Council, including the

The view north from Claygate Lane footpath over Avondale Avenue, 2002.

General view north from Claygate Lane footpath, 2002.

View north over Hinchley Close, from Claygate Lane footpath, 2002.

The southern slopes of Telegraph Hill, 2002.

The top of Telegraph Hill, looking south, with the Royston Pike memorial on the left, 2002.

The southern view from Telegraph Hill, to Claygate and Ruxley Tower, 2002.

cost of fencing, making footpaths, and compensation to the dispossessed farmers, was £6,400. It was plainly a considerable sum of money of the day: but has public money ever been better spent?

There was much praise for their action at the time. "Might we not have that testimonial framed? It is not often that Councillors have any praise for what they do," said a Councillor on hearing at a Council meeting that a ratepayer had written thanking the Council for preserving Telegraph Hill. The letter observed that future generations would thank the Council and their respected Surveyor and Clerk for what they had done to preserve this open space.

The Council applied to Surrey County and to London County Councils for financial help with the purchase of Telegraph Hill. This was declined: Esher was (and remains) exceptionally well endowed with commons and Surrey County Council clearly felt there was no pressing 'open space' need. But we should recall that in this era the County Council was bearing a heavy burden of road improvement costs. This makes Esher Council's decision to go it alone and buy The Hill all the more meritorious.

By the time all the formalities had been sorted out, it was October 1930 that the purchase was completed, just

as the new railway station was about to open and just as the first residents were moving in to their new homes on the first Berg estate. The Council took on the obligation to erect boundary fences and to divert footpaths so that they were consistent with public access. More permanently, the Council covenanted with the previous owners not to use the land for the erection of any dwelling houses or to use the land for any purpose except a "public park".

Horses had been causing problems in 1932. The Council's surveyor reported that horse riders galloping over the top of the hill were doing damage. To stop this he proposed to have a gate erected at once at the bottom end of the "20 feet access road" off Manor Road South which had been created when the land was brought into public ownership. That gate, or at least its successor, is still there.

In 1938 there was a report of negotiations being started, by Esher Council, with a view to acquiring additional land at Telegraph Hill to be added to the public open space. This land, which would have doubled the space open to the public, was located on the eastern side towards Claygate Lane. Sadly, no more was heard of this: perhaps with the war coming, land for agriculture was more important than public open space. Ultimately, this land was placed in the "Green Belt" but it has never come into public ownership.

The dairy business

When the Council acquired the land, a Mr. Richards lived with his family in Semaphore House, from which he conducted a dairy business as a tenant on an annual agreement. An additional 10 acres on top of the hill was let to Mr. Richards at a rent which Esher Council's Surveyor told the members was fair because "the public will have access over the land". Whether it was fair or not, Mr. Richards had the notion that paying rent was a voluntary activity: the minutes of Esher Council are littered with references to his unpaid rent. By 1935 he was two years in arrears and an offer to pay it off at a discount was accepted by the Council; the next year he was in arrears again!

The Council seems to have been on the wrong end of dealings with that tenant of Semaphore House. In 1933 there were problems with the water supply which was, of course, critical to the dairy business. The Council spent £21 on a deep well pump that could bring water up from 40 feet below the surface. Later that year the rent which Mr. Richards hadn't paid on his additional grazing land was reduced by a half. No one I have ever met remembers seeing cows on The Hill. In 1937 Mr. Richards moved out and this was almost certainly the end of the dairy business and may have been the last time cows were seen.

Demolish Semaphore House?

It would appear that Semaphore House was vacant for a while after Mr. Richards moved out for there was a frightful fuss over the Council's decision to find a new tenant and a suggestion that they allow the use of the house as a tea room. The Hinchley Wood Residents' Association didn't like the idea at all and at their autumn general meeting in November 1937 they passed a most extraordinary resolution. The meeting resolved to ask the Council to reverse its decision and to pull down Semaphore House! Demolish Semaphore House? Can you imagine? This resolution does not look good in print. It is quite the worst position that the Hinchley Wood Residents' Association took on any matter I have seen: for I can find nothing in mitigation.

HINCHLEY WOOD

RESIDENTS PROTEST TO COUNCIL

◆

Objection to Semaphore House
as Tea Room

Surrey Comet: 22 November 1937

I suppose there must have been some reason why the meeting worked itself up into such a frenzy. It was an aberrational error which in a way gives insight into the mind-set of the Association at that time: "lowering the tone of the district" as one resident said famously, but revealingly, when six candidates were put up for election in 1933. Happily, the Council took no notice: how could they take the idea of institutional vandalism seriously? Ultimately, the house was preserved by the listing process: in 1984 its grade of importance in heritage terms was elevated to Grade II*. so there can be no thought of demolition. In my dreams I can see at Semaphore House a tearoom serving homemade cakes on summer Sunday afternoons!

Semaphore House today

In due course, Semaphore House was let to Fred Bristow who was employed by the Council and who, amongst other things, did maintenance work on the public open space. He lived there from 1938, with his family (in the 1950s he had a very disagreeable dog) until 1980. The house was then left empty and subjected to vandalism of the more familiar kind. This kind of behaviour is as old as time and the Council was in error in taking so long to find a long-term solution: and in consequence leaving a remote and isolated, but important property vulnerable to violation (our attitude to such things is more rigorous today).

Semaphore House from Telegraph Hill, 2002.

In time, the Council decided that the best course was to sell the property for owner occupation. Even as the process of disposal by tender was being conducted, further material damage was done to the house. The only way to stop the decline was to get the premises occupied. The tender of Mr. Beverley Abbey was accepted and in May 1982 the transaction was completed. The house at that time was scarcely habitable: after considerable recovery work, Mr. Abbey and his wife, Hilary, were able to move in with their children in the following year. Much restoration work was achieved even later, for Semaphore House was in a very poor state: now, it has become a cherished family home of great charm. The house has a feel of great presence; obviously very old in its bearing: the original flagstones and wide oak floorboards give the floors an attractive patina; and the high ceilings a stately air. The Abbeys have made their own luck in living in and owning one of the most interesting family homes in the county, a house with an enchanting history and amazing views.

Semaphore House from Surbiton golf course, 2002.

There is no remaining evidence in the house of its former use as a semaphore tower except for the huge beam in the first floor ceiling, which carried the semaphore mast's weight. It is encased but both its dimension, and the fact that it runs across the house at an unexpected angle, give the clue that it had a special purpose: which is unconnected with the normal structural needs of a house. When doing some reinstatement work under the floor of the front steps to the house, Mr. Abbey found a large array of old bottles of a shape and vernacular blowing that suggest that they have been in the floor for a very long time: discarded there by a building crew. Many of the bottles have the mark of T H Hawkes of Thames Ditton in relief: others have the name R White. Both these names are very old soft drinks businesses. Hawkes is a business which was founded in Thames Ditton High Street in the 19th century but finally closed in the 1960s. R White was founded in 1845 in Camberwell, but had a depot in Thames Ditton.

An array of mid to late 19th century bottles found at Semaphore House, 2002. Photo: courtesy of Mr. Beverley Abbey

A "Hawkes" mineral water bottle, from Thames Ditton, of mid to late 19th century, found at Semaphore House, 2002.
Photo: courtesy of Mr. Beverley Abbey

Expert forensic work by Rachel Witton of the Bass Museum, Burton on Trent, has established that the bottles are from the mid to late 19th century. This allows the speculation that they were left on the premises during some early refurbishment work. The Semaphore Line was closed in 1847 when, with the railway now being driven through to Portsmouth, the electric telegraph made semaphore obsolete: Semaphore House was sold by the Admiralty when the station closed. By whatever means the bottles came to be abandoned in Semaphore House, it is intriguing to imagine some thirsty person walking to Thames Ditton to get supplies: because deposits on bottles didn't come in until the Great War, it was a one way journey for the bottles.

Royston Pike memories

Royston Pike loved Telegraph Hill and he often wrote about it: for example, in somewhat dated language he wrote:

"Overlooking the modern township of Hinchley Wood are the shadowy slopes of Telegraph Hill. For many years now most of the hill has been a Public Open Space, and day by day it is visited by numbers of people (and their dogs) that come from near and far to enjoy the opportunities it affords for "air and exercise".

It is an area of wild woodland and grassy plain, of oak copses and groves of chestnut and sycamore, where in spring the banks are crowded with nodding bluebells and in autumn and winter the ground is covered with a thick carpet of leafy accumulations, almost noiseless to the tread.

Whichever way you may come, from Hinchley Wood where there are two entrances, in Hillcrest Gardens and Manor Road South, or up Telegraph Lane from Claygate

on the other side of the hill, you may expect to reach the summit in 10 minutes or a quarter of an hour, but why be in such a hurry? If it's the view you are after, it won't run away, take your time, and associate every moment with a happy memory. You will find that half an hour is pretty good going, but an hour is ever so much better, especially if you do as I do, slow down and stop every now and again, just to stand and stare."

Here is another reference to the views which as I noted above have been lost to the growth of trees. In Royston Pike's day he tells of views of Hampton Court Palace, Claremont House, Christ Church, Esher; these have now largely disappeared behind the trees. It is such a pity.

Telegraph Hill is an obvious name but it did not appear on the Ordnance Survey maps until 1937; on earlier maps the name was given as Coopers Hill but no one seems to know about the origin and meaning of this name. It was still known as Coopers Hill when the Council bought it.

"Having entered the woods from Hillcrest Gardens," said Royston Pike, "wherever we look are trees of all shapes and sizes and of many different species. This is the 'Hinchley Wood' from which the settlement derives its name. It is a rectangle of woodland, occupying the northern slopes of Telegraph Hill. It has been here since the Middle Ages, and possibly long before."

According to Royston Pike, the earliest mention seems to have been in 1241, when the name appears as Hengesteshill. He wrote "In the language of our Anglo-Saxon forefathers 'Hengest' meant 'a stallion', … For hundreds of years this idea of 'the stallion's hill' has persisted in a succession of spellings, from Hynxhulle in 1332 and Hynkeshill in 1539 to Hinslet Wood on Bryant's Surrey map of 1823 and Hinks Hill Wood 20 years later, to its final form of Hinchley Wood, as printed in the Ordnance Survey maps of the 1860s."

Royston Pike tells us also of what to his mind was the most remarkable feature of Telegraph Hill, i.e. "the ditch". He describes it: "This runs along the brow of the hill facing Esher across the valley. Winter is the best time

"Lara" in the pre-historic ditch, 2002.

to see it, when the scrub has died down; it is still plain to see – an obviously man-made earthwork, four or five feet wide and a foot or so deep, with a mound or rampart on one side. It is not an agricultural ditch. It is a boundary ditch, as is plain enough when we see it forming the southern boundary of the wood." Royston Pike thought

"Cleo" in Royston Pike's pond, much silted-up, 2002.

it is much older than the Middle Ages: "It is ancient, quite possibly prehistoric," he said. The present owner of Semaphore House, Mr. Abbey, asserts that the earthworks are not a boundary at all but the remaining parts of an extensive series of fortifications. Mr. Abbey has uncovered earthworks on his own land near Semaphore House which, in Royston Pike's day were uncleared and probably unnoticed. I am attracted to Mr. Abbey's fortification theory not least because The Hill is so obviously defensible.

The pre-historic ditch, 2002.

In other writings of Royston Pike he tells us that: "Up the slope from Hillcrest Gardens to where on the left there is a glade of chestnuts backed by a massive fallen oak, there is a pond. So well hidden away is it that few people seem to be aware of its existence." To tell the truth it is not much of a pond any more. But, according to Royston Pike it is very old, and there was a kind of sullen beauty about the place that grew on you. This, I fear, was the site of the most spectacular use of the garage-made gunpowder in the 1950s referred to earlier; well we had just seen '*The Dambusters*' at the cinema!

Telegraph Hill in the Great War

Writing in the newsletter of the Esher District Local History Society*, Terry Gale tells of the fascinating former uses of the land on Telegraph Hill up the slope from the former College of Estate Management in Manor Road South. This land, says Gale, was in use as a brickfield in the 19th century and the early part of the 20th. There is a reference on maps to "Oaken Lane Brickfields". In common with other brickfields in the south east, it was taken over by the War Office during the 1914-18 war. Brickfields were used extensively at this time as ammunition dumps. In this case, however, the War Office, whether additionally or alternatively, used the land as a testing ground for tunnelling machines for military mining.

The Channel Tunnel connection

In 1919 the Channel Tunnel Co purchased for £6,150 a 12-ft diameter machine following a visit to the War Office Testing Ground on The Hill, where a similar machine had undergone tests during the war. It was felt it would strengthen the hand of the Channel Tunnel Co. if in possession of such a machine when negotiating with Parliament. Between June 1922 and September 1923 this machine cut 480 feet of tunnel at Folkestone Warren and, according to Gale, the remains of the machine can still be seen above the Martello Tower on the Folkestone-Dover Railway line.

The College of Estate Management took over the site in 1932 as a sports field and surveying ground. They say that one of the tunnels is said to have passed right under The Hill to emerge on the far side of Claygate village. They also say that when the Military left, they blew up

the tunnels' entrances with dynamite. According to them traces of these entrances were still visible, and members of their staff cleared away the soil from the largest tunnel entrance and exposed the timbers and strutting. These, however, were so rotten that any further exploration was stopped and the earth shovelled back to hide the entrance. A year or two later, after a very wet season, two or three large depressions appeared on the slopes of the hill where the pit props had rotted away and allowed the roof to fall in. This apparently made it easy to see the direction, which the line of the tunnel must have taken. Examination of the land today shows signs of extensive digging, either Military or from the brickwork days, but the untutored eye cannot discern the difference.

The Royston Pike memorial

After Royston Pike died in June 1980, the officers of Hinchley Wood Residents' Association cast around for a fitting memorial to the man who had been at the centre of the origins of Hinchley Wood. In November of that year, in a ceremony attended by a small group of Royston Pike's relations, the tablet in his memory, on top of The Hill, was dedicated. There was no other more fitting place. It is worth going to gaze upon it for, although Royston Pike could claim no part in the acquisition of The Hill, he merely enjoyed its charms for 50 years, the existence of it as public open space is a permanent example of the best in public service.

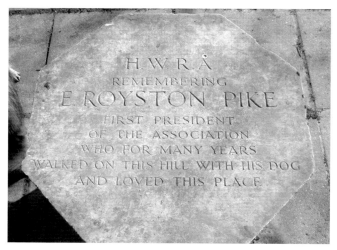

The Royston Pike memorial on top of Telegraph Hill, 2002.

* Esher District Local History Society, Newsletter, February 1985

CHAPTER 9: MORE ON BY-PASSES

The Kingston by-pass was a continuing story of the whole of the 1930's and it occupied a major part of the Residents' Association agenda; serious injuries were commonplace and there were deaths on the road virtually every month throughout that period. It was so bad that it was obvious to the authorities that something radical had to be done: additionally, in 1935 the Ministry of Transport raised the subject of a by-pass for Esher: in a way which was to be echoed in the 1960s and 1970s, the Residents' Association was considerably exercised by this subject.

The road system can't cope with the traffic

The inadequacy of the original design of the Kingston by-pass was compounded by the increase in traffic levels which, as they still do, took everyone by surprise. The by-pass, in a forerunner of the now well-known phenomenon, had created its own traffic through widespread development around its numerous junctions. The sheer closeness of these junctions brought upon the road a strain for which it had not been designed. It was even said at the time that the smart motorist was driving through Kingston in order to avoid congestion on the by-pass.

The increase in traffic was not just a local affair; it was not even just associated with the new by-pass. In every part of the country, except in North Wales and Scotland, traffic levels grew in the five years from 1930 by very nearly 50%. These census figures were reflected in the Surrey Comet's report in October 1935 on the growing traffic levels and congestion on the Portsmouth Road. Something needed to be done about the Portsmouth Road as well as the by-pass. For anyone who was familiar with the Portsmouth Road in the early post-war years, ie when it was nothing other than a very pretty winding route without much scope for overtaking, they can only be amazed at how narrow it must

have been in its early 1930s life before the pre-war widening schemes. But the traffic in Esher was mounting to unmanageable levels: something had to be done

"Hands off the Commons!"

It was in 1935 that the question of a by-pass for Esher came into serious consideration and, not surprisingly it became the biggest local issue of the whole of the second half of the 1930s. The whole business was very badly handled from the public sector point of view and the various debates got off to a confused start: the great obstacle to rational discussion was the passionate feeling that people had then, as later when the subject re-emerged after the war, for the defence of the Commons. Democracy, it would seem was advancing: when the railways came they drew their lines, as had the Romans, and that was that (more or less). In the 1930s no reconciliation had been made between the car and the environment; it hasn't been made even yet either, but in the 1930s it was not at all clear that the two could not co-exist. "Why?" people were asking, "do we need an Esher by-pass when all this money is being spent on the widening of the Portsmouth Road?" This was of course a huge red herring: as we saw in Chapter 2, Col. Butler of Esher Council spotted the flaw in the Kingston by-pass not circumventing Esher in the first place. The widening of the Portsmouth Road would never eliminate the need for a by-pass of Esher.

What was done was both inflammatory and easy to fault: was it the Ministry or was it Surrey County Council, or even the officers of Esher Council who conceived the route which was the most easy to hate? In October 1935, a proposal was put to Esher Council that a new by-pass should be routed to start, can you believe it? at the Marquis of Granby (where the Hampton Court Way had recently joined the junction of the Portsmouth Road and the Kingston by-pass – a junction now known as the "Scilly Isles"), to cut across the Commons and back to the Portsmouth Road south of Esher.

Accidents on the Kingston by-pass were commonplace: this one at the Manor Road junction was in 1939. Photo: Hulton Archive

ESHER & DISTRICT

BY-PASS ACROSS COMMONS

◆

Tentative Enquiry Arouses Protests
in Council

◆

COUNTY COUNCIL BEHIND SCHEME?

Surrey Comet: 2 November 1935

One outraged resident of Esher was quick to write to the Surrey Comet, under whose headline "Ghastly Proposal", he said: "… at the meeting of Esher Council, one of the most amazing suggestions that has ever been made was laid before the members. It was reported that tentative proposals had been made to build a by-pass road for Esher. It is suggested that the road would go across Littleworth Common, across Arbrook Common, and across Esher Common."

It seems almost incredible today that such an outrageous scheme should even have been considered, but they actually went further than that and recommended the Council "to proceed with discussions on the matter with those who have brought forward the proposals." Our spirited correspondent went on: "There is another aspect which requires some explanation. During the past year the Surrey County Council have spent large sums of money on the widening of the Portsmouth Road through Esher. Actually the work is not yet completed, and yet, although there has been no chance to test the results of the widening, the Surrey County Council now propose to by-pass Esher!" With a retort which was to be echoed for the rest of the 1930s, and when the Esher by-pass subject was revived in the 1960s, our correspondent concluded: "… to be told that if the Ministry of Transport has made up its mind to carry through this project and that nothing can stop it is a 'throw up the sponge' policy. Other authorities have fought and fought successfully any attempt to build by-pass roads across their commons. It would almost appear as if the little matter of "Hands off the Commons" which occurred about twelve years ago [in relation to the Kingston by-pass] has been forgotten by those who have inspired this plan."

Thus was resuscitated the slogan "Hands off the Commons" that was both appealing and enduring: but because it made no concession to the fact that, sooner or later, the traffic position in Esher would become untenable, it missed the vital point which was not: whether a by-pass is necessary, because it was going to become unavoidable, but: in all the circumstances, which is the least damaging route. It is interesting to note that the 1935 proposal was a forerunner of the equally hated 'link road' to the proposed Esher by-pass 30 years later.

An outraged public caused the authorities to think again. The proposal was modified later in the 1930s and in 1939 a public enquiry was held. This gave the local residents' associations the chance to cooperate and achieve a common voice at the enquiry. The joint association action group appealed for funds so that Counsel could be briefed: the point on which all associations were agreed was to defend the new route (which was much as eventually built) against all objectors for fear that, on grounds of economy, the Ministry would favour the Littleworth Common route: in preference to the unaffordable long route which by-passed Ripley as well. It is interesting to note that Claygate joined in this policy, by the Esher and Claygate Open Spaces Protection Association, a predecessor body to Claygate Village Residents' Association;

whereas, after the war, Claygate and Hinchley Wood failed to find any concordat on the same issue.

The public enquiry duly assembled in April 1939, but as is well known, the war stopped the project until it was resurrected in the 1960s.

The first dualling

Back in 1936 attention had reverted to the existing problems with the Kingston by-pass when the question of dualling the carriageways came under consideration. New concepts of road design were emerging. In November 1936 it was announced that the Ministry of Transport had authorised the first re-building of the by-pass with a 2½ mile dualling between New Malden and Tolworth. To remind the reader, as first constructed the single carriageway track was 30 feet wide. In the planning phase of the dualling project, the revised standards for highway width were changing quickly. At first, two 20 feet wide carriageways were specified (with cycle tracks and footpaths): then 22 feet wide: then in 1937, with work already in progress, the Ministry insisted on them being 30 feet wide. This exactly doubled the carriageway capacity compared with the original design: with no need, now, to consider oncoming traffic, vehicles could now approach the road junctions at their top speeds with their drivers only dimly aware of the impact of the extra speed on braking distances. This could not continue; the design evolution would have to go on.

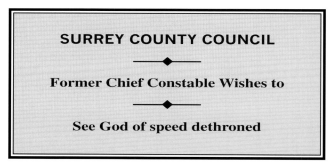

SURREY COUNTY COUNCIL

◆

Former Chief Constable Wishes to

◆

See God of speed dethroned

Surrey Comet 1937

Danger to pedestrians

During the 1930s the Pedestrians' Association became active. The Surrey Comet reported in January 1937 an Esher Council meeting at which there had been reported an alleged official admission that the "by-pass was a failure". A delegation from the Pedestrians' Association had been received by the Parliamentary Secretary to the Minister of Transport who was alleged to have admitted that: "The Kingston by-pass was the most dangerous experiment the Ministry of Transport had ever made. It had been a failure in every respect." Whether he said it, or not, doesn't matter; it was reported and everyone agreed anyway! As the member of Esher Council said, of Hinchley Wood: "There was a large residential area on one side of the road, and the shopping centre, schools and Church were on the other." Evidently, the

In 1937 the Kingston by-pass dualling began.   Photo: Surrey Comet

vehicles an hour negotiating with each other: 2,500 an hour on the by-pass and 1,500 an hour across it and it was proposed to separate these conflicting movements by the construction of a fly-under which was essentially like the one that was eventually built in the 1950s. The arguments which were ranged against the scheme at the enquiry do not look good in print now, motivated as they may well have been by some vested interest in relation to the loss of land. The most spectacularly wrong argument was to plead that an under-pass would be dangerous! The inspector was having none of it: "Every one knows" he quipped to the amusement of the hearing: "The Kingston by-pass was conceived in sin."

Ministry was not in favour of speed limits on that sort of road: because they could not be enforced. Instead, the Ministry view was: "… to favour pedestrian operated lights, islands, bridges and subways." The Hinchley Wood Residents' Association put up a continuous fight through the 1930s for safety improvements: their successes were short lived because new problems overtook old solutions.

The first fly-under

By the summer of 1938 a radical solution to the problem at the Ace of Spades junction at Hook had been proposed, a roundabout having already been built in 1933. A public enquiry was held to consider a 'fly-under': The German autobahn experience (which by now was very extensive) had established that vehicles wishing to leave or join a high-speed road had to have their own path along which to do it. We saw in Chapter 1 that the railways had discovered the same solution of fly-overs and unders, more than a generation earlier. This design feature was now to be used at Hook.

BY-PASS SUBWAY AND FLY OVER

———

Scheme Criticised by Surveyor at
Surbiton Inquiry

———

WILL LEAD TO EVEN MORE ACCIDENTS?

Surrey Comet: 4 June 1938

The 1938 public enquiry into the matter was told that in the 28 weeks to May 1938 there had been 28 people killed or injured on one two-mile stretch of the road. The high accident record of the by-pass was attributed to: the large number of premises which (incredibly) had direct access to the by-pass; the lack of facilities for pedestrians to cross; the inadequacy of the 30 foot single carriageway; and the variety of traffic using the same piece of road.

At the Hook roundabout junction there were 4,000

KINGSTON BY-PASS "FLY-UNDER"

———

Work to Start Within Few Months?

———

COMPULSORY PURCHASE ORDER APPROVED

During the next few months it is likely that a start will be made on the "fly-under" crossing, the first of its kind in Britain, which is to be installed on the Kingston by-pass at its junction with the Leatherhead-Hook Road.

The Minister of Transport has signed the order for the compulsory purchase of the necessary land and the "fly-under" is included among the works to be put in hand in the current financial year.

The fly-under was not built until the mid 1950s.
Surrey Comet: 31 August 1938

In 1933, a roundabout was built at the Hook intersection of the Kingston by-pass.
Photo: Surrey Comet

59

A roundabout at the Malden intersection c1936: still single track; notice the handcart. Photo: Surrey Comet

In August 1938 it was announced that the construction of the under-pass was to proceed. Unhappily, the war broke out before work could start, so another project was shelved. In the post-war years, once traffic levels had recovered to their pre-war scale, and new growth had commenced, the pressure on the Hook roundabout became chronic. I remember, on summer Sunday evenings in the mid 1950s, homebound traffic would often be backed up at Claygate Lane as it waited its turn at the Hook roundabout. The pre-war scheme, one of the first to be built, was brought off the shelf and finally built nearly 20 years after its conception.

...and congestion was becoming a problem, as this 1950s shot in Hinchley Wood shows. Photo: courtesy of Gerry Hall

CHAPTER 10:
THE LAND BETWEEN THE RAILWAY LINES

This 1930 shot of the early works to Hinchley Wood Station, shows the "land between the railway lines" under agricultural use. Photo: Surrey Comet

The story of the land between the railway lines is a long and difficult one which started in 1934; was resolved in part in 1939; but which did not end, after some unexpected twists caused by the war, until 1958. It ended very well for the Residents' Association, for they won their long battle to have at least some of the land dedicated to recreational use by the public.

The origins of the site

We saw in Chapter 1 how, when the New Line to Guildford was laid down, the junction with the main line carried both the up and the down lines. The tunnel under the main line, which was made to divert the up line so that it did not disrupt main line traffic, was opened in 1908. This diversion created a 35 acre triangular shaped parcel of land the boundaries of which were the main line and the up and the down branch lines: the only part of the boundary to this land which was not railway land was a thirty yard stretch where Lynwood Road now joins Claygate Lane and where is located the scout and guide joint headquarters.

Since the 1920s, when Esher Council bought eight acres of land from the Speer Estate, there had been allotments on this land next to Claygate Lane. This meant that there was no effective means of access to the land. The lack of a right of access, and the cost of building a bridge, if that was what it would take to open the land up, had ensured that this land was neglected when the Hinchley Wood town plan was worked up in 1929. It was not for want of trying by Southern Railway that it remained undeveloped until 1939.

The site was farmed before and after the railway company bought it. Quite why they needed to continue to own the spare land is not recorded. We saw in Chapter 4 how the railway companies were, on the one hand, piqued at not being able to benefit from the increase in land values brought about from their own investment in railway infrastructure and obliged to sell surplus land. Somehow, they had managed to retain a holding of 27 acres of land between the railway lines. Now that the 1930s housing boom had arrived, the Southern Railway was keen to cash in: but how?

The key was access: how could a road be built to give

access to a housing development when the Council owned the only land through which it could be driven? In the 1930s Southern Railway became anxious to realise the development value of their land and put forward the expensive idea of a bridge over the railway line.

The public open space between the railway lines (opened 1958): the 16.50 Waterloo to Guildford, fast, is on the down line; with Royston Court and Gibson Court in the background, 2002.

Development or public open space?

At a meeting of the committee of the Residents' Association in 1934, even before the Southern Railway scheme emerged, the prospect of building on "the meadows between the railway lines" was causing concern: the Association's councillor, Dr. Macdonald was asked to oppose vigorously any action by the Council aimed at facilitating development. The Association had in mind that the land should be dedicated to recreational use by the public.

Events seemed at first to be favourable. There was in 1934 a report of Esher Council discussing a proposition of a land swap to enable Southern Railway to develop their land. Several members at that time seemed keen for the Council to buy some or all of the land for public open space. Esher Rugby Club let it be known that they were interested in leasing some land if the Council acquired it. A few months later, as a way of rationalising its unwillingness to grant the rugby club a long lease, it was reported that the Council had no intention of buying the land: this was somewhat disingenuous for they wanted the land for public (not private) open space.

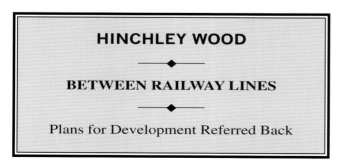

HINCHLEY WOOD

◆

BETWEEN RAILWAY LINES

◆

Plans for Development Referred Back

Surrey Comet: 28 November 1936

By 1936 nothing tangible had happened and the affair now took an ugly turn. At an emergency meeting of the planning committee of the Council, held in the holiday season giving the impression that a motion had been slipped through, it had resolved to allow the development of 216 houses on the site and, in order to get access to it, the building of a bridge and a ramp to it, from Manor Road North: but what was the Council getting in return for this compliance? It was never recorded just where this ramp and bridge was to be located but it would have been, wherever it was, unusually ugly and very intrusive.

The residents rose as one at their 1936 general meeting and unanimously resolved that a petition should be organised. It was couched in temperate terms and, for the most part, was entirely rational. In addition to presenting the petition to the Council, the committee was mandated to lobby support from the County Council and the Ministry of Agriculture (which backfired) and other associations which had as their aim, the preservation of open space. There was even talk at this meeting of public subscription to help fund the purchase but nothing came of this.

More of the public open space, looking north, 2002.

The Council takes note

The petition was successful in persuading the Council not to back the "bridge" scheme for development of about 200 houses. The full Council, mindful of the scale of objections, and led it would appear by some good debating by Hinchley Wood's Councillors who made much of the need for public open space, referred the scheme back to where it had come from, and into oblivion from where it never emerged.

Following this debate in Council, Royston Pike moved that the Surveyor be instructed to enter negotiations for the purchase of the land as an open space. This was carried and subsequently he reported back. The problem now was one of cost. The land had acquired a development value and the Southern Railway (who probably still owned the land) wanted their pound of flesh. The Council had no power, as it might in modern times, of arranging affairs so that the development value fell away. It was going to cost £600 per acre; a figure far higher than the Council had ever paid for open space (they had paid about £270 per acre for Telegraph Hill). Serious questions of affordability would now arise, but Royston Pike had a plan.

HINCHLEY WOOD

◆

LAND BETWEEN RAILWAY LINES

◆

Question Re-opened of
Preservation as Open Space

Surrey Comet: 30 June 1937

At a general meeting of the Residents' Association, Royston Pike explained that the Hinchley Wood Councillors had successfully moved a motion that the Council should go ahead and pay the price. But some juggling of the conflicting uses of the land had to be achieved so that

a solution could be found whereby the land could be divided between the competing uses of allotments, open space and development. Because of financial restraints, there was no way to finance the purchase, and end up with about 14 acres of open space unless the ransom value of the allotment site was realised: this would mean selling that land and moving the allotments to another part of the site. There then followed a long, and looked at from today's perspective, a very silly debate about how undesirable it was to relocate the allotments to near the station; obviously times have changed and in the 1930s, tending an allotment was not seen as a suitable middle class activity. Where they were to be moved to remained in doubt; what was now certain was that, in spite of their protests, the allotment holders were going to have to move; the ransom value of their site had to be realised. But no! The Ministry of Agriculture cavalry rode over the hill to rescue them: they refused permission for the allotments to be moved. This threw the whole project into confusion.

Later in 1937, the Residents' Association regrouped and the Council considered their representation that they should reconsider purchasing the site and that they should approach the County Council for a grant for the

Aerial photo of the newly built Surtax Office in 1948. It illustrates a number of points in relation to the land between the railway lines: the fly-under of the up line to Waterloo: the old boundary lines shown by the mature trees: land under organised food production: the large scale of the site.

Photo: Aerial Films, courtesy of Mr. Roger Davy

purpose. In the meantime the owner of the land asked for zoning density to be increased from eight to twelve houses to the acre; this the Council declined to do. At the autumn general meeting of the Residents' Association in November 1937, Royston Pike explained that the new intention of the Council was to sell only a part of the allotment land so as to make possible the construction of an access road from Claygate Lane which would allow a small housing estate to be accommodated between the allotments and the recreation ground.

Then came the gloomy news that, in spite of the offer of a grant of £1,000 from the County, Esher Council proposed no further action in relation to the land. This was probably not their true position but it did induce the landowner to think again and improve the deal for the Council. When the subject came up again in Council the Clerk reported that a contract for the purchase of the land at a total cost of £17,000 was "on the point of being signed". Esher Councillors debated for an hour and a half whether or not they should complete the purchase of the land, but finally they ducked it.

Royston Pike then moved that in view of the decision of the Minister of Agriculture, the land should be bought as an open space and that previous resolutions inconsistent with this should be rescinded. He said that now an entirely new factor had entered into the matter when it was reported by the Surrey Comet that the land to the east of Hinchley Wood and between it and Tolworth was to be sold for building. "Three thousand houses were to be erected there," he said, "and even Surbiton Golf Club was threatened." He was referring to the news of the proposed development of 700 acres of the Lovelace Estate (see Chapter 12). Royston Pike was clearly taking the line that the preferred option would be to eliminate the risk of more development, by the Council buying the land. This spirited proposal fell because it couldn't be funded.

A scheme is approved, but the war intervenes

A year later a scheme had been all worked out which appeared to satisfy some points of view; sadly, the means by which it was all thrashed out are not recorded. In July 1938 the Council approved a proposal for the development of 186 houses. The allotments must have been moved somewhere else (they are of course still there on a different site) and Lynwood Road was driven through (with Woodfield Road off it), to give access to the site. It rather looks as though Southern Railway had sold their land by now because, according to Anita Witten, the developer of Lynwood Road was Cuddington Estates Ltd, which had been building at Stoneleigh and Worcester Park.

In the event, because of the delay in bringing this land into a developable state, the war intervened to prevent any more than about 15 mostly semi-detached houses being built. The houses were probably first occupied in 1940. The developer must have been badly caught out by the coming of the war: he still owned land for 170 houses.

The prisoners-of-war camp

During the war the undeveloped land was used for food production, but several ironic twists were to come. In 1944 the Residents' Association emerged from its wartime dormancy and called a public meeting: the Ministry of Works had requisitioned the land between the railway lines for the construction of temporary offices. Esher Council had unanimously opposed this action, but it went ahead all the same. Then the Ministry changed its mind about the use to which it was to be put: the new plan was to house Italian prisoners of war on the site. It was time for another residents' petition to which Esher Council gave their full backing, with Royston Pike being reported as saying in emphatic manner that: "we didn't want Italian prisoners-of-war in Hinchley Wood!" I don't think this looks very good in print but he was successful: the plan to house Italian prisoners was dropped – Germans came instead!

This happened after the war was over, from mid 1945 until 1947. No protest would be considered by the authorities: gradually the message sank in. The prisoners had work to do and they were engaged, amongst other things, on clearing bomb damage, specially in Kingston.

Post-war developments

In 1947 the prisoners went home. On the site of the camp were built the temporary offices that the Ministry had requisitioned the site for in the first place. In 1948 the Inland Revenue moved in to the "temporary" headquarters of the Surtax Office which was built by men who had been displaced by the war. The temporary use lasted until just a few years ago to make way for more housing development following an extension to Lynwood Road into Bourne Close and Wessex Close. In their day, some 1,500 people worked in these offices.

I suspect that in the early post-war years, much of the land continued to be used for food production. It is also obscure who owned the land, but we can say with certainty that the recreation ground still did not exist. It was not until 1955 that the topic came back routinely on to the agenda of the Residents' Association which made

Close-up of Lynwood Road and Woodfield Road, 1948.
Photo: Aerial Films, courtesy of Mr. Roger Davy

considerable effort to have the land made over for children's recreation: but budget restraints got in the way until, finally, by 1958, the land was dedicated to public open space and the recreational facility which exists now. It had taken 25 years but the Residents' Association had finally achieved its aim.

There has always been a kind of separateness to this island site: the character of the pre-war houses is quite different from, say, the Montgomery estate semi-detached houses. If anyone lamented the use of part of the site for offices they were, ultimately, to be satisfied by the change of use from temporary offices back to houses. If nothing else the story illustrates very well the difficulties in the 1930s for local authorities to plan with any sort of secure legislative support.

Close-up of three huts of the Surtax Office, post-war austerity design, 1948.　　　Photo: Aerial Films, courtesy of Mr. Roger Davy

CHAPTER 11: SCHOOLS

War-time picture (note gas masks) of children leaving Mrs Betty Ashby's school at her home in Claygate Lane: Ann Ashby is in the centre; to the right, holding the "traffic" is her brother, John.

Photo: courtesy of Ann Ashby

The subject of schools was another whose story slips out of the 1930s, into the 1940s, it not being completed until the infants' school opened in 1951. It is not a story which reflects very well on either the authorities, or it has to be said, the early residents of Hinchley Wood. Royston Pike's record on the subject is good: famously, he said that some residents regarded schools like fever hospitals: "I suppose we have to have them, but can they be somewhere else, please?" When the builders were busy pushing the locational advantages of Hinchley Wood, on the subject of schools, they had less to say. In this chapter we examine the evidence, uncomfortable as some of it is: and finally, recall the impact of war-time conditions on Hinchley Wood's County school in the hard years of 1940 and 1941, followed by the Doodlebug summer of 1944.

No provision in the 'town plan'

I have already written in praise of Hinchley Wood in the context of its town planning being well ahead of its 1930s peers, but on the lack of provision for a site for schools,

Esher Council was at fault. When, in the late 1920s, the Council was having no qualms about zoning large tracts of land for housing development and local shopping facilities appropriate to it, not a thought was given to the zoning of land for schools (and, as we shall see, nor for a church site either). It was Surrey County Council's responsibility to plan for the expansion of school rolls and the evidence suggests that in the early days of Hinchley Wood, the condition of the Council's finances did not allow the issue to be addressed as early as it might have been. Between them, Esher as the planning authority and Surrey as the education authority, failed to plan at an early stage for the impact that a thousand new families in the settlement would have on either school rolls or, if their was no local provision, the movements of children out of Hinchley Wood in order to attend school. This omission was a long time in the remedy.

No organised data is available to tell us about the growth in the numbers of children involved, but in 1945 it is thought that there were 68 children of primary school age who were travelling to school variously to

Esher, Long Ditton and Thames Ditton This statistic tells us nothing useful about the population of primary school age children because, as we shall see, a large number of the children of Hinchley Wood were educated privately.

The Residents' Association position

What is the answer to this question? Did Hinchley Wood attract the type of residents who were likely to educate their children in the private sector? Or, did the new Hinchley Wood residents, finding that there was no prospect of local public sector provision, take the private sector route because it was available? It is beyond the scope of this book to enquire into this question, but it is instructive that there was no widespread community clamouring for a primary school until after 1945. Was this because of all the difficult travelling the young children had had to undertake during the war: travelling which was at times dangerous? Or was a social change taking place? A post-war family growing up in the 1944 Education Act era might have had different expectations; and they may not have found private education as affordable as it was in the 1930s.

In 1933, Royston Pike tried to take a leadership position on the subject of public provision of schools in Hinchley Wood: Surrey County Council had already informed the Residents' Association that no new school was contemplated. At the 1933 annual general meeting, Royston Pike urged that the meeting should take a position on this fact. The desultory response, varied from: "not necessary yet", through "put it in Thames Ditton" to "the country can't afford it". In the absence of public opinion, no community leader can be strong in pressing a case. The subject lay dormant.

In 1935, Royston Pike felt able to raise the subject again because a number of residents had mentioned the need of a Council school. He used this fact as a platform to go public on the issue: he wrote an open letter in the Hinchley Wood Times asking for residents to express their views. Clearly, he had less than full support from the committee for the minutes of their meeting record that if there was sufficient evidence of support, "endeavours *might* be made" (author's italics). Only six letters were received.

As the numbers of residents grew, more support arrived. The subject came up again at the 1936 annual general meeting. Support was not at all without objections: Royston Pike, it would appear, became tetchy; the minutes record him as having made "pungent" remarks about the selfishness of many residents. His leadership won the day: to the great credit of Royston Pike the meeting achieved an overwhelming majority for the committee to continue its efforts to achieve the provision of a primary school in Hinchley Wood. The committee wrote to Surrey County Council saying that it had a mandate from the residents of Hinchley Wood to press for a primary school. In 1951, 15 years later and after stronger pressure from residents, the primary school opened: it was late not just because of the war; it was late because the early residents of Hinchley Wood generally weren't interested.

The private school response

Unsurprisingly, the situation in the 1930s created a demand for private schooling within Hinchley Wood and a number of kindergarten and minor preparatory schools were started by local residents to meet the demand. Betty Ashby, a faithful, life-long worshipper at St Christopher's, moved into 96 Claygate Lane when the house was new and stayed there for the rest of her life: she started an infants' school there in the 1930s and, later, expanded into one of the Sunspan houses in Southwood Gardens. Clanricarde House School at 92 Manor Road North received planning permission in 1931, The Hill Preparatory School in Manor Drive in 1934, and House of St Nicholas at 94 Hillcrest Gardens in 1937. Mrs. Audrey Watson started a pre-preparatory school in 1948 which she called "Granchester House" in an allusion to the poet Rupert Brooke whose work she admired. The school is housed still in a property in Hinchley Way which was originally built as a hotel. The school started a close relationship with St Christopher's Church which is maintained to this day with annual nativity plays performed in the Church and services of harvest thanksgiving: moreover, one of the decorated windows in the Church (a nativity scene) was donated by the school: and after Mrs Watson died, as a tribute to her and as a mark of the school's lasting relationship with the Church, another window, opposite the other one given when the Church was built, was decorated in her memory.

After pre-school and preparatory school, these privately educated children would have gone on either to boarding schools or day schools in the private sector. Very few parents in Hinchley Wood in the 1930s would have been considering the local County schools in Claygate and the Dittons, which, ultimately, Surrey County Council decided to combine and locate in Hinchley Wood.

Squabbles over sites

While it fell to Surrey County Council to decide whether to build a school, to finance it and staff it, it was for Esher Council to choose a site and zone it. The first discussion of a site by the Council is thought to have been in December 1931. That this was too late is a point that has already been made: the result of being too late is that squabbles arose about where the site for schools should be located. Initially, the suggestion was that a site in Manor Road would be suitable: we don't know where. Perhaps it was the site which was developed after the war by Esher Council on which was built Manordene Close. In May 1932 it was reported that Rose had objected to the site, but why would he? Perhaps he was manoeuvring to keep the schools well away from his pet Cumberland Drive/ Chesterfield Drive/Claygate Lane schemes: was it Rose who suggested the schools should be sited on the Montgomery estate land, much of which, at the by-pass side, was not yet developed?

Naturally, Montgomery was going to object to that,

and this was reported to the Council in October 1932. Montgomery, evidently, suggested a site on Littleworth Common but this was easy to reject. The problem for Esher Council was how to accommodate the schools without changing the town plan. Is this the reason that in December 1932 it was announced that Esher Council had chosen Claygate Lane as a site for the schools? This was not an ideal site: it was as far as anywhere in Hinchley Wood could be from the station and, thanks to the original residents of Manor Road, there were no buses down that road (they had objected to a double-decker route because it would infringe the rural ambiance: the route had been suggested so that it could avoid the long arch on the Portsmouth Road), and therefore none that could be easily diverted to the school, as the 471 route does today.

Claygate Lane, both north and south of the by-pass marked the eastern boundary of Hinchley Wood and that is how the town plan had it. In the light of the other sites all having their objectors it was easier for the Council to allow the projection of the boundary eastwards to accommodate schools instead of cows.

Two schools on one site

As the 1930s progressed, Surrey County Council's attitude towards school provision changed. Perversely, Hinchley Wood was to be the site of a brand new central school, but there was to be no primary school. In October 1938 the Surrey Comet announced that a contract had been let for £51,000 for the construction of the "Hinchley Wood Central Schools" on the Claygate Lane site. There were to be two separate schools on the same site: one for Kingston Day Commercial School, the other for Hinchley Wood Central Council School; and separate buildings were erected for each, side by side. In September 1947 these two schools were merged to form Hinchley Wood County Secondary School. The building facilities have expanded over the years including a connecting building to join the two school buildings physically, to reflect their institutional merger some years earlier. Neither of the two secondary schools, newly opened in Claygate Lane, is to be confused with the primary school, built after the war, on its own site on the southern boundary of what was, by then, the merged secondary school.

Kingston Day Commercial School was an existing school, which, as its name suggests, moved from Kingston to be one of the two schools which started in Hinchley Wood in 1940. (In those days Kingston was in Surrey, so the site was the concern of only one Education Authority.) It became, after the 1947 merger, the Commercial Department of the County Secondary School. The other school was the mixed Hinchley Wood Central Council School: this was a brand-new school which drew about 360 boys and girls from five different local schools: Thames Ditton and Claygate Council Schools (both of which had separate boys' and girls' schools), and the mixed Long Ditton Church of England School.

Hinchley Wood Central Council School

The regulations provided that every school head should keep a bare record of the events which constitute the history of the school. The log was to be stoutly bound and contain not less than 300 ruled pages and was to be kept at the school. He or she was to enter in it, from time to time, such events that deserved to be recorded. The log was for the purpose of recording statements of fact only with no opinions, but for the historian, to have a complete record of significant contemporary events recorded chronologically is a rare aid.

The entries for example were to be made as required to explain the reason for the closing of the school on all occasions; record all important variations in attendance and deviations from the ordinary routine of the school. This was to be a great asset in writing up the impact of the war on the school, a brief account of which I give later.

The school log of Hinchley Wood County School, opened in 1940.

The Central Council School opened on 4 March 1940. The children were organised into nine forms of 40 to a class. The ages of the children were 10 to 14, the latter age being the statutory minimum school leaving age at that time. The headmaster was Mr. P N Hallifax who had a complement of 12 permanent teaching staff.

The children's first day at school was occupied by copying out their timetables and receiving 'stock'; very little of this had been delivered, except stationery, on account of the war conditions. Mr. C S Clayton, the chairman of the school managers (we would call them governors today) was an early visitor: he attended morning assembly on the third day. Five of the characters of our story were also school managers: the successive Curates-in-charge at St Christopher's: the Revs Robins and Vallins and, later, the Vicar, the Rev Newton Jones: Marion Barker of EFS and Royston Pike. On the fourth day of school came air raid drill: for the boys in shelter trenches (in any weather) in the playing field, and shared with the boys of the Commercial School: but the girls had special areas within the school building, specially reinforced for the purpose during construction, in which to shelter: As the school settled down to its routine, if anyone thought that the air raid practice was tedious, it was nothing to what was to come.

The log has been dutifully written up by the head teacher, as required, with the bare facts: deviations from the routine; official visits; any special circumstances of the day and any reasons for closure. It creates the foundation of a social history, for example:

"Mrs Bull is absent today. I received a telegram this morning that gave the reason as illness."

"Mrs Bryant telephoned to say her husband's home leave had been extended by one week."

"Miss George (His Majesty's Inspector) visited the school today."

"Miss Woods (Health Visitor) came today and saw all the girls present. Two girls were excluded suffering from scabies and one with a verminous head."

"Boys born in 1929 were medically examined today."

"Miss Kathleen Vallins [the daughter of Rev Hedley Vallins] *of 44 Greenwood Road started today a four week period of teaching practice prior to attending Training College."*

"All the girls were assembled in the hall today in order that Miss Lenton might talk to them on matters which are peculiarly the concern of the girls."

"Joy Champion became ill with a fit. Dr. Glyn of Hinchley Wood was sent for."

"Miss Shaw is absent today. I have so far received no explanation."

"Rev Robins [of St Christopher's], *school manager, visited today and stayed to have dinner with the children in the canteen."*

"Miss Tyler absent this afternoon. She received a telegram this morning from her parents in South Wales asking her to return immediately."

Thus were minor deviations from the routine of the school recorded. Sometimes there was an incident to be recorded.

"Colin Bradford (aged 13) was brought to school today by his mother. He had had a very bad record of attendance. He was seen by the Assistant MO last week who stated he was fit to attend school. Today, he ran away from his mother and left the school premises."

Evidently, another boy was sent to follow him, which he did as far as Woodstock Lane, where a policeman found them. What a to-do!

I spent about three hours at one sitting reading the whole log from 4 March 1940 to September 1945. I found it quite the most exhausting of experiences (yet thrilling) for I was utterly drained, emotionally, by the time I reached the end. It was written, as it was supposed to be, as a bare fact record with no literary embellishment, no adjectives to colour the text; there is no wearied turn of phrase: neither praise nor blame; neither despair nor happiness. Consider the entry for Thursday 10 May 1945:

"The last two days May 8 and 9 have been public holidays to celebrate the unconditional surrender of Germany and the end of the war in Europe. The school has been closed."

Street party in Greenways to celebrate VE Day, May 1945.
Photo: Elmbridge Museum

The most destructive war ever waged has just ended: the nation has survived; everyone has done their bit but there is not even a place in the log for a muffled "hurrah"! It is the very understated, unwearied economical use of language, prosaic but sublime, which the head teacher uses to record the periods of exhausting air raid activity, which reduced me to tears.

1940 and the Blitz

It may not be part of the story of the origins of Hinchley Wood but I am sure I will be forgiven for giving the following brief account of war-time life in the school: a testament to the selfless application to duty which characterises the teachers of children. The first sign of what was to come is the unusual entry for Tuesday, 14 May 1940 (France had just been invaded and Churchill, now prime minister, made his famous speech offering nothing but 'blood, toil, tears and sweat' broadcast on the previous Trinity Sunday evening).

"14 May 1940: School reopened at 9 a.m. as a result of broadcast instructions from the government that all schools would reopen today. All staff were present and 303 of 344 children."

Air raid drill had been practised at least once a week but now it was real.

"28 June 1940: The low attendance this week (89%) is mainly due to air raid alarms during the night having resulted in children losing sleep and being absent the following mornings."

The unusual circumstances of the nation (the fall of France and the return via Dunkirk of the British Expeditionary Force) brought a big change to the routine.

"24 July 1940: School closed for one week rest period. Owing to the war, the usual summer holiday is abandoned."

On 5 August the school reopened to a routine of lessons interrupted by air raid warnings (and dental inspections). There was now to begin a period of intense air raid warnings (the Battle of Britain was beginning to enter its critical phase).

"16 August 1940: Air Raid siren sounded today 12.20 p.m. while children were at lunch. All present proceeded to shelter immediately with staff. All Clear sounded after 45 minutes when children returned to canteen to finish their lunch."

The same thing happened on 26 August, at lunch and at 3.10 p.m. when the chairman of the managers, who was visiting, shared the shelter trench. Attendance on that day was 55% owing to *"the disturbance of night air raid warnings"*. This was to become commonplace.

"27 August 1940: Attendance very low this morning, 30%. Reason: Air Raid alarms lasting till 4 this morning. Many children have arrived late. Registers have been marked and left open until 10 a.m. All staff present. Dental inspection this a.m. Attendance p.m. 49%. School closed 3 p.m. today to enable children to get home and get some sleep."

"28 August 1940: Air Raid alarms lasted till 1.15 this morning. School opened at 10 a.m. Attendance 58% a.m., 67% p.m. Absentees for previous inspections were seen by dentist this a.m."

I have made the point already: the log is for deviations from routine without embellishment; an air raid and a visit by the dentist get the same weight in the record.

"29 August 1940: Air Raid alarms lasting till after 4 a.m. have caused children to lose sleep; registers were kept open until 11 a.m. Today is the last day of the extra term inserted in the year owing to the absence of summer holidays."

The school reopened on 2 September from which day there were one or more air raid warnings every day, bar seven, that the school was open until it broke up for Christmas on 20 December. The disruption became chronic: in the week ending 20 September there were 11 air raids in school time.

"16 September 1940:
Air Raid alarm   10.05 a.m.   :   All Clear 10.40
Air Raid alarm   11.00 a.m.   :   All Clear 11.45
Air Raid alarm   12.10 p.m.   :   All Clear 12.50
Dinners were served to the children in shelters, by the school staff.
Air Raid alarm   2.10 p.m.   :   All Clear 6 p.m."

"17 September 1940: Air Raid alarms in the area to 5.30 a.m. last night. Another alarm sounded at about 8 a.m. All clear, 8.50 a.m. Yet another alarm at 9.10 a.m. Most of the staff were present and about 60 children. All went to the shelter until the All Clear at 10.15 a.m. After leaving shelters the children went to their own form rooms till 10.40. Children arriving up to 10.40 were marked present. Usual timetable worked after break. All staff present by 10.30. Air Raid alarm 2.45 p.m. All Clear 4.30 p.m."

This continued all week. On Thursday:

"Arrangements have now been made for some work to be done by the children in shelters. The boys are handicapped by lack of light in their shelter."

The Battle of Britain is celebrated as having been won on 15 September 1940; on the above evidence you could not have known it at the time.

The following week there were 11 more air raid alarms and on

"27 September 1940: Heavy gunfire and many aircraft have been heard over the school today."

The following week saw a big event, which I expect caused the boys at least, to go home boasting about 'their bomb'. The head teacher again:

"2 October 1940: I received a message (at home) from the caretaker early this morning that there was an unexploded bomb on the school field. I came to school immediately and found that the bomb was a few yards from the air raid shelters. Children who had arrived were sent home with instructions that they would be notified if the school was to reopen before Monday next [this was Wednesday]."

"The school reopened on 16 October, the bomb having been exploded by the military the previous day." We can only guess why it took so long.

"On account of the extreme disruption generally, an official County Hall circular instructed the hours of the school to be changed to: 10 - 12 a.m. and 12.45 – 2.45 p.m. Parents were told that their children could stay at school and, if required, could be supervised from 9 a.m."

In the dire circumstances even this truncated day couldn't be made to work; daily school life could not be maintained. On 18 October the authorities directed all schools to close until 30 October, but on the same day, and to keep everyone's interest up:

"A land mine is being exploded in Thames Ditton this afternoon by the military authorities. As some children come from homes which have been evacuated while the mine is being exploded, I have kept them in school until their parents have called for them or until they can be taken to their parents when it has been ascertained where they are."

On 31 October there was something else new. In the afternoon, because heavy gunfire could be heard locally and because the electricity had failed, the children were taken to the shelters for fear the sirens wouldn't be working. Mr. Hallifax phoned the Esher Control centre to ask for a telephoned 'All Clear', which came well after school closing time.

"Parents called for some children. Others were escorted to their homes by teachers."

On 4 November the school hours were changed again to 9.30 a.m. to 3.15 p.m. with a ¾ hour break for a meal. This fitted with the government's decision to continue summer-time throughout the winter and to the fact that, generally, parents had agreed to allow their children to be escorted home when the All Clear had not been given by the time of school closing. Meanwhile, on a rare day with no air raid, four children took the entrance examination for Kingston Day Commercial School.

The pattern continued and was resumed unabated for the new school year on 6 January 1941:

"40 children from Claygate have today been convoyed to and from school by coach. This will continue daily for 6 months."

The following day the All Clear did not sound before school closing time and

"The children were convoyed home in parties other than the seniors who, with parental authority, were allowed to make their own way home."

We are now well into the period known as 'The Blitz' and there was a new worry for the authorities: fire was a menace bigger than high explosive and for the greater part of the rest of the war, fire watching parties were organised to be alert to the risk. So it was with schools: a County circular provided that for every night from 14 January 1941 four members of staff were to remain on the premises all night. This meant 'every' night and the task was shared with staff from the Commercial School.

Life had to go on and the bureaucracy was not to be stopped. On 20 January the vicars of Claygate, Thames Ditton, Weston Green and Hinchley Wood called at the school (during an air raid alert) to discuss the future implementation of Section 12 of the 1936 Education Act which allowed children to be withdrawn from school for religious instruction.

There now started a particularly intense period of air raid activity. After a quiet day on Monday, on Tuesday 28 January there were three air raid alarms, each lasting 25 minutes, between 11 a.m. and 1.15 p.m. A fourth sounded at 2.05 p.m. but because no 'All Clear' had sounded by close of school the children *"were convoyed home by parents and teachers in parties"*. After one alert on Wednesday, Thursday was to be a repeat of Tuesday with four alerts and with no 'All Clear' to the last one, the convoy home again. On Friday there were three alerts in the morning, the first being at 9.30 a.m., the third at 12.20 was still in force three hours later when the school was to close: the children were escorted home again: *"They had spent all day in the shelters."*

On Monday 3 February, there was no coke for the boilers, it having been ordered but *"not having been delivered"*. Mr. Hallifax telephoned the authorities at County Hall and agreed to close the school for the afternoon session, the children having spent the morning in their overcoats.

At the end of March 1941 the air raid alerts petered out. By May, swimming lessons at Kingston baths could be organised. In July Mr. Edwards was *"absent this p.m. to keep an appointment in London in connection with his possible employment on strategic work of national importance"*. In August, in the new school year, the first air raid practice since over a year earlier was held; all the others in that period had been real. Staff came and went; hours reverted to normal and 1941 passed into 1942. The new Curate-in-charge of St. Christopher's, the Rev Headley Vallins, called at the school again to discuss the workings of the arrangements for the withdrawal of children and Section 12 of the Education Act (which started on 13 January 1942): 75 children had been withdrawn from the scripture period and had attended at St Christopher's Hall until 9.35.

The routine of the school was re-established and was only occasionally deranged by isolated air raid alerts from the spring of 1941 to 1944. Each year from 1940, on 3 September, the timetable was interrupted at 10.45 a.m. in order for the school to assemble and join in the broadcast national day of prayer on the anniversaries of the outbreak of war. The problem of staffing became increasingly tight. Healthy male teachers would join the forces: married lady teachers were given automatic leave of absence for the whole duration of their husband's home leave. All this put tremendous pressure on the rest of the staff.

The Doodlebug summer

On 16 June 1944, there started a new phase of air attack which was to last for three months and which, in the derangement it caused to school life, and probably in its wearisome toll, was even worse than the badly disruptive period of 1940 and 1941. This, of course, was the period of the V1 pilotless bomber or 'Doodlebug'. The numbers that were launched were so many that, even though a large proportion was destroyed, the defences were overwhelmed. Each one that escaped the protective screen caused its own air raid alert in front of its path, until, when it ran out of fuel at a random moment, it fell to earth. The bombs were aimed at central London but in order to protect it, clever deception by the authorities induced the enemy to alter its aim. As a result, many bombs fell on the suburbs or overflew them; the disruption to school life of these continuous attacks was frightful.

There were alerts every day. On 29 June there were six Alerts and All Clears on the one day. School life was impossible; attendances dwindled. The log is gripping in its day-by-day account

"In view of Home Secretary's advice in the House of Commons and broadcast in the news advising all people to keep under cover if possible, all children convoyed home."

"51 of our 353 children came to school today: all staff were present."

"186 attended today; all staff present."

"A large explosion occurred very soon after the children were in the shelter, breaking windows in the school, no children injured."

"Lessons are organised in the field near the shelters: all staff were present."

"Sports day postponed due to air raids; 33 children present."

"Dinners taken to the shelters and eaten there; 119 children present; all staff present."

The following log entry is set out below with no comment by me: the few words have their own eloquence.

"3 July 1944: 74 children and all staff present a.m., 64 children and all staff present p.m.
Alert in force at 9 a.m., All Clear 9.30 a.m.
Alert in force at 9.50 a.m., All Clear 10.10 a.m.
Alert in force 10.30 a.m., All Clear 11.30 a.m.
Alert in force 12.5 p.m.
Dinners were served by the staff in the shelters and children remained in the shelter until close of school, when those whose parents had sent written agreement to this course were sent home during quiet periods.

Other children were kept in the shelters with members of the staff until fetched by their parents or until the All Clear had sounded. Some children travelling to Claygate by train were taken by a mistress and others convoyed by members of the staff living in the same direction. The last child was taken home at 6 p.m."

The next day was much the same: *"83 children and all staff present"*. There were five alerts, one of which started before and lasted well past the lunch break: *"Dinners were served in two shifts in the indoor shelters, near the dining room"*.

On 5 July: 78 children were present: *"All staff present."* On 6 July: *"All staff present,"* but two had been delayed *"owing to a bomb falling on the railway line in front of the train."*

It was not just the schools which were suffering: on 6 July an official called at the school *"in connection with arrangements to use the school as a Registration Centre for the evacuation of homeless people due to bombing"*. The calm recording of events with no subjective embellishment could not disguise the fact that very serious measures were to come. A breakdown of daily life was at hand.

The air raid siren held dominion over school life: it could be no other way. Most adults, after they had become familiar with the nature of the Doodlebug, went about their daily lives content to play a kind of Russian roulette: they adopted a self confident certainty that the droning pest would over-fly them, each indulging a selfish wish that the destruction, which was surely to come soon, was destined for somewhere else further along the bug's route; or if this hope failed, they were content to take their chance that, even as the drone cut out, there would be a ditch or something else in which to shelter from the blast which followed, seconds after the fateful

silence as its engine cut out; randomly, but venomously. But the children could not possibly be included in this game of chance. Thousands of V1s were launched, each one tracked by radar as it approached our shores, and each setting forth a progression of alerts along its predicted route; and each one sending the children to their shelters. Daily life at school could not be sustained in the face of such attacks. (As for the adults, the statistics were on their side as they took more risk: as far as death is concerned the tally was only one death per one bomb launched; but the blast caused very serious damage to property owing to the fact that they were designed to explode before penetration of the ground.)

In 1944 a Doodlebug destroyed some houses in Greenways and damaged these (one of them was the home of St Christoper's Sacristan, Mr. Christoper Gill. Photo: courtesy of Elmbridge Museum

The new phase started on Saturday 8 July 1944, when the school was opened for the commencement of the daily registration of children to be evacuated under the government scheme. On the next Tuesday the first party left for Exeter. By Wednesday 63 children had been registered, followed by 17 more later in the week and three more one week later; 50 had been evacuated by private arrangement. The evacuation party was led by Mr. Henderson, with five other teachers accompanying the children: Mrs. Bull, Miss Harvey, Miss Cordery, Miss Menzies and Mrs. Henderson. On 13 July the head teacher received telegrams informing him that the party had arrived safely in Exeter, and another in Wales.

On 14 July the school closed for the summer holiday and reopened on 14 August when 78 children were present. Because of the bomb damage in the locality, gangs of building operatives were being billeted in the next door Commercial School. They were fed in the Central School canteen and temporary arrangements to feed the children had to be made via containers from a central kitchen. On 30 August came the news, reflecting continuing serious damage if not loss of life, that the numbers of building operatives to be billeted in the school was to be doubled to 120.

The attendance figures were now down to between 80 and 100 and as a response to more or less unabated air raid alerts, lessons were taken in the open air, near the shelters. With many teachers now away on evacuation duty, the staff problems of Mr. Hallifax were becoming impossible: he had to resort to exceptional measures. Two members of the WRVS who were on the premises daily were assigned to help out the teachers. The only staff available to Mr. Hallifax were five, two of whom were teachers of either handicraft or domestic science. Recording this fact unpleadingly in his log, Mr. Hallifax reports that he has written to the Chief Education Officer asking for the recall of two of the teachers from the evacuation party. In accordance with his schedule the dentist turned up to do his inspections.

The staffing difficulties became even worse. On 30 August, Mr. Hallifax records that: *"Mrs Stagg absent today owing to the sudden return of her husband on leave. Mrs Stagg will be absent for 14 days – the duration of her husband's leave."* The record adds: *"No supply teachers are available."*

By mid-September we can infer from his log entries that Mr. Hallifax was in despair: daily attendances were now over 130; the authorities could neither supply any additional teachers nor recall any that were on evacuation duty. Mr. Hallifax records, with no hint of distress, that he telephoned the head teacher of another school and arranged to borrow a teacher for a week. Meanwhile, classes were reorganised to meet the new circumstances which included the disruption to and exclusion from parts of the two schools because of the continuing billeting of building operatives. As September drew to a close, the attendances reached 150 and on 29 September as the school closed for the autumn holiday, the building operatives left.

The new term saw attendances rise to over 200 and a deviation in the routine of the school of an extraordinary, but in the lives of the boys involved, memorable new activity: ten senior boys went potato picking at Thorkhill Nurseries. All the official exemptions in relation to child labour were given: the bureaucrats were satisfied, for these were exceptional times. The people had to be fed and labour was scarce. The boys worked from 9 a.m. to 12 noon and, after eating at school, from 2 p.m. to 5 p.m.

On 2 November *"an incident locally as a result of enemy air action*"* caused about 200 windows of the school to be broken as well as damage to doors and locks. Later in the month the various evacuation parties returned. On 27 November the normal timetable was resumed: prosaically, the log records that: *"The head teacher was late in arriving at school today, having visited a dentist for urgent treatment."* The storm had passed; life became normal again.

As this period of endurance passed into history, two points must be made. We know that, as a nation, we survived this terror attack; it was never going to lose us the war because it had no influence on the battle raging in Normandy: but for how long would it last? A week; a month; six months? That was the unknown that might have broken lesser spirits; the new form of attack imposed a burden worse than the air attacks of 1940 and 1941; the strain lasted much of the day; the dawn or cloud gave no relief; the helplessness of the people on the ground against the impersonal attack was unrequited. That the randomness of the destruction and terror wrought by the "revenge" weapon could never be decisive was no comfort: the people of Greater London would just have to tough it out: but for how long?

The second point is particular to log. In reading the account of disruption to school life I am inspired by the repetitive entry of three words; the unembellished three words: *"All Staff Present."*

---

* This euphemism concealed a new menace: the damage referred to was caused by a V2 rocket bomb which hit the earth near the Hampton Court Junction railway viaduct. Against this new weapon there was neither warning nor defence. Happily, the victorious armies, having fought their way from Normandy, over-ran the launching sites.

CHAPTER 12:
THE LOVELACE ESTATE – A CATASTROPHE AVERTED

---

10 MILES FROM LONDON
FORMERLY PART OF THE LOVELACE ESTATE
COMPRISING ABOUT
650 ACRES adjoining Surbiton
Hook, Claygate and Hinchley Wood
believed to be
THE FINEST BUILDLING ESTATE IN THE MARKET
1¹/₂ MILES OF FRONTAGE TO THE KINGSTON BY-PASS
Over three miles of frontage to existing highways and
Over two miles of frontage to roads already town-planned

The Estate is developed up to the boundary on all sides, and zoned in densities
of four, six, eight and twelve houses per acre for residential areas, and seven general
business areas, and includes SURBITON GOLF COURSE

MAIN SERVICES AVAILABLE
MAIN WATER IS LAID THROUGH PART OF THE ESTATE

The Levels and layout of the land are eminently suitable for economical development,
and the Estate, when the Chessington line of the Southern Railway is opened, will
be served by FOUR FIRST-CLASS RAILWAY STATIONS and ample bus services

The Freehold Estate will be offered for Sale by Auction by
Messrs. KNIGHT, FRANK & RUTLEY
In conjunction with
Messrs. HATCHWELLS
in suitable Lots, in the Tudor Room at Messrs. Bentalls, Kingston-on-
Thames, on July 14th, 1937, at 3 p.m. (unless previously sold)

Solicitor: A. J. NEWSOME Esq., Old Palace Yard, Earl Street, Coventry.
Auctioneers: Messrs. Hatchwells, 8-10, London Road, Kingston; Messrs. Knight,
Frank & Rutley, 20, Hanover Square, W.1.

Surrey Comet: 10 July 1937

The story of the attempted development of the Lovelace Estate land ran from 1937 to the mid 1950s, when Severn Drive and Hill Rise were built on a small part of the it: the story of the development of those roads belongs in the next chapter, on the post-war completion of the development of Hinchley Wood. Now we must consider the development of the great Lovelace Estate, which, if it had happened, would have been a planning catastrophe.

The Surrey Comet's dismay and despair

It was with a discernible sense of dismay and despair that the Surrey Comet reported in July 1937 the forthcoming sale by auction of 650 acres of land (about twice the size of Hinchley Wood) which was formerly part of the Lovelace Estate. The estate had been assembled over 200 years previously and at one time had extended to 15,000 acres of woodland and meadows stretching from the Earl of Lovelace's seat at Ockham Park, Ripley to Surbiton. The auction was to be held at Bentall's Tudor Restaurant on 14 July 1937. The land that was being offered had been the last remaining land from that great estate. But it was not the Lovelace Estate that was the vendor at the auction. They had cashed in two years earlier to a speculator called Gillitt. According to Anita Witten, Gillitt bought the land from Lovelace in 1935. Having worked up a development scheme, Gillitt parcelled up the land for auction in 73 lots.

As the Surrey Comet lamented: "Neither the buyers nor the auctioneer will be concerned with historical sentiment or the beauties of the great expanse of land, the miles of leafy lanes, the snug little farm houses, the still pools overhung with lovely trees and the bright, clear running streams, which may all - or very nearly all - disappear as the result of a few taps from the hammer."

The land extended eastwards from Hinchley Wood on both sides of the by-pass with the greater part, which included Surbiton golf course, on the south side. It was that vital part of green countryside which entitled Hinchley Wood to claim that it was in the country: in keeping Long Ditton, Hook, and Chessington separated from Hinchley Wood by a green lung, which had the effect of averting London's reach, it gave vivid illustration of what was needed: a legally sustainable "Green Belt". If the development had happened, the entire stretch of land from Claygate Lane to Hook would have been covered with houses.

The Surrey Comet didn't hold back, telling its readers the land has to be: "… sold to the highest bidders, and over 500 acres of this land may soon be covered with anything up to 3,000 houses. Love Lane and Woodstock Lane, as we know them at present, will gradually become memories. Sweet memories to many, but one by one they will fall by the hammer. Great oaks and stately elms that have stood for longer than the life of man must bow their heads, and maybe one day become smart little dining room suites in some modern suburban villas."

The Surrey Comet explained: "Among the lots for sale is the land known for years as Hook Common, which the inhabitants have come to call their own. Ditton Hill Farm, Manor Farm, Claygate, and Manor Farm, Hook will all meet the same fate." Most of the land was in Esher district but some 100 acres were in Surbiton (now Kingston).

The auction

The advertisement giving notice of the sale was naked in its advancement of the quality of the land to be sold. "The finest building estate in the market" trumpeted the advert: "1½ miles of frontage to the Kingston by-pass" it added. The auctioneers were Knight, Frank and Rutley, a surveying firm which lives on at the same Mayfair address today.

In the biggest land sale in the district in memory there were about 300 people present at the auction. The Surrey Comet offered its view that because "well known building developers" were among the purchasers and bidders the indication was that there was "the probability of early building and the creation of a great new residential area". The auctioneer created the atmosphere by opening the sale with the overstated announcement that: "This sale of such an important freehold estate is a unique occasion", and forecast that; " … the sale would mark a new era in the development of the district." His rhetoric continued ominously: "Surbiton had practically become attached to London. All the way from London to Surbiton it was houses, houses, houses. The estate was the only unbuilt-

on area of any considerable size from that point to London." We can't blame the auctioneer for his professional pride in bringing this estate under the hammer. If he thought he was doing anyone a favour, other than his client, it was those people who might move into new homes on the estate; the very people we considered in examining the 1930s housing boom in Chapter 3. This market-driven view was typical of the era: but it was not to be. The land was to be spared from development, with no apparent effort by the Residents' Association, by the onset of war: but in 1937, with the housing boom still going on, it seemed inevitable that Hinchley Wood was going to be joined to Hook.

Unexpectedly (were people put off by the Esher by-pass issue which had broken?) not all the lots on offer fell under the hammer. The most notable lot to fail to find a bidder at £20,000 was the 135 acres of land on which Surbiton golf course had been laid out in 1895. This was just an early part of what was to become a long, and at times near fatal, saga for members of Surbiton Golf Club. Those Hinchley Wood residents who had bought houses in Old Claygate Lane, which shared a boundary with the golf course, were also threatened with their loss of amenity. That the golf course would have survived without being developed can be traced to a trade-off two years later between Esher Council and the would-be developer of the Lovelace Estate land. In order to gain some advantage, the developer offered to sterilise the golf course land, by agreeing to its being zoned as private open space.

Esher Council

On 4 June 1937 Esher Council had granted interim permission for the land to be developed: thus was the land, now pregnant with development opportunity, brought to auction. The Council actually zoned the land for residential development and granted interim permission for its development because they had no effective power to stop it. There is no evidence to suggest that they actually wanted the development, but we can surmise that the zoning decision was made because the Council wanted to exercise some control over it. As we saw in Chapter 3, in the general review of the planning regime in the 1930s, the Council was not in a position to refuse permission without burdensome compensation having to be paid. Because they zoned the land they gave themselves some leverage in negotiations over density and other issues. These negotiations took time: in fact it was time, much assisted by frantic arguments over the routing of the Esher by-pass, that was the great redeemer. It was to be two years later, in 1939, that definitive planning proposals came before Esher Council, at which time, wearying of the developer's style, it reversed its decision and decided to disallow the proposals. Some members had wanted to duck the decision while the war was on (the meeting in September1939, took place three days after war had been declared): this couldn't be done, lawfully, but in practice the result was the same. Hitler's invasion of Poland gave this land its reprieve from development: the

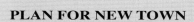

ESHER & DISTRICT

◆

PLAN FOR NEW TOWN

◆

3,000 Houses Between Hinchley Wood and Surbiton

◆

COUNCIL OPPOSE DEVELOPER'S DENSITY PROPOSALS

The building of what would be virtually an entirely new town - 3,000 houses of the small villa type for a population of 12,000 – between Hinchley Wood and the Surbiton boundary is causing anxiety to members of Esher Council. The proposal is to erect these houses on the Lovelace estate, about 520 acres of which would be involved, on either side of Kingston by-pass road and on either side of Woodstock Lane. There would be three shopping areas. It would have the effect of doing away with the whole of the open land between Hinchley Wood and Chessington, except for the 130 acres at Surbiton Golf Club.

Surrey Comet: 1 July 1939

NEW TOWNSHIP PROJECT FOR ESHER AREA

———

Council Rejects Plans for Over 2,500 Houses on Lovelace Estate

———

STAND TAKEN ON TOWN PLAN ZONING

The fate of 530 acres of land adjacent to Kingston By-pass between Hinchley Wood and Chessington was considered by Esher Council at a special meeting on Wednesday.
The land, formerly part of the Lovelace estate, has been bought by Mr. H. N. Gillitt, who wants to erect over 2,000 houses and several shopping areas there. Plans he has submitted to the council show 2,705 houses on the estate if the new Esher by-pass crosses the land, and 2,564 if the road takes another route.

A special report had been prepared by the Surveyor, and this, together with the plans was considered on Wednesday. Several members of the council were for adjourning consideration of the plans while the war was on, but when it was found this could not be done the proposals were rejected.

Surrey Comet: Saturday, 9 September 1939

1947 Town and Country Planning Act allowed it to be designated 'Green Belt'.

Hinchley Wood Residents' Association: where did it stand?

Where was the Residents' Association in all this: what was their attitude? Years later Royston Pike claimed that the Association had fought a great fight against it. Maybe, but the minutes of the Association are silent on the issue from when the news broke through the whole of the relevant period; it is as if the subject did not exist! Why was there this silence? The minutes of the autumn general meeting held a couple of months after the news broke, in July 1937, illustrate the point.

The meeting was chaired by Mr. W G V Vaughan, who had recently joined Royston Pike as a member of the Council. Four topics were ventilated at the meeting: the Esher by-pass; the tea room on Telegraph Hill; the land between the railway lines; and official preparations in the context of Air Raid Precautions, for the recruitment and training of wardens. There is no mention of the Lovelace Estate land and the proposed development on it. This is very strange and inexplicable, as indeed is the missing page in the minute book from early 1938!

Post-war planning

With the arrival of the war all thoughts of developing the former Lovelace Estate land were shelved. The wholesale revision of the planning legislation had to wait until 1947. It is interesting to note, however, that even when heavy fighting was taking place during the war, the government was able to allocate resources to thinking about the post-war period. (Another example is R A Butler's 1944 Education Act.) In 1944 Professor Abercrombie presented his Greater London Development Plan which he had prepared at the request of the government and which followed on from the Barlow report of 1940. He recommended the dispersal of people from overcrowded town centres, not to the suburbs, in the unrestrained fashion of the 1930s, but to new towns comprehensively planned for work, leisure and living, well outside the conurbations. By leap-frogging the suburbs, a Green Belt could be placed round London. And so it happened: it is almost literally true to say that the present day urban sprawl of London stops where the builders left off in 1939. The Town and Country Planning Act, 1947, gave Abercrombie's blueprint the statutory force which local planning authorities needed to protect green land from development.

Abercrombie's gaze fell on Hinchley Wood: in his Greater London Development Plan, the Lovelace Estate land was identified as the key green land by which Hinchley Wood, and points west, could be saved from annexation by London: the catastrophe which had been averted in 1939 was to be made safe by the great high-grade thinking about post-war planning: but the question of compensation had to be settled.

The 1946 public enquiry

The 1946 public enquiry was more about compensation than an attempt to overcome the planning refusal. The 1947 planning reform had not yet come into force but the straws were in the wind. Plainly, the landowner could see that the Green Belt was coming. The enquiry was to into the Council's application to make an order revoking the interim permission, which it had granted in 1937. The enquiry broke up on the third day, with the consent of all the parties, to enable the Council to determine their attitude to the question of compensation.

It didn't take long and the Council resolved to follow the guidance of their Clerk: in the most robust of terms, the Council declared that: the revocation of permission to develop was necessary in the interests of Greater London at large, as proclaimed in the Abercrombie plan: further, that the question of compensation should fall on the Exchequer and not on the ratepayers of Esher and that copies of the resolution should be sent to all parties concerned. This was great stuff: "we have done what we have done for the greater good and we are not to be expected to pay for it." All the signs are that Esher won the day, because, on the evidence of the Council minutes, nothing more of the issue was heard.

CHAPTER 13:
THE POST-WAR COMPLETION AND A RETROSPECT

Looking south, across the by-pass in 1957: single carriageway and no access to Claygate Lane North.   Photo: Surrey Comet

As we have seen, the coming of war left several aspects of the development of Hinchley Wood unfinished: the speed at which everything had happened in the 1930s ensured that the stamp of that decade was imprinted, even though the original conception was not completed until late in the 1950s. We must now sweep up the post-war work on completing the 1930s settlement, taking the opportunity to look back in retrospect.

The post-war completion

When the war came all civilian building stopped, everywhere. This left the Medina Avenue, Heathside, Harefield estate stranded; it left Station Approach, Greenways and Greenwood Close unfinished and the land between the railway lines in limbo. After the war, Frank Montgomery tired of the endless control over and delay to the finishing off of his Medina Avenue estate: the land was released piecemeal, development on it having been frozen while the great post-war regional plans (stemming from Abercrombie) for roads and other development were considered. Building started again in the 1950s and ran on into the next decade.

Building on Station Approach had stopped pre-war at a point which proved to be the viable limit of shopping provision. Crouch still owned the undeveloped land and when he proposed offices, the Residents' Association quickly countered with a preference for flats. These were built in the late 1950s or early 1960s and gave a good architectural treatment to round off the shops. Moreover, it was the first development of non-family housing in Hinchley Wood and represented, therefore, a welcome diversification of the housing stock which until then had been all family housing.

The post-war housing shortage saw Esher Council respond with their development of Manordene Close in the late 1940s and Bankside Drive in the early 1950s. This, together with Severn Drive, discussed below, completed the eastern part of the settlement, much of it post-war but all of it outwith the 1929 town plan of Hinchley Wood.

Severn Drive, Hill Rise

Although the plan to develop the Lovelace Estate land was finally kicked into touch, there was one tongue of land over which a later public enquiry was to be held. Many readers will remember cows grazing on this land to the north of the by-pass, south of the primary school and having its western boundary on Claygate Lane. Here was to be built the last development of green land in Hinchley Wood: Severn Drive and Hill Rise. (Harefield was built later but was planned before the war.)

Severn Drive today: one of the last good street scenes, 2002.

In 1953 there was a new proposal for the encroachment on to Green Belt land: this was something different from the former pre-war attempt to build on the Lovelace Estate land, even though it was on a small part of that land. The 11 acres of land had passed into the ownership of Davis Estates Ltd. whose application to build on it had been refused, on Green Belt grounds, by Esher Council: Davis Estates appealed and a public enquiry was held on 10 November 1953. The Residents' Association adopted a position of opposition to the development and to consider how best to give its support to the Council. A new resolution was passed to the effect that: Hinchley Wood Residents' Association, being anxious to do all in its power to preserve the amenities of the district, urges the retention of the land in the Green Belt. Moreover, and here was a tangible point of objection, the objection was based on road safety issues: the development would create new traffic problems at what was then a dangerous spot on the Kingston by-pass. Lt. Col. A J Cousin of Hinchley Way, and a member of the committee, was appointed to present Hinchley Wood's case to the enquiry at which members of the public were urged to attend (of which about 30 duly did).

It was all to no avail: the public enquiry heard all the arguments but gave permission to build, the decision being announced in April 1954. In allowing the incursion into the Green Belt, the Inspector had been influenced by a side issue which had been raised by the Inspector who had heard the 1946 enquiry: it had been said then that the parcel of land on which Severn Drive and Hill rise were built was included in the Green Belt questionably. The point of view which prevailed at the 1953 enquiry was that the land could be regarded as an acceptable infilling which justified taking it out of the Green Belt: certainly the land was an anomalous projection and its development tidied up the eastern end of the settlement.

The decision to allow the development brought about a new problem which exercised the Residents' Association for the next couple of years. At that time there was no northern access to or egress from the by-pass to Claygate Lane: it had been closed many years earlier; access from the second Berg estate to Claygate Lane North, was achieved (amazing though it will seem today) by a right turn off the by-pass into Hinchley Way: and, it is important to stress, there was no speed limit on the by-pass. On account of the new development, the Claygate Lane junction would have to be opened up to allow traffic in

Bankside Drive, 1950.   Photo: Esher Council

and out of the northern section of the road: to rely on the existing access via Hinchley Way would be untenable; as a consequence, the Residents' Association pressed for island refuges to be built. The problems of this junction continued and were not solved until the present round-about was built in conjunction with the dualling of the by-pass and a speed limit.

So, Severn Drive and Hill Rise were built and in 1956 and 1957 the new residents moved in, with one of the new residents joining the committee of the Residents' Association. This was to be the start of a very significant contribution which Severn Drive has made to community life over the years. The road has supplied two members of Elmbridge Council; several members of the Parochial Church Council of St Christopher's; one Churchwarden and the present chairman of the Residents' Association and himself a former Councillor, Mr. Peter Highley.

After all the objections over Green Belt encroachment, a very pleasant development was created: the gentle rise in the land has been brilliantly exploited by curves in the roads; this, together with the unusually long front drives, now fully matured, have given a streetscape of quite exceptional quality. In fact, I know of no other post-war development that can match Severn Drive's streetscape and its varied house designs; it is, perhaps the last of the best post-war developments.

A retrospect

In his definitive work on the development of London and its suburbs up to 1939 (*Semi-Detached London*), Jackson reaches his conclusion with a very gloomy assessment of the builders' contribution: "That the outer layer of London which emerged from all this activity was neither well balanced in its constituents nor visually and psychologically satisfying is common ground" he writes: when thinking of Hinchley Wood we must disagree. "It happened" according to Jackson, "largely because there was no positive planning on a regional scale, and was worse

than it might have been because such planning powers as did exist were not properly used by most of the local authorities": we would have to exclude Esher Council, in fair measure, from the generality of this criticism. Jackson cites learned evidence given in 1938: "...the devastating onrush of the speculative builder..." which no local authority "even pretended to regulate and guide for the common good": this cannot be said of Esher Council.

The evidence given in 1938 included the widespread truth: that the peace of rural surroundings, so eagerly sought by migrating householders, was in many cases destroyed by the development that accommodated them: to Esher Council belongs every atom of credit for saving Telegraph Hill for public enjoyment; but only after considerable effort from the Hinchley Wood Residents' Association was Esher Council, ultimately, able to save some land for recreation between the railway lines. But it was the timing of the start of the war which allowed the Lovelace Estate to escape from development: an event which would have made Jackson's gloomy analysis apply in full force because Hinchley Wood would have been annexed by London's suburbs: its discrete individuality as a settlement was saved.

There was at the time a dearth of properly trained planning advisers which makes Horace Fread's work (he was the long serving Surveyor of Esher Council) on the town planning scheme (and the Telegraph Hill purchase) all the more praiseworthy: the sudden, wide ranging onslaught of the private developers through the 1930s, says Jackson, "...was little affected by the pitifully inadequate planning measures" which were described briefly in Chapter 3. In large measure Fread was ahead of the game and Jackson's general criticism, valid though it is, cannot be levelled at him.

In one of Jackson's last words on the subject, he referred to "... the shallowness of local allegiance and a lack of community spirit found almost everywhere in the outer suburban belt, characteristics which very largely stem from the haphazard and often dormitory nature ..." of development. That this observation, whatever its wider general truth, does not apply to Hinchley Wood can, in my analysis, be attributed to three things: the station, around which the identity of the settlement was created: Royston Pike, who as we have seen epitomised community life; and St Christopher's Church for without this, even non-worshippers would agree, a community is not worthy of the name. From the very beginning, Hinchley Wood was embraced: newcomers in the 1930s did not say, "I am going to live in a part of Thames Ditton". The reality preceded the official position because what they said was: "I am going to live in a nice new place called Hinchley Wood."

The vast majority of the newcomers to Hinchley Wood found that Royston Pike was already in action, leading the new community. Spiritual leadership for the community came from a separate direction. Separate: yes, but it is intriguing that, Royston Pike apart, so many of the leading figures in the Church and the Residents' Association were the same people, the one example I give

Station Approach wasn't finished until the late 1950s, early 1960s.   Photo: courtesy Elmbridge Museum

here is that both the Churchwardens, at the time St Christopher's Church was consecrated, were active members of the Residents' Association and one was a member of Esher Council.

Even before the countryside was protected by the Green Belt, Horace Fread and Esher Council were in the vanguard in protecting open space, both by zoning and the purchase of Telegraph Hill. The Green Belt has served Hinchley Wood well: it is well protected by Littleworth Common, Ditton Marsh, Telegraph Hill, Surbiton golf course and the land either side of the Kingston by-pass to the east of Severn Drive.

I must state now, lest it be thought that I am an unalloyed admirer of Hinchley Wood, that fault can be found. Horace Fread (and Crouch) set out to build a dormitory settlement around the station and that is exactly what they got. In 1937, Royston Pike asserted that the development of Hinchley Wood had been controlled. "It was not a model village", he said, "but it was most certainly a good example of suburban town planning." Let us examine this.

Although sitting astride the railway, Hinchley Wood was the child of the Kingston by-pass: it would never be able to shake off that incubus by which it was conceived. By 1956, after all the deluge of criticism that had been levelled at the by-pass in the 1930s, a Hinchley Wood resident referred to it as: "a tortuous, twisting little alley: a wicked road and a scar across Surrey". It is unproductive to lament the by-pass's intrusion: it is there; Hinchley Wood is there because of it and the arrangements for living with it are the best that can reasonably be made.

Sensibly, most of the houses which have contiguous boundaries with the road have turned their backs on it: that Hinchley Way did not, and had a service road which initially gave it its street address of the unlovable "By-pass Road" was, in my opinion, a mistake. Manor Drive, Hinchley Way, Medina Avenue and Avondale Avenue: all these properly turned their backs. The fact that Hinchley Way did not, may have been caused by the site layout plan for Cumberland Drive, Chesterfield Drive as well as Hinchley Way, being severely constrained by a large tongue of land, perhaps 150-200 yards long, projecting back from 'The Woodlands', the early 19th century house in Manor Road North. Southmont Road also faces the by-pass, albeit with a large amount of dead ground, now well wooded, between the two roads.

Horace Fread got hold of the density restraint for development, the road widths and building lines, possibly also influencing the curving lines that many of the roads take. There are no grids in Hinchley Wood, like there are in Stoneleigh, for example. The density of development in Hinchley Wood was, in its generosity, a matter of pride for Horace Fread: but there is a paradox here. The Berg estates are as fine an example of the best mass housing of the 1930s as is possible to find: nothing better came afterwards, and yet the most offered criticism of them is that they are built just a bit too closely together. In an overall sense, the density to which Hinchley Wood was built was generous: but it was not a uniform density. The very long plots on Manor Road North, for example, have allowed contemporary in-filling whereas the Bergs estates are tightly built. Royston and Gibson Courts were built on infill land: great names; good diversification of

Manor Road North and the shops, 1960s.   Photo: Courtesy, Anita Witten and Peter Hanna

the housing stock, but illustrating the disbalance of the original layout in the town plan.

Crouch (I am almost certain) modified the shopping area layout so that it did not straddle the railway, which it does to bizarre effect in Stoneleigh. Station Approach and the shopping area works reasonably well. Ideally, the road width would be a little more generous in Station Approach to facilitate more easy one way working and shoppers' parking: when it was designed, and until the 1960s, it was for two-way traffic.

A commuter settlement: waiting for the 8.13 c1960.
                    Photo: St Christopher's Church

When Hinchley Wood was planned, apart from the hotel and the shops, no provision was made for anything except houses: it was planned as a dormitory and its leaders have reflected public opinion in doing their best to keep it that way. There was no thought given to schools and we have seen how, ultimately, this was rescued. Open space was thought of, as we have also seen in relation to Telegraph Hill, but magnificent though this acquisition was, it was no answer to a community's need for flat land for organised games.

Horace Fread's grand plan made no provision for the site for a church, whether by neglect or mistake, and probably deliberately, it made no provision for employment use of land. I think this was a mistake: the land between the railway lines could have accommodated both offices and recreational use. As we have seen, offices came by accident (and against the wishes of the Residents' Association). When the Milk Marketing Board sought to develop offices in Claygate Lane (I don't know where), there was the Residents' Association, ready to object. Where better for offices than between the railway lines with its railway station connection? No: everyone wanted a dormitory; and now that all the offices have gone, or are going, this is what we've got, albeit a very good one.

My final note on a retrospect is to lament the decline and then the going of the Hinchley Wood Hotel. For a village to have neither a public house nor a family eating facility is a pity; the absence of a good pub (no-one would miss a bad one) is a lacuna which I greatly regret.

CHAPTER 14:
CHURCH LIFE IN THE EARLY DAYS

The Hall Church set out for Harvest Festival, 1949.   Photo: St Christopher's Church

In this chapter is given the early history of St Christopher's Church, and its various early phases: the separation of Weston and Hinchley Wood from their mother Church, St Nicholas, Thames Ditton in 1932; the start of Christian worship at Esher Filling Station in 1933; the informal separation of Hinchley Wood from Weston and the appoinment of the Rev Robins as Curate-in-charge in 1935; his six years in office including the establishment of Hinchley Wood as a "conventional district" followed by his replacement by the Rev Vallins in the years 1941 to 1945: which point I have taken as the start of the story of the permanent Church which is described in the final chapter.

Thames Ditton and Weston

For ecclesiastical purposes, as well as civic, Hinchley Wood was, at first, indistinguishable from Thames Ditton; the early residents found themselves parishioners of St Nicholas. It had been the same for Claygate a century earlier when, until Holy Trinity Church was consecrated in 1840, it also had been in the parish of Thames Ditton. It was the same for residents of Weston Green who, as Hinchley Wood started, were also parishioners of St Nicholas: but unlike in Hinchley Wood, where there was not yet any organised body of church people, in Weston

an embryo church had already existed since 1885. By 1900 these people had built a hall Church but by the early 1930s, with the population expansion, All Saints' Weston was beginning to need its own identity.

The year 1932 was destined to mark the point where the decisions were made which shaped the future for All Saints' Weston and its future daughter church, St Christopher's. The situation was this: the worshipping community of Weston Green, although organised, had grown too big to be served adequately by Thames Ditton while the needs of Hinchley Wood had not yet been addressed. The expansion of Thames Ditton and the changing character of the outlying parts of the parish had caused anxiety to the Vicar of Thames Ditton, the Rev Jacob Blackbourne, and something had to be done. The first recorded indication of his attention to Hinchley Wood is in January 1932, when he wrote in his parish magazine that he had been able to arrange for it to be offered for sale at the new post office at Hinchley Wood. Soon after a Commission was appointed by the Bishop of Guildford to judge how the growing spiritual needs of Thames Ditton and its satellites could best be met. This Commission included the second of the two men to whom this book is dedicated; we shall hear much of Bishop Cyril Golding-Bird.

The issue for the Commission was, of course, how to

accommodate the problems of growth. To remind the reader, the diocese of Guildford was itself very young: it had emerged out of the diocese of Winchester in 1927; and its people knew about change and growth: the foundation stone of its own Cathedral was laid in 1936: but it was to be 25 years before the Cathedral was consecrated and replaced the temporary Cathedral of Holy Trinity in Guildford High Street.

The Commission proposed the division of Thames Ditton parish into two: Weston Green and Hinchley Wood together were to be placed in the Conventional District of Weston. The proposal was presented to the annual parochial meeting of St Nicholas on 6 April 1932 and agreed by it. When it came into effect on 1 July 1932, the district included about 1,000 homes (of which about 250 were in Hinchley Wood) and had 430 names on the electoral roll. The formation of a conventional district was a step towards the establishment of a separate parish, which would happen if it were able to show that it had a sustainable church life. Hinchley Wood now left the orbit of Thames Ditton and came under the wing of All Saints'. As a mother church, All Saints' Weston, was exemplary in its recognition of the separate spiritual needs of the newly developing community of Hinchley Wood; ultimately, it gave support to the development of Hinchley Wood's own place of worship; in having it recognised as a conventional district, followed ultimately by its acquisition of parish status. To the Rev John Matthews, Curate-in-charge, and later Vicar of Weston, and to his Churchwardens Mr. Hill and Lt. Col. Rees, go the credit for much of what was achieved by Hinchley Wood in its separate development in the 1930s.

Before the story moves on from All Saints', we should just note here that, reflecting its new parish status, it celebrated the foundation stone laying of its new Church, at its site by Marney's Pond, on 9 October 1938 followed by the consecration on 24 June 1939: a Church designed by Edward Maufe who had also, by this time, designed Guildford Cathedral.

Esher Filling Station

Once again, Esher Filling station was to play a role in our story. As we saw in Chapter 6, it was reported in June 1932 that on account of there being no early prospect of a community hall, Marion Barker was minded to create a facility for hire to local groups. The population was by now growing rapidly and reports from the magazines of neighbouring parishes speak of good numbers of people attending services at Christmas 1932. Just prior to this the Vicar of Thames Ditton was writing in his parish magazine that of the many problems clamouring for solution, not least was the provision of some sort of facility for worship in Hinchley Wood. Responsibility for the development of church life in Hinchley Wood at this time rested, of course, with Rev Matthews who, conscientiously, was visiting the new homes of Hinchley Wood. Hearing of Miss Barker's new hall, he approached her and she agreed gladly to its use for services.

A dance had been held on the Saturday night prior to

the first service: at midnight the music stopped; the room was cleared and the chairs arranged, and then a table was set up for the service on the following morning. On Easter Day, 16 April 1933 (just one month after Dr. Macdonald had won his seat on Esher Council) the first celebration of Holy Communion in Hinchley Wood took place in the ballroom of Esher Filling Station.

Part of the stained glass window in the Lady Chapel of St Christopher's Church, showing the petrol pumps.

This was indeed an extraordinary beginning: Easter Day being a propitious day for the start of church life but, even as communion was being celebrated, petrol was being served to those indulging themselves in the fashionable activity of the time, a drive in the country. Quite who suggested St Christopher, the patron saint of travellers, for the dedication of Hinchley Wood's Church isn't recorded: the allusion to the activity where church life began is plain, and the name was adopted. Easter Day 1933 proved so encouraging to the Rev Matthews that it was decided at once to make arrangements for regular monthly services at the filling station. This combination: of the secular and the spiritual side by side, was to be normal in Hinchley Wood for twenty years. When the permanent Church was built in 1953, with the connection with Esher Filling Station still well within memory, a stained glass window in the Lady Chapel was endowed with the atmospheric scene: a townscape including the image of some petrol pumps: a thematic reminder of the natal connections of Esher Filling Station with St Christopher's.

The Hall Church: where and how?

Two and a half years elapsed, only, between the generative start of church services at the filling station and the opening of the Hall Church (the present parish hall) on 22

FIRST HARVEST FESTIVAL

The first harvest festival to be held in Hinchley Wood took place on Sunday in a room at Esher Filling Station, which is used for church services. Three services were held during the day, including one in the afternoon for children, and they were all well attended. Many harvest offerings were brought, and these were afterwards sent to Thames Ditton Cottage Hospital. The Rev. J.E. Matthews (Vicar of All Saints', Weston) officiated at all services, and his brother, the Rev. W.D. Matthews (curate-in-charge of Burgh Heath) preached in the morning.

Source: Surrey Comet, 13 October 1934

September 1935. That the community was able to spring from its makeshift start to its own freehold hall in such a relatively short time was due to the leadership and inspiration of Bishop Golding-Bird and not to any effective help from the Residents' Association: being non-sectarian, as well as non-political, the Association adopted a neutral stance on the issue. The problem of where to locate a church was one where the worshipping community and its leaders achieved their goals by self-help. Certainly, the Rev Matthews was invited to address the early general meetings of the Association but he could have gained no encouragement from them. At the autumn general meeting in September 1933 he explained the position as regards the proposed Hall Church and the difficulties which were being experienced in obtaining a suitable site and raising the necessary funds, but to no effect.

Separately from the Residents' Association, a public meeting was called at Esher Filling Station on 21 February 1934 to consider the prospects for the building of a church: it was presided over by the Rev Matthews from Weston Green and addressed by Bishop Golding-Bird.

HINCHLEY WOOD

◆

The piece of land at Manor Road, Hinchley Wood which has been given by Mrs. Litchfield Speer as a site for a church in Hinchley Wood, has been made available for immediate use by an arrangement whereby the present tenant will waive the remaining period of his lease. It is probable that building operations will begin before the end of the year.

Source: Surrey Comet, 5 May 1934.

John Matthews was able to report that: "Hinchley Wood was one of the districts marked *'urgent'* on the list of the new areas requiring churches." The meeting considered the various options for a site; all of which, save one which had been offered as a gift, were going to cost formidable amounts. Evidently, Crouch (who as the entrepreneur who started Hinchley Wood, knew of the merits of reinforcing the centre of the new settlement) took an interest in the problem and he offered a site near the station and shops, but not as a gift.

Mrs. Litchfield Speer offered to donate a site, which was part of Manor Farm, on which to locate a Hall Church in Claygate Lane. She was a descendant of the Lord of the Manor of Weston and, as we have already seen, the Speer Estate was a major local landowner and much of Hinchley Wood was built on its land: *noblesse oblige!* There is no doubt that considerable debate took place at the time, and continued for nearly twenty years in relation to the permanent Church, on whether the location of the Claygate Lane site was ideal. As I have already lamented (Chapter 13), no provision was made in the town plan for a site for a church. Bishop Golding-Bird led the discussion of the merits of the various sites, but the meeting could not lightly reject Mrs. Litchfield Speer's offer of a gift: it sat comfortably with the impoverished atmosphere in the room. The meeting decided to establish how soon the offered land would be available. At the time it was grazed by Mr. Keen's dairy herd (we saw in Chapter 6 how he had a dairy business in Station Approach supplied from Manor Farm); his lease over the land in question was not due to expire until 1940. When it was found that he was willing to negotiate the waiver of his lease, the prospects brightened at once: the die was now cast so far as location was concerned: not the best, but free.

The availability of the land was discussed at the first annual parochial meeting of the new parish of All Saints',

Lt. Col. Rees, Churchwarden, All Saints', Weston: who did so much to help St Christopher's in the early days.   Photo: St Christopher's Church

The Rev Albert E Robins, first Curate-in-charge, St Christopher's.
Photo: courtesy Surrey History Centre

Cranleighans sports ground to raise funds for All Saints' new Church: "I am always pleased to give a leg up to people helping themselves, as you are doing", he said. The Rev Matthews spoke of the corporate life of the Guildford diocese being at its beginning, which in 1934 it was indeed, and the inability, yet, of some parishes to achieve their essential place in it. "Parishioners of Weston Green must", he said, "work hard for the building of their parish church": as ever and almost in the same breath, there were encouraging words for those present from Hinchley Wood who could, he said, "look to receive help with funding their own new church".

The Reverend Albert Edward Robins

During the time discussed above, Holy Communion continued to be celebrated monthly at the filling station; in October 1934 the first harvest festival service in Hinchley Wood was held, from which point weekly Sunday services began. A Sunday school had been started in the home of two residents. With the growing activity, a curate was needed. Early in 1935, Bishop Golding-Bird persuaded the Ecclesiastical Commissioners to

Weston, in April 1934. Bishop Golding-Bird said that a church must be built in Hinchley Wood but, of course, All Saints' needed their own new permanent church too, so the two projects had to be accommodated side by side; in five years Weston would have All Saints', but the permanent church for St Christopher's was still nearly 20 years away. The diocese was busy raising funds for its new cathedral as well as for new churches and Lt Col Rees, a Weston Churchwarden, gave some hope that access to these funds might be possible: in the meantime, the vital need was to start local fundraising.

At its meeting on 12 July 1934, the decision to accept the site in Claygate Lane was made by the Weston Church Council. The following Sunday week, the Church of England took possession. By holding the first Evensong ever held in Hinchley Wood the occasion was marked: it was conducted on the site in a barn near Claygate Lane (about where the foundation stone of the permanent St Christopher's now lies).

On 15 October 1934, another meeting was called to encourage local people to join in the work to be done, it being obvious that in the absence of self help, the people of Hinchley Wood could not rely reasonably on their supporters at All Saints'. Twenty-two people attended, and ten were chosen to co-operate with Weston Church Council to plan the building of a temporary Hall Church. This was a key event. At the first sign of local interest, the diocese promised £1,000 and Bishop Golding-Bird secured a further £1,000 from funds given by a wealthy donor, Charles Gaston, who had left money to the diocesan new churches fund: with this core funding in place, plans for building the Hall Church could now be made. Spirited attempts to raise money locally carried the prospect of early reward from the diocese.

Self help had been the theme of Lord Ashcombe (Lord Lieutenant of Surrey) when opening a fête at the Old

---

GUILDFORD DIOCESE CATHEDRAL AND NEW CHURCHES FUND.

———

PARISH OF WESTON

———

ORDER OF SERVICE FOR

BLESSING AND LAYING THE FOUNDATION STONE

OF THE

MISSION HALL CHURCH

AT

HINCHLEY WOOD

on

Sunday, July 28th, 1935 at 4 p.m.

by

The Right Reverend
CYRIL H. GOLDING-BIRD, D.D.
Assistant Bishop of Guildford

In the presence of
The Rev. Canon H.J.F. Tringham, M.A., Rural Dean
The Rev. John E. Matthews, B.A., Vicar of Weston
The Rev. Albert E. Robins, B.A., Curate in charge
Representatives of the Clergy of the Diocese
Civic Representatives
The Parishioners
Councillor Albert H. Hill) Churchwardens
Lt.Col. E.T. Rees, D.S.O., M.C.) of Weston
Miss Mary F. Rigg, A.R.I.B.A., Architect
Messrs. Gaze Ltd., Kingston – Contractors
Mr. R.B. Harding, Foreman

Source: Surrey History Centre, Woking

allocate £120 p.a. towards the stipend of a Curate-in-charge: this was supplemented by a grant of £150 p.a. from the diocese, making £270 p.a., being then the salary of a curate.

In May 1935, a young priest, the Reverend Albert Edward Robins, offered himself for the work in Hinchley Wood. He was an assistant curate at Dorking and the Secretary of the Diocesan Council of Youth. He was to serve the fortunate people of Hinchley Wood from before the Hall Church was built in 1935 through the formative years which followed until, having given spiritual leadership to his people through the early dark days of the war, left in July 1941 to take up his appointment as Vicar of Onslow. It was a ministry which marks St Christopher's history for its devotion and record of solid achievement.

The foundation stone of the Hall Church.

It had only been in May of 1935 that Bishop Golding-Bird and the Council of All Saints', Weston, had decided to go ahead with the two building projects: first, the purchase of the site at Marney's pond for the permanent church of All Saints' for Weston and, secondly, the building of the temporary church for St Christopher's. Now, in July, the foundation stone had been laid and the Rev Robins took up his duties on 15 September. Hinchley Wood was, of course, still part of the parish of Weston and his appointment, technically, was as assistant curate to that parish. However, Bishop Golding-Bird had arranged that the Rev Robins should have, as far as possible, an entirely free hand and be, effectively, "Curate-in-charge" of St Christopher's.

HINCHLEY WOOD

◆

INTRODUCTORY OCCASION

The Rev. A.E. Robins, who is to be Curate-in-charge of Hinchley Wood when the new church hall is opened in September, was introduced to his future parishioners at a social gathering at Hinchley Wood Lawn Tennis Club on Wednesday. With him was his fiancée, Miss Pickford. The Assistant Bishop of Guildford (The Rt. Rev. C.H. Golding-Bird) attended, and the Rev. J.E. Matthews (Vicar of Weston), organised the social.

The foundation stone of the church hall will be laid by the Assistant Bishop at 4 p.m. tomorrow week, Mr. Robins will commence his duties on September 15, the following Sunday he will be licensed, and the church hall will be formally dedicated on September 29.

Source: Surrey Comet, 20 July 1935

The ten representatives who took responsibility for the new Hall Church were busy too. In June 1935, tenders were invited and that of Gaze of Kingston (later well known for their hard tennis courts) accepted. The speed at which things now happened is remarkable. On 17 July the Rev Robins and his fiancée were introduced to his future parishioners, by Bishop Golding-Bird and the Rev Matthews from All Saints', at a social gathering at Hinchley Wood Lawn Tennis Club. On 28 July was held the ceremony for the laying of the foundation stone of the Hall Church by Bishop Golding-Bird who said, aptly: "O God our Heavenly Father who dost choose men to be the stewards of Thy mysteries, Bless the work of our fellowship in the Church of St Christopher that we may build up Thy Kingdom in this our own district of Hinchley Wood."

HINCHLEY WOOD

◆

VIGIL OF CURATE-IN-CHARGE

◆

All Day in Church Receiving Gifts for New Building

Parishioners of St. Christopher's, Hinchley Wood, contributed £32 towards their new church fund on gift day last Saturday. The Rev. A.E. Robins (Curate-in-charge) sat in church from 8 a.m. until 8 p.m., leaving only for his meals which he had in the kitchen that adjoins the building. The fund now stands at £52 11s. 6d., which is a satisfactory sum considering that the church was opened only in September.

Source: Surrey Comet, 9 May 1936

The Jubilee of King George V had been celebrated in May 1935. The last service at Esher Filling Station was held in June. In September the Hinchley Wood Times told its readers: "It has been a matter of great concern to many of the residents of Hinchley Wood for some time past that they have had no place of worship of their own.

They will be very pleased to hear that the new Hall Church, St Christopher's, is now complete. Situated in Claygate Lane behind Manor Farm, it is a building of which they may be justly proud and which reflects the greatest credit upon all who have taken part in erecting it. As the Guildford diocese New Churches Fund has borne the cost of the new building, it is hoped that the people of Hinchley Wood will make a generous response for the new fabric fund."

If the ministry in Hinchley Wood began on Easter Day 1933, it received permanent continuation on 22 September 1935 when, at the first service held in the Hall Church, the Rev Robins was licensed by Bishop Golding-Bird. The licence document, a difficult piece of prose, enshrines the tradition of the ancient church by which under ancient law, the authority of the Bishop is given to what we might call, the man at grass roots level: it refers to the authority of Parliament and emphasises the position of the Church of England as the Established Church. The Vicar of Weston conducted the service, it being a matter of some relief for him to see a good man relieve him from a burden, while Bishop Golding-Bird, busily as ever in his shepherding, gave the address. The choir of All Saints' led the singing.

Albert Robins had arrived: we can sympathise with the young priest, newly wed, and given responsibility for a new district which had no money and a mere handful of followers, but he lost no time in warming to his task: in a letter to every household in Hinchley Wood he asked for support: "When I consider", he wrote, "the task which lies ahead – men and women to be brought together to worship God, children to be instructed, in short, a new corner of God's vineyard to be tilled – I feel very inadequate, but with God's help and your goodwill, this task can be accomplished."

The first full Sunday services held in the Hall Church were on 29 September. In the parish magazine of St Nicholas, separate notes for Hinchley Wood appeared in October 1935 for the first time. Reflecting on the role of the Church in the new settlement of Hinchley Wood, the Rev Robins thought two courses were open: the first was to aim at building a church to meet the needs of a minority who desire to worship in a particular tradition; the second was to consider the needs of the whole community. It was on the second course that the Rev Robins set St Christopher's, for he thought that from its success might flow the impetus of a growing group of worshippers to build a church. Boldly, he made known the requirements which he thought the Church should fulfil in Hinchley Wood, which were: to hand down to generations the basic tenets of Christianity, the Bible, the Creed and the Sacraments: to educate children in the Christian faith: to care for the weak, the sick and the dispossessed in what he described as the "ambulance work" of the Church, and to make possible the true fellowship of the Church. How far St Christopher's may have realised these ideals is not judged here: but when we come to consider the purposeful response in 1951/52 of the hundreds of people of Hinchley Wood who gave substance for the new Church building, even where some of them were not active

churchgoers, we may surmise that, deep within them, they would not have the witness of the Church fail; if this is true Albert Robins' wisdom of approach can be attested.

On 17 October 1935. the Hall Church was dedicated to St Christopher. The Lord Bishop of Guildford performed the ceremony and was accompanied by Bishop Golding-Bird who had done so much to make the building possible. The Bishop preached on the meaning of the words "Thanksgiving, Dedication and Fellowship". In his references to the new Hall Church he emphasised its intended use for all purposes, fellowship in worship and fellowship on secular occasions. The hall was used on weekdays for various community groups and contributed much to the growth of village life.

For the community to move into its new Hall Church was a little like moving into a new home. Complete though the structure may be, the occupants find many things unsuspected to be done and paid for. A little money from the £2,000 given by the diocese to build the Hall Church was left over for furnishings but much still had to be done. The Altar was given by the Rev Mother Superior of the Home of Compassion at Thames Ditton and the Sanctuary carpet came from Bagshot Church. There were chairs to be bought and parishioners were invited to buy one each at a cost of 6/-. Psalters and hymnbooks were wanted and as a temporary measure many people gave spare prayer books from their homes. There was an appeal for Altar curtains in the liturgical colours, white, red, green and violet, and for the rails on which to hang them. The need for curtains led to the formation of a ladies' sewing party, who also made garments: from the proceeds of their sale were bought the first surplices for the choirboys.

The legal position of the Church was anomalous, for St Christopher's remained part of Weston parish until December 1938. However, from the beginning Albert Robins was able to act as if he were, actually, Curate-in-charge: and the laity set about forming its own administration with a Church Council, called at first a "Committee", with its own wardens. These arrangements were with the full agreement of Weston Parochial Church Council, the body legally responsible for Hinchley Wood in ecclesiastical administration. Indeed there was a certain eagerness, naturally enough, on the part of Weston to be relieved of responsibility. Even, before the Hall Church was built, Weston had sought and obtained from the Bishop an undertaking, recognising their freedom from any financial responsibility for it or for the stipend of the Curate.

Nor was future maintenance of the services at Hinchley Wood to be a charge upon them: Weston had enough financial problems of its own, for it was facing the cost of building its own permanent Church. But the worshipping community of Weston had had nearly fifty years to grow up and seek finally its independence of St Nicholas. Hinchley Wood had no such period of maternal guidance nor time for the development of a strong, local church body. Even into the 1950s it was thought possible that the fellowship suffered for having been so precipitately thrown on its own resources. The diocese had been generous in providing the Hall Church and Mrs Litchfield Speer in giving the land, but there was no wealthy family in Hinchley Wood to endow a church, as was common in older times: St Christopher's began with a bare treasury cupboard and the struggle to grow the ministry had few to share the burden.

Thus left to fend for themselves, the few got to work. The first Church "Committee" (it had no legal status yet) met in October 1935, at the Rev Robins' home. This date may therefore be taken as the birthday of the Parochial Church Council. Mr. Marsh, who with his wife had done so much at their home in Claygate Lane to build up a Sunday school, was chosen as "Curate's Warden". Mr. Boyd Watson was elected as "People's Warden" and thus for the first time in Hinchley Wood the offices of Churchwarden were filled. Mr. Luck became the first Secretary and Treasurer. One of the first tasks of the Committee was formally to record gratitude to the Rev Matthews, the Vicar of Weston, who had worked so hard, single handed in the early days, to recruit support in bringing the ministry to Hinchley Wood.

Finance was an immediate problem, but despite the pressing needs of the infant Church, it was decided to allot one collection each month to overseas missions and it stands to the credit of St Christopher's that from its inception the wider responsibilities of the Anglican Church were remembered. Albert Robins' uncompromising approach is well illustrated by his appeal in September 1937 for the founding of a Youth Fellowship. This was his letter:

*"Will young people between the ages of 16 and 30 think over these questions? What exactly does the Church mean to me? Do I need it? Does it need me? If you are not very satisfied with your answer to the first and can say 'Yes' to either or both of the last two, will you be a member of a Youth Fellowship which it is hoped to form in October? I should like to say at the outset that a Youth Fellowship is **not** just a Social Club but it is a means by which young people can also study and discuss the important things of life, and so be more fitted to take an intelligent and active part as members of the Church in the reconstruction of Society. That sounds rather stiff and highbrow I'm afraid but I won't scratch it out now. Don't be daunted: if you like to listen and think, no one will ask any more from you if you prefer not to speak. – A. E. Robins."*

The Youth Fellowship was founded in 1937. It flourished until the war came in 1939 to snuff it out.

Baptisms

The first baptism at St Christopher's was on 19 May 1935, before even the Hall Church was built. The new member was the infant son of Mr. Luck, the first Treasurer of the Church. The christening, by the Rev Matthews, took place in the old barn, which formerly stood on the site of the new Church building in Claygate Lane. The font used was a milk pan lent by Mr. Keen, the dairyman. The first baptisms in the Hall Church were: -

27 October 1935	Diane Evelyn Singleton.
17 November 1935	Ann Elizabeth Ashby.
11 January 1936	Jennifer Jane Foster and Malcom Graham Wheeler.

For these babies a "pocket" font was used as it was not until April 1936 that the present stone font was dedicated and given by the Vicar and people of Claygate. Ann Ashby, a member of the choir of St Christopher's, has lived in Hinchley Wood and worshipped there for the whole of her life: she has contributed several items to this account.

There have been two notable 'Christophers' baptised at St Christopher's: Christopher Edward Robins, baptised on 25 September 1938, and Christopher Vallins, on Palm Sunday 1943; both the sons of successive Curates-in-charge.

1936: the first full year

In 1936, the church magazine which had hitherto been a joint publication by All Saints' Weston and St Nicholas, Thames Ditton, became a joint Weston and Hinchley Wood issue, severing connection with the mother parish of St Nicholas. Hinchley Wood now had its own separate district news and its own local advertisers began to appear: these included Mr. Wallis Jones' pharmacy and Mr. Montgomery's housing estate; both these men gave support to St Christopher's over the years.

On 20 January King George V died and a week later a memorial service was held at St Christopher's at which a good congregation was present. On 29 January the Rev Robins presided at the first annual general meeting, at which the Churchwardens who had been appointed temporarily in the previous September, were confirmed in their offices. The existing Church "Committee" which had done so much to get things started, was elected *en-bloc*, as the first Church Council. The first Electoral Roll of the Church was approved. It contained some sixty names, mostly transferred from the Weston Roll on which it had been necessary for Hinchley Wood people to register previously. The Sunday school report was encouraging with the names of 81 children on the register out of an estimated 120 children in the district.

In February the newly elected Council met for the first time. Methods of appeal for the New Church Fund were discussed and the idea of a Gift Day was suggested. Whist and Bridge Drives were also approved despite some objections about "card games". One member undertook to make and erect a signpost to the Church in Claygate Lane: at that time it was just a lane, not at all open to view as it is now. Lighting of the entrance was also a problem: hurricane lamps were purchased, the expense of more elaborate lighting being postponed as the new road in Claygate Lane was soon to be built.

An appeal was launched for the funding of the permanent Church; £20 had been subscribed at that date. The Bishop had urged the beginning of fund raising and had promised that if a certain proportion of the sum needed

Claygate Lane c1951: looking south at the junction with Manor Road (Geoffrey Tregaskes standing in Claygate Lane).
Photo: Surrey History Centre

Claygate Lane c1953: looking north to Manor Road.
Photo: Surrey History Centre

for a permanent Church was provided locally, the diocese would find the rest. In May the first Gift Day was held. The Rev Robins kept a vigil in the Church from 8 a.m. to 8 p.m. so that people could respond to his gesture by making donations. The children took part by laying a line of pennies from one end of the Church to the other. Over £30 was given, a very large sum for at this time the average Sunday collection was 30/-. In June the first of many successful garden parties was held in a parishioner's garden where over £25 was raised for the New Church Fund. It was the policy to invest every £25 in Savings Certificates, and by the end of the year the Church had purchased £375. About this time the Hinchley Wood Players were producing dramatic entertainments in aid of the Church Building Fund. The group started as an offshoot of the Tennis Club and had a strong and enthusiastic membership working entirely for charitable objects.

On 22 July an important event took place: a contingent from St Christopher's attended the laying of the foundation stone of the new Cathedral at Guildford by the Archbishop of Canterbury, Dr. Cosmo Lang. Three days later St Christopher's celebrated the first patronal festival of St Christopher's with a special service of Evensong and the Rev Matthews came over from Weston to preach.

In 1936, a programme of social occasions began: until then, these had been the sole province of the Residents' Association and the Tennis Club. A Brownie pack and Guide company were started which, apart from a break during the war, continued to flourish. In October 1936, a branch of the Mothers' Union was inaugurated. Perhaps most successful of the social groups was the Badminton Club begun in July 1936. Enthusiasts secured permission for the use of the Hall Church; play was continued until the outbreak of war; it was resumed afterwards and, although discontinued now, the court lines can still be seen on the hall floor.

Albert Robins thought that the first Easter at St Christopher's was a time of great joy: the Church was beautifully decorated and there were 170 communicants on Easter Day when many Hinchley Wood people came

to the Church for the first time. On Trinity Sunday, the first candidates from St Christopher's were confirmed by the Bishop at Weston Green. These children were Betty Ainsworth, Pat Campbell, Kathleen Dann, Grace Griffen, Estelle Mayer, Zanthi Porter, Victor Broadribb, Peter Hoard and Kenneth Holden. Grace Griffen had the misfortune to be killed in an air raid during the war.

The first Harvest Festival at St Christopher's in October was a great occasion. The Archdeacon of Dorking preached and for the first time 38 spare chairs hitherto stored in the loft had to be brought into use for the Church was full. In December a Nativity Play was produced, and a Carol Party of Church members began what has become an annual and popular tradition in Hinchley Wood.

In 1937, in the first service of Confirmation to be held in St Christopher's own Hall Church, fourteen candidates were presented to Bishop Golding-Bird who was assisted by Canon Hyde, who had come to live in Hinchley Wood in 1934. The young people confirmed in 1937 were Jack Butcher, Douglas Suter, Kevin Noble, Dudley Cowderoy, Bernard Weaver, Leslie Rendell, Myrtle Bailey, Valerie and Vivyenne Underhill, Muriel Kingsnorth, Joy Parker, Josephine Brand, Joan Bosley and Nancy Stone.

Music

Albert Robins was a music lover and he soon encouraged the start of a choir by appealing for men and boys to join, but before it was established, members of the congregation turned up half-an-hour before Evensong on Sundays to practise: "so that our worship might be made reverently and with understanding". It was several weeks after Albert Robins arrived, and after much careful preparation by congregational practices at 10.30 on Sunday mornings that a Sung Eucharist became possible as a regular service. Music was provided by a "wheezy" harmonium, on which the first organist, Mr. C N Longhurst, "performed feats of great endurance". It was impossible to keep the wind in the instrument for long; tunes requiring very sustained chords had to be avoided so that the organist could "keep the wind in". After a few weeks the harmonium was given up as a bad job and a grand piano was obtained and this continued in use until the electric Hammond organ replaced it.

Perhaps the boldest financial decision in the early days was to purchase an organ. The grand piano had been better than the harmonium but it was felt that an organ would be more atmospheric. The problem was to find the money. Rev Robins, with the support of several members of the Council, was determined to explore the possibility of buying a Hammond organ which could be used also for the permanent church when it was built. The thought of embarking on an expenditure of £400 was, for those responsible for the slender finances of the Church at this time, easy to resist, so it was inevitable that the project was keenly debated. Some were for keeping the piano and others for getting the harmonium repaired. But, undaunted by caution, the visionaries proceeded with their plans and paid a visit to the Church of St James, Kennington, where a Hammond organ was in use. From this they took fresh courage and quite unconstitutionally, they decided to buy an instrument from Boosey and Hawkes. Donations came from many and often unexpected quarters: it was paid for quickly, allowing an organist, Mr. Birchall of Ewell, to be appointed at a salary of £30 per annum. In due course the Hammond organ was moved to the permanent Church where it served until the present organ was installed in 1970.

St Christopher's: a "conventional district"

In 1937 thoughts turned to seeking the status of "conventional" district for St Christopher's, as All Saints' had done five years earlier. At the annual meeting for the year, the Rev Robins reported the steady increase in the congregations since the Church opened in 1935. All parish activities were progressing with over 100 children on the Sunday school roll. In spite of his achievements, the Rev Robins had to report that the Church Council's ambition to seek the status of "conventional district" was regarded by the authorities as premature: this must have been very disappointing to the young man. The Electoral Roll of the Church had grown to 93 names: was this sufficient to sustain St Christopher's independence of All Saints'?

The following year, 1938, the question was asked again, but this time it was thought that separate legal status in ecclesiastical matters should be given to Hinchley Wood. Up to then, during the three years since the licensing of its Curate-in-charge, although St Christopher's had managed its own affairs with its own Churchwardens and a Church "Council", this had been possible only due to the goodwill of Weston parish of which Hinchley Wood was still a legal part. Now an application to the Ecclesiastical Commissioners and to the Crown was submitted by the Bishop to have Hinchley Wood defined as a "conventional district". In December 1938, the application was sealed and so the conventional district was formed and at a special service of Evensong, in a form

much like that for the induction of an incumbent, the licence was handed to Albert Robins. The Archdeacon of Dorking conducted the service in the presence of the Rural Dean of Emly.

The establishment of a legal basis for St Christopher's allows us to pause to consider a boundary issue. A practical result of the original delegation of responsibility (in 1935) had been the need to decide on an unofficial and ad hoc sub-division of Weston, and to allot to St Christopher's its own space on the map. The rationale behind how this division was drawn is a mystery. It has led to a curious anomaly which was not corrected at the time St Christopher's was given separate legal status nor has it been addressed since. A glance at the map demonstrates the natural boundary created by the Portsmouth Road: yet Couchmore Avenue and Westmont Road, on its south side, were left in Weston. It was said that the two roads were included in Weston at the time in order to make up the Weston population figure to support its application for parochial status. Expedient, perhaps, but it was not a good reason for drawing a parochial boundary, which ought to reflect geography as well as natural communities. The north western boundary of St Christopher's parish has a bulge of Weston intruding into it to capture two roads of Hinchley Wood. The bizarre anomaly has endured to the present day: perhaps the issue only needs to be addressed for it to be rationalised. (The anomaly is now compounded by the civil boundary of Hinchley Wood having migrated to the north of the Portsmouth Road: which is equally bizarre.)

It was fortunate that the conventional district was formed when it was. No one could have foreseen that within twelve months the country would be plunged into the greatest war in history and that such high hopes for the local development of the Church would remain unrealised for over a decade.

A site for the permanent Church

Following the achievement of conventional district status, thoughts turned to the building of a permanent Church. It may seem surprising now, but there was never in the 1930s nor later after the war, a total acceptance that the permanent church should be built on the present site: in spite of the fact that it was available and that this is where the Hall Church was: the old worries about it not being sufficiently centrally located surfaced again.

Writing in All Saints' parish magazine in 1939, the Rev Robins said: "When do you think the new church will be started? I wish I could answer the question. It will cost approximately £10,000 and we are raising £300 per annum. If a big appeal were made in Hinchley Wood we might raise £1,000, giving us £2,000 in hand. If the Diocese gave us another £2,000 we could build the chancel of the Church and a part of the nave, or the nave and a temporary chancel. So that if all goes well and people do their utmost we might have a part of the new Church by the end of 1941 or early 1942. But the problem is rendered difficult by another point. The site in front of the Hall Church is geographically a bad one. When we build we build for a long future and the Church will be expected to minister to the needs of many thousands of people, keen and apathetic. The work of future Vicars among these last must be considered. While there is any possibility of a better site we must not let our natural desire to build a Church as soon as possible lead us to take a step of such importance which other generations will condemn as short-sighted."

Opinion was divided: Albert Robins and, evidently, the Church Council, longed for a site in the central area near the station and shops. The Residents' Association did its best, and was successful before and after the war, to prevent the building of St Christopher's Church on what is now the memorial gardens in Station Approach. At the 1938 autumn general meeting of the Association, consideration was given to correspondence with the Rev Robins: he had requested the support of the Association to an application which the Church authorities had made to Esher Council for the purchase of a site for use as a church. The Association maintained their po-faced attitude of being in favour of the site, which at the time was a nursery, being purchased by the Council for public open space; this was an ambition in which they were ultimately successful in the form of the memorial gardens.

The Memorial Gardens, 2002.

I find myself at odds with the Residents' Association generally on the issue of a church site; they may not have been wrong, specifically, about the memorial gardens site for I am not sure it was quite big enough to accommodate a church and its associated facilities and to avoid spoiling the general feel of space. The Residents' Association fell back on the town plan in rationalising their objection: it was the town plan which was wrong in the first place for, as I pointed out in Chapter 13, absolutely no provision was made in it for a site for a church. Here was the error made and here must lie the blame: but the evidence is not comfortable for the Residents' Association, or perhaps the residents they represented, for the lack of their concern about any alternative site.

Albert Robins considered other sites, but with no support from the Residents' Association for any of them, we

can imagine his despair. The Bishop rejected one site which was available because of its proximity to the bypass. Other sites near Station Approach, whilst suitable, had to be rejected because they weren't available at the time (the town plan problem).

It is necessary to break from chronology, for a moment, so that the post-war part of the story on the church site can be completed here. In 1948 there was considerable support at St Christopher's for moving the whole church presence, lock, stock and barrel, from its Claygate Lane site to the location of the Hinchley Wood Lawn Tennis Club which was on land owned by Mr. Symonds, somewhere on the present site of the builders' merchant. Mr. Symonds was prepared to sell the site of the Tennis Club for £7500: but how could such a sum be raised? The essence of a funding scheme was to sell the undeveloped land (on which, eventually the church was to be built) and, in an inspired thought, sell the Hall Church to the Education Authority, whose school site was contiguous with it. Everything went well except the numbers: even though the school needed the extra space, the gap between what the Claygate Lane site could be sold for, and what Mr. Symonds wanted for the Tennis Club site, could not be breached. The scheme had to be dropped: Mr. Symonds used the land for a builders' merchant which, initially, traded under his name. The Tennis Club closed in 1949 but not without a most praiseworthy valedictory gesture: on liquidation of the club, the residual funds were given to St Christopher's to promote the resurrection of the youth work in the parish, started by Albert Robins, but moribund for ten years since the outbreak of war.

The story of the church site was to have one last twist before, wearying of ever finding an alternative, the Church Council, decided to build on the site it owned. In 1950 the idea of building a church at Station Approach was resurrected and the Residents' Association was to receive a severe rebuke from the Esher News when they renewed their objection to a church on that site. "Probably for the first time in its useful life", wrote the paper, "Hinchley Wood Residents' Association has shown itself out of step with current thought in its locality by opposing the suggestion that a church should be built in Station Approach" (on which neither the flats nor the memorial gardens had yet been built). How this sharp criticism was received isn't known: the minutes of the Association are silent on the issue. How different it may have been if Royston Pike had been a supporter of the Church: if a man of his leadership skills in civic affairs, the monuments to which are beyond doubt and recorded at length in this book, had been actively *for* the Church; inevitably, he would have encouraged resources of thought and reasoning to be applied to the problem. If Royston Pike had wanted better provision for a church site in the 1930s and again after the war, he would have led public opinion towards it: he didn't, and the Church had to have what it could get.

Returning to the pre-war time, the Hall Church was much in use, during the week, for the social life of the community: it was used also for air raid training. There began a movement to have the Hall set aside purely for use as a Church. The Church Council gave much thought to this and steps were taken to try and provide separate premises at the Claygate Lane site, with the object of using this for social work. The cost was estimated to be £300 and for some months the project was freely canvassed. By June 1939, however, after consultation with the diocese, it seemed likely that in the normal course of things the new permanent Church would be built by 1941 or 1942. The completion and consecration of All Saints' on 24 June 1939 had shown what could be done and hopes for St Christopher's were high. So the immediate expenditure on a further temporary building seemed unjustified. But the idea of reserving the Hall Church only for worship was a pointer to the feelings of the time: there were a number of people who found difficulty in using the Hall as a place of worship and private prayer. The need for a consecrated building was keenly felt and its absence added greatly to the difficulties of Albert Robins' ministry.

Albert Robins leaves – Hedley James Vallins arrives

The Rev Albert Robins' farewell letter to his parishioners in June 1941, was one of a character in which the man's warmth towards his fellows and his affection for the work he was to leave behind can be felt, 60 years later. Of course, the war had spoiled for him any vision of a permanent church, and much more besides. He was only a young man and he had had the tough job of leading church life for the six years since the Hall Church had been built: an increasingly gloomy period which at its beginning brought the sense that war might be coming, through the realisation that it was inevitable and now, in 1941, having emerged from its very darkest period came the madman's invasion of the Soviet Union: and brighter hope. As Churchill had said, as he warmed to the Soviets: "If Hitler invaded Hell, I would at least make a favourable reference to the Devil." More prosaically, Albert Robins wrote: "My last Sunday will be on 13 July when there will be a parade service for the Home Guard at which I shall close a very happy though short time among them as their padré." He left to become Vicar of Onslow Village.

The Rev Hedley Vallins was the Curate-in-charge from 1941 to 1945. Probably on account of the whole of his time in Hinchley Wood being during the war years, very little has been written about him. He had been a schoolmaster at Farnham Grammar School before training for the ministry at Chichester Theological College. He was ordained in Godalming, and had curacies in Bromley and Fleet before coming to Hinchley Wood. Later he was Rural Dean of Chertsey and Canon of Guildford Cathedral. It was the Rev Hedley Vallins who conducted the first marriage ceremony in St Christopher's (until then it had not been licensed for marriages which were conducted at All Saints') when on 9 October 1942 James Andrews of Manor Road North married Miss Fay Winter of Colwyn Bay.

As the worst days of the war passed, and it was clear that the survival of Christian life was secure, thoughts of the building of a permanent church after the war's end could be accommodated. Hedley Vallins was able to leave an indelible stamp on the story of St Christopher's, because, on 1 July 1942 the Parochial Church Council was informed that an architect friend of his, Mr. Samuel Beverley, had inspected the proposed site for the new church and had offered to make preliminary drawings in order to help advance the project in the minds of the congregation. On this evidence the story of the Church as ultimately built, to the design of Mr. Beverley, dates from 1942 and Hedley Vallins' name is permanently linked with it.

As someone with no consciousness of the war years: only the rationing which continued after it; I am deeply impressed how the contemporary records of parish and Church Council meetings are consistently full of hope: not even in the darkest days is there a hint of foreboding: how strong those people must have been. Even in 1941, Hedley Vallins was encouraging his people to settle on the Claygate Lane site (we have seen, however, that the issue was not finally settled until after the war); he was always looking to the war's end and his dream of what we now have. In 1943 the plans which Mr. Beverley had drawn up were put to the diocese as a basis for planning the post-war building. In January 1945, Mr. Beverley was contracted as architect for the new church. These high hopes were to receive their set-backs, not least on the financial front; to give colour to how poor the country was and the conditions in which these bright hopes were clasped, the minute books tell us that, as an economy measure, they were turned about so that pages already used could be re-used. Post-war shortages were to be a problem.

Except at a distance, Hedley Vallins was not to see how the people of Hinchley Wood responded, after the war, to the financial demands which the new church were to put on them; later in 1945, he left Hinchley Wood to take up the appointment as Vicar of Englefield Green.

An early sketch c1944 of the permanent church by the architect, Mr. Samuel Beverley.   Photo: St Christopher's Church

The Parish Hall in 2002, showing the 1983 extensions.

Hinchley Wood Home Guard.   Photo: courtesy Elmbridge Museum

Hedley Vallins' contribution to Hinchley Wood was recognised after he left. He came back in 1951 to take part in the ceremonial cutting of the first turf for the permanent Church: and again in 1958, when he dedicated the gates and railings to the Church, which had been given by two anonymous donors, to mark the 25th anniversary of Church life in Hinchley Wood*. His son, Christopher, entered the ministry and is Chaplain of Epsom Hospital.

---

* As this book was going to press, it emerged that one of these donors was Bill Lawson, a Churchwarden in the 1950s

AIR RAID WARDENS

———

A number of part time Air Raid Wardens urgently required for Hinchley Wood. For particulars of Service, Training, etc., apply to your nearest Warden's Post, or to the District Warden.

Wardens are particularly required for short periods of duty during the day-time.

Source: Hinchley Wood Times, February 1940
(Elmbridge Museum)

The Hall Church on the occasion of the last service to be held, February 1953.   Photo: St Christopher's Church

A vignette of wartime Hinchley Wood

To reflect the sombre days of the Rev Hedley Vallins' wartime ministry I reproduce below a poem by Mrs. Cecily Pile of Thames Ditton, who wrote in 1979 to Esher District Local History Society: "Re-reading Mr. Royston Pike's article on Hinchley Wood, I am reminded that in the early 40s the side of the hill facing the railway station was in use by a farmer. I used to catch an evening train and waiting on the station admired the scene, complete with haystack. I wrote the following:

Hinchley Wood, 1941

A smudge of blue smoke
Against the green wood,
Dimmed in the dusk
But coloured and clear.

Thatched is the stack
On the height of the hill,
And fallow the fields
To the turn of the year.

CHAPTER 15:
THE PERMANENT CHURCH

The turf-cutting ceremony, 22 July 1951: the Ven Newill (Archdeacon of Dorking) has the spade; the Rev Vallins looks on from the left of the picture, with the Rev Newton Jones from the right. Councillor Kerr, Churchwarden is in the centre.   Photo: courtesy, Ann Ashby

In this final chapter we see the building and consecration of the Parish Church of St Christopher's in 1953: the remaining piece of the jigsaw puzzle in the story of Hinchley Wood: the origins of a 1930s settlement.

The Rev Newton Jones

The Rev Newton Jones came to St Christopher's in 1945 and was inducted as the Curate-in-charge on 3 November. A Welshman, he came to Surrey from Liverpool in 1928, having held posts in Godalming and Bookham. He spent 21 years in the parish. It was he who was present to hear Mr. Samuel Beverley, the architect, tell the Parochial Church Council on 6 July 1949 about the plans for the new Church, and again on 3 November 1950 when the plans had been approved by the diocesan authorities and planning consent had been given by Esher Council. He was to be the incumbent who would see the realisation of the permanent Church so longed for by Alfred Robins and Hedley Vallins.

He was an active man, not known for bright sermons, but extremely dutiful: in calling quickly on newcomers to

Hinchley Wood and, so to say, gathering them, he was exemplary. He actively supported youth activities and it was he who reformed the youth group after the war, the Young Communicants' Guild, helped by the Tennis Club funds referred to in the previous chapter. He was a great harvester of support: writing, calling, prompting and persuading: as he was loved, so he succeeded.

He would be the first to say that by the election of two special Churchwardens in 1949 he, and the Church, were blessed with fortune: these two men gave stout contribution to the huge work, and achievement, of the next four years, which did not end with the consecration but was marked by that momentous point: these two men were Councillor W Kerr and Mr. J H Jordan.

In that same year, on 29 September, was gazetted the decision of the Court at Buckingham Palace that, once the Church had been built, St Christopher's would be a new parish in the archdeanery of Dorking and in the rural deanery of Emly. This was quickly followed by the public licensing of Newton Jones on 15 December 1949.

1950 was a busy year: it saw the purchase for £400 of the site for the vicarage in Manor Road North and the

The Rev Newton Jones.   Photo: courtesy, Ann Ashby

Part of the first post-war new church fund raising activity.
Source: St Christopher's Church

granting of planning permission (but not yet the grant of a building licence): and, as already noted, Samuel Beverley presenting his plans for the Church. Well might Newton Jones quote Nehemiah 2:18 in his Christmas message of 1950: "Let us rise up and build, so they strengthened their hands for the good work."

Newton Jones worked vigorously to support fundraising for the new Church. In July 1951, the tireless Vicar installed himself in Station Approach from 9 a.m. until 3 p.m. to receive gifts from the people of Hinchley Wood for the Church building fund: this act was the echo of the Rev Albert Robins' vigil in the Hall Church in July 1936, also to raise money for the Church. In 1951 the estimated cost of the new Church was £22,000: £7,000 had been collected already over the years since the Hall Church was built and the parishioners had been told that £3,000 would come from the diocese; this was to be a matter of grave concern a year later when doubt was raised about whether it would be forthcoming (see below). There was a gap of £12,000 to be bridged as Newton Jones first visited the homes of Hinchley Wood, then sat in Station Approach to collect gifts of cash and promises by covenant to pay in the future: by December 1951 over £5,000 had been raised from this initiative.

Newton Jones arranged a big programme of events around the St Christopher's Day patronal festival of 1951. He wanted to cover the whole community with the good news and preside over the debut of the new Church, which, only the month before, had been licensed to over-

come the post-war building restrictions: now, if the funding gap could be closed, the Church could be built. On the Friday he led a big group to the annual service on Stag Hill, the construction site of Guildford Cathedral (construction had been suspended because of the war, but now work had recommenced): on the Saturday was the receiving of gifts in Station Approach: on the Sunday was the ceremony of cutting the first turf, followed by Evensong conducted, in a thoughtful touch on the part of Newton Jones, by the Rural Dean of Chertsey, St Christopher's own Hedley Vallins. Then, on Wednesday 25 July 1951, the day of St Christopher, the patron saint of travellers, Newton Jones presented to the people of Hinchley Wood the plans for their new Church, which if the funding gap could be closed, would be built.

Councillor Bill Kerr and Mr. John Jordan

Bill Kerr and John Jordan were the two Churchwardens who were in place at the critical time to help the tireless Newton Jones, and by their talents and faith, guide the final years of striving, ultimately to see the realisation of 20 years of aspiration: the consecration of St Christopher's Church. These three men, assisted by Bill Lawson as Treasurer and Bill Tregaskes as Secretary to the Covenant Fund, were the driving force of that achievement; Bill Lawson and Bill Tregaskes were to be the next Churchwardens.

Bill Kerr and his family had moved to Hinchley Wood before the war from Barnes, where he had been a member of the Parochial Church Council and a sidesman at the Church of St Michael and All Angels. He became active at St Christopher's and in the Residents' Association where, being a Christian, his influence in Hinchley Wood's civic life provided a counterweight to the godless Royston Pike. He became chairman of the Residents' Association in 1947, and was elected to Esher Council in the following year. Bill Kerr had the first distinction, emulated twice since, of serving on the civic Council and as a Churchwarden of St Christopher's. (The latest ones are Norman Phillips and Jack Mulder. Two other members of St Christopher's congregation who have held elective office as Councillors Mr. Peter Highley and Mrs. Janet Turner, who is a sitting member now.)

Churchwarden John Jordan.
Photo: courtesy, Mrs. Pat Gregory, Mr. Jordan's daughter

John Jordan and his family came to live in Hinchley Wood during the war, living at first in Avondale Avenue, and later, Manor Road North. One of his fortés was fund raising ideas and organising people to this end. His original notes, roughly penned on the front of a small brown envelope have survived [see photograph on this page]. Most of the items on the notes have achieved historical status and are referred to in the late Will Williams 1987

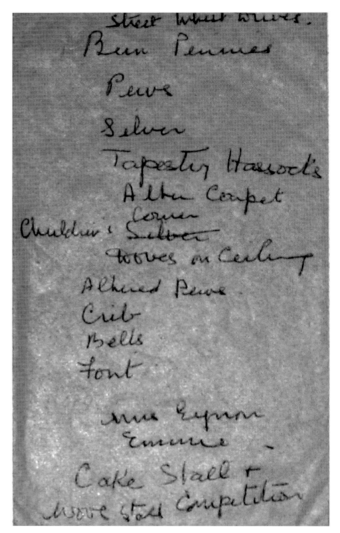

The 1950 brown envelope containing Churchwarden John Jordan's notes on fundraising ideas.
Source: Mrs. Pat Gregory, Mr. Jordan's daughter

description of the Church which is given as an Appendix to this book (reference to this is recommended for it is a valuable record of the source of many items in the Church's inventory). Special mention should be made of a few items. In December 1951 Mr. Jordan announced an appeal for second-hand silver, which after melting down could be fashioned into candlesticks, an altar cross and other items for the new Church. This appeal, which was cast widely, was very successful. Large numbers of people, many from outside the parish, notably because the invitation was cast so widely, responded to this appeal which touched a sentimental spot: all sorts of silver items were given, to provide altar ornaments worthy of the new Church. The processional cross was used for the first time at the dedication of the vicarage. The ciborium was made at a later date from silver presented by Mrs. Wells, being sporting trophies of her late brother, and in his memory. It was an inspired idea to appeal so widely: whether the item given was loved, as many were, or unloved, every donor was able to feel blessed by the creation of something so valued and otherwise unaffordable.

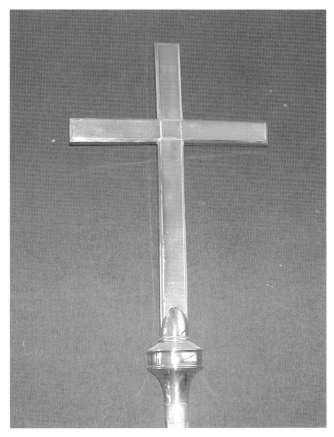

The processional cross of St Christopher's: made from donated silver.

One of the 14 doves on the ceiling of the Church.

There is an attractive story about the doves on the ceiling of the Church (the idea of the architect, Mr. Beverley, and which are described in the Appendix). After they had been supplied but before they were fitted, they sat for a while on Mr. and Mrs. Jordan's dining table; to have one dove would be remarkable, but 17! Equally homespun is the story of Mr. Jordan's work with tapestry. In the earlier part of the war, before the Jordan family moved to Hinchley Wood, they were living in Liverpool, a city which endured particularly cruel bombing raids. Boring of the long hours spent in the shelters, John Jordan, became intrigued by his shelter companions: ladies who, in the manner of such creatures, could not possibly allow

the tyrant to waste their time while sheltering from his bombs: they knitted; and while they knitted, John Jordan learnt to knit. Working as he did with textiles (for the NAAFI) he had a ready supply of odds and ends of wool: he became a very proficient knitter. The reader may guess that when the question arose of: what about hassocks? there was Mr. Jordan, now supervising ladies, so good had been his tutors, organising the sewing parties.

The final reference here to John Jordan's way-marking list; so symbolic of fertile thought across a range of fund raising ideas which were captured is the reference to 'Bun Pennies'.

The "Bun Penny and Ship Halfpenny" pew

Visitors to the Church should notice the front pew where a small plate records this name. The idea was born in June 1952, when the Church was being built and appeals went out for its furnishing. Mrs. Gladys Bentley, who had some years previously organised a collection of bun pennies to help build King George's Hall, Esher, came forward with the idea of organising a similar collection to include the ship halfpenny to provide funds for a pew. Mrs. Bentley improvised a number of collecting jars which were issued to over 30 homes who had volunteered to take part in the scheme. Each month Mrs. Bentley set forth on her bicycle to collect the full jars and deposit empties. The coins were paid into the local post office and banks with the object of keeping them in local circulation! Never was there a more practical example of how casting bread on water could yield many-fold. It is hard to bring to mind the effort involved in collecting, handling and checking something like 20,000 coins. The Parochial Church Council placed on record their most grateful thanks to Mrs. Bentley and her supporters, so typical of the beehive of activity at the time, so that future generations might know how the "Bun Penny and Ship Halfpenny Pew" came to be provided.

The turf-cutting ceremony

It seems to be of another world now, but after the war building works were rationed just like other things: the rationing process was achieved by the government disallowing building work except by the positive approval of it by licence. The licence to build St Christopher's was granted in May 1951. On 22 July a service was held to mark the cutting of the first turf: the mark that the building project had started. During the early part of the afternoon lightning and heavy rain sweeping in on the wind created conditions traditionally associated with the patron saint – "Surely a good omen", commented the Rev Newton Jones.

"In a short while you will have only a small scratch in the ground, but it marks a beginning – on the foundations will be built a fine and well-designed parish Church of which you may well be proud." With these words the Ven E J Newill (Archdeacon of Dorking) opened his address at the short service which preceded the ceremony. Taking for his text "… it is more blessed to give than to receive" the Archdeacon commented that the new Church would stand as a symbol of the strong faith of the people of Hinchley Wood. The Rev Hedley Vallins was there, deservedly, to play his part in the service.

Confidence was high after the turf-cutting, that with the Church design settled; planning permission given; the building licence in hand; the funding in place or promised; the construction could commence. Considerable energy was applied in the next few months to settling the terms of a building contract.

The foundation stone is laid

Laying the foundation stone: Admiral of the Fleet, Lord Tovey, with Churchwarden Councillor Kerr. Photo: Courtesy, Geoffrey Tregaskes

---

ORDER OF SERVICE
FOR THE
LAYING AND DEDICATION
OF THE
FOUNDATION STONE
OF THE
CHURCH OF ST. CHRISTOPHER
HINCHLEY WOOD
ON
SATURDAY, 12TH JANUARY, 1952
AT 3 P.M.

S. NEWTON JONES, B.A., *Vicar.*
J. H. JORDAN
W. KERR   Churchwardens.

The excitement of the events can be imagined: in no time it seemed, the contractors were ready for the foundation stone laying ceremony: it was watched by over 400 people on 12 January 1952. Work had started on site in the previous October, the contract for the works having been let to Tom Porter Ltd. Now, with the foundations laid, Admiral of the Fleet, Lord Tovey could honour the proceedings.

Admiral of the Fleet, Lord Tovey, from "Men of Action" 1943.

The text of Lord Tovey's speech survives:

"I feel as if I am laying the keel-plate of a ship, but one far more important than the ordinary ship.

You are building a ship to embark on a tremendous adventure. You are setting out to do what our ancestors have done ever since Christians first came to our island. Through the centuries they have built Churches to the Glory of God, in which they have humbly worshipped and found comfort, courage, inspiration and the love of God.

Difficult as it is in these days to find the ways and means of building a Church, your more important and, possibly, even more difficult task is to build up in the parish a true Christian brotherhood, without which the Church itself is of little content.

How vitally important this is, becomes very obvious when you look round the world today. The appalling state of chaos with fear, suspicion and uncertainty everywhere.

It seems all wrong when one remembers that the last 100 years have been the most progressive in our history. Great discoveries in science, engineering, medicine: great advances have been seen in education and social conditions. All of which one would expect to react to the benefit of mankind, yet all we have achieved are two ghastly wars leading us to our present state of misery and chaos.

Isn't the trouble that man, full of conceit in his achievements, has come to regard himself as self-sufficient, no longer in need of God, to worship Him, humbly to offer Him our love and to seek His.

Many people with the best of intentions are seeking a solution, hoping to find the solution in solving the troubles of the moment, but with no clear vision of the ultimate object.

Probably the nearest they get is to wish for a better world: but that is too vague and so easily becomes a purely selfish object – a better world for self, family, class or nation. We fell down on it after the first war and even now six years after the second we are having to put most of our effort into staving off yet a third war.

Surely our object must be a Christian world: a world such as God wishes and intends us to have. With that as our object we have in Christ's own teaching a guide for our every thought, word and action whether as individuals, members of a family, community or nation and between nations.

In the task you have undertaken, you are seeking that object with high courage, sure faith and humbly seeking God's aid you will succeed."

(Here was a man, speaking at the time of the Korean War, who was well qualified to speak of war and fear. Before becoming a Church Commissioner, which was his qualification for the day's task, he had served in the Royal Navy, most notably as Commander in Chief, Home Fleet. Knowing fear and the price of defeat, he had run the Battle of the Atlantic: from the bridge of HMS King George V, he had commanded the fleet when it sank the Bismarck: yet here was a man of peace who could speak of community and seeking God's aid.)

The steel shortage

Any thoughts that all the problems of the venture had been identified, addressed and solved were found to be premature.

As the contract for building the Church was let in October 1951 the expectation was that the job would be finished in 10 months: even allowing for slippage, this would allow the consecration to be planned for a year later. It was not to be, for rumours began to circulate that there was a problem with materials. The austerity of the years following the war, from which the country had not yet completed its emergence, caused the divergence of resources away from domestic consumption into products for export. In 1952 there was a shortage of steel and the contractor could not get, on time, the supplies it needed for the roof: the whole programme of construction was bound to be delayed. The problem was not so much an absence of roof steel, but a queue for it: there would be a delay of three months; in consultation with the architect and contractors a new date for the consecration of the Church was set: Saturday, 7 February 1953: in Coronation Year!

The new vicarage

As if they were not busy enough, but because the building licence for the new vicarage in Manor Road North came through, work on it had to start and the foundation stone was laid by Mr. Jordan on 12 October 1952. This had not been the first site considered for a vicarage. In

Work-in-progress, 1952, standing in Claygate Lane are Mrs Tregaskes, Edith with bicycle and Geoffrey. Photo: St Christopher's Church

March 1945, discussions were held with Mr. Keen (our dairyman in Manor Farm) about the availability of his orchard on the north side of the Church with a frontage on Claygate Lane; its proximity to the Church (if that was where it was to be built), made the site ideal. Sadly, the attempts to procure the Claygate Lane site foundered: it was unaffordable at the time.

THIS STONE WAS LAID BY
J. H. JORDAN, ESQ.
THE PEOPLE'S WARDEN
12TH OCTOBER 1952

The inscription on the foundation stone of the Vicarage.

The funding crisis

A new crisis broke which, if not overcome, might have broken the staunchest spirit. Whether through miscalculation, mistake or unavoidable and severe diocesan financial strain, a grant of £3,000, which everyone at St Christopher's thought was secure, suddenly became in doubt.

It was early in 1952, after the contractor had commenced work, that this embarrassment emerged. £3,000 may not sound like such a large gap in the finances but at that time the most valuable house in Hinchley Wood might not fetch this amount: it was a big problem. With no means of bridging the gap which would be created, the loss of the grant would have left the parish unable to pay the contractor.

At the time, Bill Tregaskes, was also a member of Guildford Diocesan Board of Finance. He wrote a long letter to the Board, pleading St Christopher's case which was to be considered at its meeting on 25 April 1952. The problem which he addressed was the possible loss of the grant of £3,000. The evidence for the existence of a promise to grant £3,000 was this. Mr. Tregaskes pleaded:

"At the very first annual meeting (January 1936) the new Church fund was launched with Diocesan encouragement and the local people were told that if they raised a proportion of the sum required the Diocese would supply the rest." This early indication of help "though never precisely formulated as to amount" had always been present and "has been reiterated from time to time" in responsible quarters.

The problems which St Christopher's had overcome were recited: "With the coming of the war, the prospect of building the Church vanished"; the post war years had brought building control and other disappointments. Inflation meant that as fast as money was collected, estimates of the cost of the Church mounted. Evidently, Mr. Tregaskes said, there had been those who said the Church would never be built, and had transferred their support outside the parish. "The Church which would have cost £8,000 in 1939 is costing £22,500 today exclusive of furnishings …" Of this sum, the Parochial Church Council had raised, by gifts or loans supported by deeds of covenant, £16,750: other grants of £2,750 left the £3,000 gap. Emphasis was placed on the fact that St Christopher's was to be the first post-war Church in Surrey to be built.

The crisis passed: Bishop Golding-Bird had risen from his sick bed to plead the case for St Christopher's and he won the day, for some days later the news came that the grant would be paid. It ensured that the Bishop Golding-Bird had been involved in every critical event in St Christopher's life: from even before the first Christian worship in Hinchley Wood to the finishing of its Church: the Bishop's frail letter of acknowledgement is shown below; it is appropriate, here, to say more of him.

the parish Church of St. Christopher is about to be consecrated, pay tribute to him to whom we owe almost our existence as a Church."

To re-cap, in 1932, Dr. Golding-Bird was a member of the small Commission appointed to consult in Thames Ditton, and to consider how best the spiritual needs of the growing district could be met. In February 1934, he presided at the meeting of Hinchley Wood people to try and obtain a site for a church and to plan the erection of a temporary Church building. Largely as a result of his efforts the present site was given to the diocese by the Speer Estate and, presently, funds made available to build the Hall Church.

He secured grants to provide a stipend for a curate-in-charge, and on 28 July 1935, he laid the foundation stone of the Hall Church; on 22 September 1935, he took the service of licensing of the Curate-in-charge and in the following month, he was present when the Hall Church was dedicated.

In June 1937, candidates were presented to him at the first confirmation service held in Hinchley Wood. In December 1938, he made the application to have Hinchley Wood defined as a conventional district and to give it its first independent legal status. He had always championed the cause of the new Church building and, despite illness, he made it his business to support wholeheartedly the claims of St Christopher's. In 1953, the Parochial Church Council resolved unanimously to send Dr. Golding-Bird a message of good wishes, and a token of their affection and goodwill in his retirement. It was a great privilege, they said, to place on record their debt and gratitude to the man whose name was pre-eminent amongst the early leaders in the Church.

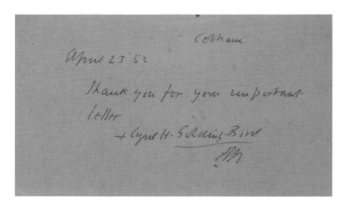

Bishop Golding-Bird wrote to acknowledge news that the funding crisis had passed.

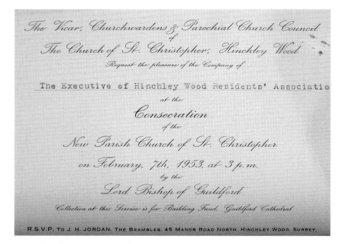

An official invitation to the Residents' Association to the Consecration of the new Church. Source: courtesy, Surrey History Centre

Bishop Golding-Bird

Bishop Golding-Bird, who had come to Guildford from Mauritius in 1930, had been Archdeacon of Dorking from 1930 to 1936 and Archdeacon of Surrey from 1936 to 1949. In 1953, through ill health, he was obliged to lay down his office; for over 20 years he had toiled for Hinchley Wood. In 1953 it was written of him, with no overstatement: "We in Hinchley Wood, at a moment when

The last service in the Hall Church

As the day of the consecration drew near, and the anticipation for the future mounted, the realisation came that the Hall Church, their place of worship for over 17 years, had reached its end: the last service was Evensong on 1

102

February 1953; in the style of the contemporary Church historian, this is what was written about what they were leaving:

Evensong – 1 February 1953

"It was as if we were bidding farewell to some great ship whereon we had voyaged many a day in fair and foul weather. We knew that she could carry us no further in our pilgrimage and that if we saw her again it would be in another and less hallowed guise. We knew too that this parting had been of our own choosing – the sort of choice which is an inevitable but bitter accompaniment of growing up.

Before she sailed leaving us to voyage anew, our minds cast back to the moment when we first stepped aboard her. 'Built to the Glory of God' – that was how her stocks were laid, just like those of the bigger St. Christopher which towered above her even as we knelt. Some of us had been in at the launching – in a world remote from the horrors of a war that came and of its aftermath. Some aboard her had been carried to their last resting places. We had seen them gently pass on. Her captains had changed too and many of her crew. But withal there remained those who knew her beginnings, her tribulations and many a joyous moment.

She had served for hallowed things and for the fellowship of daily life. She was the place where children came for games and for service - mothers too for cod liver oil and orange juice – benefits of a beneficent state when food in larders was low. Thousands upon thousands received the Lord's grace within her. Some – a half-thousand – came as infants, not knowing, to be signed with the sign of the Cross. Pledged, they were, by loving hands, to be brought in the fullness of time to be full members of her crew. There were no passengers. Some joined her for a while and left for other ships, or for no ship at all, and we sorrowed for their absence and for their waywardness in the great seas.

It was not all plain sailing. Sometimes we shrank at the prospect before us. Sometimes we felt the loneliness of our watch. Always we took fresh courage from the others. The Captain must have felt the loneliness most – his was a difficult job with such a motley crew as ours. We were free

---

DIOCESE OF GUILDFORD

———

THE ORDER OF SERVICE
for the
CONSECRATION
of the
CHURCH OF ST. CHRISTOPHER
HINCHLEY WOOD
By
THE RIGHT REVEREND
THE LORD BISHOP OF GUILDFORD

———

Saturday, 7th February, 1953 at 3 p.m.

---

men, wherein was our strength and our weakness, for we did not always rightly interpret our duties or know our loyalties.

She is safe home now and we are pledged to her greater self. We shall never forget those last moments aboard her when the trimmings of her best days had already been removed and we were back to the cleared decks of her launching.

We had always sailed under the same flag so that it was not really a new one which we took. But the bunting laid on the altar of our old love was blessed for the unfurling on our new."

The Surrey Comet reports the consecration

The Surrey Comet reporter wrote at length:

"Coronation year will be linked for ever in the hearts and minds of the people of Hinchley Wood with the consecration of their new parish Church of St. Christopher. On Saturday afternoon a crowded congregation, which included civic dignitaries, many visiting clergy from adjoining parishes, and representatives of local organisations, witnessed the ceremony, performed by the Bishop of Guildford, the Rt. Rev H.C. Montgomery-Campbell.

The interior of the new Church is tastefully finished in

The circling of the Church at the consecration.   Photo: Surrey Comet

white stone and there is a parquet floor. Multiple electric lights are suspended from wrought iron chandeliers and a flight of doves cross the ceiling from east to west. An electric Hammond organ is installed. Heating is by gas fires set high in the wall just below the upper windows.

It was bitterly cold when the Bishop's procession formed in the old Church – now the Church hall – to circle the new Church. Inside the Church the packed congregation rose to their feet as the singing outside of the 24th psalm reached them: 'The earth is the Lord's and all that therein is.' Arriving at the South Door, the procession halted, and clear to all came the three resounding knocks by the Bishop with his Pastoral Staff.

The exhortation: 'Who is the King of glory?' and the Bishop's reply: 'Even the Lord of Hosts: He is the King of glory', came clearly to the assembled people as the keys of the Church were handed to the Bishop by the people's warden, Mr. J.H. Jordan.

The procession then moved with solemn dignity up the nave of the Church to the chancel, which then presented a vivid picture: there assembled were the Cross-bearer, Apparitor, Registrar, the Bishop and Chancellor, the Bishop's Chaplain, the Archdeacon, the choir, Churchwardens, the Rev S. Newton Jones – now properly the vicar of the parish of St. Christopher, Hinchley Wood – the parochial Church council, and the visiting clergy.

Among these were the Rev E.A. Hone (rural dean of Emly), and the Rev A.E. Robins (rural dean of Epsom) and the Rev H.J. Vallins (rural dean of Chertsey) – both former priests-in-charge at Hinchley Wood.

The ceremony of consecration then proceeded with the singing of a further psalm and the hymn, 'Come Holy Ghost, our souls inspire'. The Bishop traced the sign of the Cross upon the pavement, in token that he took possession in the name of Christ of the ground upon which the Church stands.

The procession then re-formed to visit the font and other places appointed. At the font the Lection was recited by Major V.G. Rayner; in the children's corner by Miss P. Jordan; at the chancel steps by Mr. H.E.R. Leggatt; and again at the same place – to hallow future marriage services – by Mr. A.M. Houghton; at the lectern by Mr. R.S. Weatherley; at the pulpit by Mr. W.H. Tregaskes; in the Lady Chapel by Mrs. R. Eynon; and in the midst of the choir by Mr. C.J. Highwood.

Then followed the act of consecration at the altar, the Bishop laying his hands on the fair linen cloth, the ornaments and vessels, and tracing the sign of the Cross at the four corners and in the centre of the Holy Table.

At the completion the organ sounded a joyful chord and the choir sang the 84th psalm: 'O how amiable are Thy dwellings; thou Lord of Hosts!'. The eight candles were lighted and, suddenly, the Church lights were switched on, and on this bleak winter's day they caught the fluted oak screen behind the altar and reflected them.

The Bishop seated himself, and the Chancellor stepped with stately tread to the chancel steps, where he read the Sentence of Consecration. The Bishop, having satisfied himself that all was in order, signed the Sentence and gave directions for its safe custody.

Then, in a loud voice, he commanded: 'Let the congregation stand', and formally informed those assembled that 'We do now declare the Church to be consecrated and for ever set apart from profane, common and ordinary uses...'.

Taking as his text: 'Ascribe unto the Lord the honour due unto His Name; bring presents, and come into His courts', the Bishop spoke of the need for attendance in the House of God.

'Our minds have been led once again to the underlying principles of the Church as a building; what it stands for and what it is meant to do', he said. 'Clearly a very grave responsibility rests upon the shoulders for those who are the first members of this Church.'

'What you make of it will stamp it for very many years to come. It is your privilege and your firm responsibility to set a mark on it which will endure for all time. Remember that it is not the skill of the architect, not the diligence of the builders, nor is it the particular and entire duty of the priest of the parish, but on you yourselves that the future of this Church depends.'

There were three things the Bishop wished to emphasise: that the Church was built first and foremost for the worship of God; that it stood for an increase in the knowledge of God; and that it stood for the conversion of others that were outside the Church.

'A charge is laid against us – not altogether fairly – that we are self-satisfied people', he stressed. 'That must not be so here. This Church must be a power-house of Christianity. It is your concern that men and women outside its walls may be given the opportunity to love and serve the Lord.'

Then followed the hymn: 'the Church's one foundation', further prayers and the Bishop's blessing. St. Christopher's had joined the living Church.

The collection during the service amounted to £42, and will go towards the cathedral fund.

On Sunday morning the Bishop conducted Holy Communion and then a confirmation service."

A touching gesture

The brick from the Chapel of Chelsea Old Church, destroyed by bombing during the war, set in the tower of St Christopher's.

The Surrey Comet reporter discovered this story: it touched him and it was published.

"Ancient and Modern – A Touching Gesture
A Tudor brick from the bombed chapel of Chelsea Old Church, given after the bombing to a Hinchley Wood couple who were married there, has been incorporated in the new Church of St. Christopher at Hinchley Wood, and can be seen just above the first lintel in the tower. This lovely little story reached me quite casually when I attended the consecration ceremony on Saturday; and I think it just one more example of the family feeling and pride of achievement and possession which is abroad in Hinchley Wood. Apart from magnificent financial support, the new Church has received gifts in kind from young and old, rich and poor, publicly and anonymously. The brick, to my mind, symbolises all of these gifts.
Chelsea Old Church was destroyed by a German land-

mine in April 1941. The original structure was 14th century and this was extended and enlarged in the 17th century. The Church is famous and revered as a shrine, for it was in the older part of the building that Sir Thomas More worshipped. On the morning following the bombing a brick from the rubble was given to the Hinchley Wood couple by the then incumbent as a keepsake of the fact that they were married there."

The new St Christopher's

Reading the contemporary accounts of the new Church, one can't escape the infectious enthusiasm which the people felt: how could it be otherwise? These were the people who had seen their dream turn to reality; it is only right to allow the words of Bill Tregaskes, written 50 years ago to describe it; the language is of a different grain, but here is what he wrote:

"Coming home in the train we saw lights in the windows of the building, the floodlit tower and the West front with its great cross. Through the murkiness of an early February evening we saw the new St. Christopher's set in a scene with which we had grown so familiar. As the train left the main line and swung on to the branch the signals were against us and we had time to pick up the detail, the lights also from homes round about. The mother Church had come to her people.

Later, down Manor Road North we went through the mud of Claygate Lane. What a buzz of activity there was within and without the building in those last crowded hours. How well the Architect, the contractors, the master builder, craftsmen and labourers had worked. It was cold outside with a North wind and we shivered at the remembrance of the great floods and the sadness in another part of our country. [This was a reference to the East Coast flood disaster which, even as the Church was consecrated had cost nearly 300 lives when, after severe storms, the sea defences failed.] *But here within, the gas-heaters, high in the walls, glowed and warmed the building into life.* [These have since been removed.] *For weeks before, men, women and children had come to see the progress made; to admire, to declaim, to criticise and to give thanks. For the Vicar and Churchwardens it was an anxious time with much to think about and to do, with great calls upon their patience and goodwill in the exhorting of some and the placating of others; for in the work of the Church it is voluntary free labour which has to be harnessed and co-ordinated with toleration and love.*

On the Wednesday, members of the Church Council came to arrange final details for the ceremony. Beforehand we heard, for the first time, the organ in its new setting and wondered at its majesty and loveliness. The Vicar, wedded to his harmonies, had played the organ with the workmen singing at their labours. Now the choir came to rehearsal and the notes of well-loved psalms sounded.

Coming into the Church and seeing it resplendent for the first time was an experience never to be forgotten. We sat awhile. This was the house which we would come to know – an architect's splendid conception – built to the greater glory of God, for worship, light, knowledge of the strivings and the days of sacrifice and devotion that had gone to its fulfilment. Some might revile it. None could love it more than we who had striven.

We should hear familiar words from the Book oft repeated. We should on dark mornings of winter and in the gay easy mornings of summer come here for the breaking of bread. The sun would set on many an evensong. It was possible that the windows – so light they were – might be darkened against the enemy. Here might we be brought in our own last journey.

The great red carpet was unrolled – right down the aisle from font to chancel, spelling out the road of our pilgrimage. Within the sanctuary another lovely carpet was laid. The frontals and hangings of the altar were fitted.

We loved those last evenings ere the building passed from the hands of those who made it. It was thus, God worked through men and women, and it was so obvious to see.

And so the great day came. The morning hours were spent busy with the finishing touches. Chairs had to be brought from the school because all the pews had not arrived. 340 seats were provided with extra temporary little stools in front for the Brownies and small Sunday School children. Flowers were arranged – four big bowls of them. The printed service sheets were distributed. The doors were locked against the appointed time of consecration. The flag of the Church with its cross of St. George flew at the masthead supreme.

The service itself we shall never forget. Men not given to emotion were moved by its simplicity and its grandeur. The order of service caught up the tradition of centuries. It was a happy thought of the Vicar's to allow laymen and laywomen to do their part with clergy and Bishop and representatives of the Ecclesiastical Courts to the formal offering of the building and its several parts.

Guests were there representative of the Civil power, the Diocesan authority and parishes in the ancient Emly Deanery. There too were the former priests in charge now Rural Deans in the Diocese. Also was the widow of the first Vicar of Weston who had taken the first Celebration in Hinchley Wood at the Filling Station 20 years ago. There too, in a place kept, was the oldest member of our congregation, a figure dear to us all. No seats were otherwise reserved and thanks to the efficient stewarding and its interpretation with goodwill, those who had faithfully come through the years were there for the day of fulfilment. All along the aisles and at the back of the Church, people stood. The young gave up their seats for the old. The alms were given for the building of the Cathedral in the Diocese. So our latest daughter Church was linked with the great mother Church which is to be.

It was a proud day for hundreds who had in some way, great or small, given of themselves for St. Christopher's. There was no doubt about our debt to the Vicar and the Churchwardens who had borne responsibility over the long months of building. Each in his measure and according to the special opportunities which he enjoyed had given of more than his best. Their reward was for all to see.

The sacring was not truly complete until the Sunday

morning when the Bishop celebrated our first Communion and later received for Confirmation many loved members of the fellowship. The prayer then uttered was for us all in the new Church: 'Defend, O Lord, these thy servants with thy heavenly Grace, that they may continue thine forever: and daily increase in thy Holy Spirit more and more, until they come into Thy everlasting Kingdom'.

The Rev Newton Jones already had a parish; now he had a Church. It was commented upon by the chairman of the Hinchley Wood Residents' Association: in his report to the annual general meeting held in April 1953, Mr. Martin described the completion of the building of St Christopher's Church as "the most momentous happening of the year". Looking back at the archive material, which gives colour to those natal years, one can sense, even at the distance of 50 years, the emotions of clergy and laity alike at that time: the unalloyed joy as they entered their new Church: their monument to endeavour; an epic; the end of the beginning; a Church entire; fledged; bequeathed by the toil and treasure of one gen-

A view of St Christopher's from the north-west (which today is partially obscured). Photo: St Christopher's Church

eration to all of those to come. It was by the efforts of these people: indomitable; sure of themselves; part of a generation which had seen and survived bad times, and which had not yet seen the good, that the origins of Hinchley Wood, a 1930s settlement, were impressed into history.

Now with a church and two schools where there were formerly fields, alongside a pot-holed road, Claygate Lane, Hinchley Wood, has become a modern street bounded by wide pavements.

Source: Surrey Comet, 1 January 1955

106

APPENDIX

THE PARISH CHURCH OF ST CHRISTOPHER, HINCHLEY WOOD
A Brief Guide compiled in 1987 by William Vaughan Williams (with later additions by Howard Mallinson, who added the photographs)

Early history

The Parish of St Christopher, Hinchley Wood, was formerly part of the Parish of All Saints, Weston, which itself had been formed out of the Parish of St Nicholas, Thames Ditton in 1932. The first Vicar of Weston became responsible for the development of the Church in the new settlement of Hinchley Wood, and services were held in a room in the Esher Filling Station, the first being held on Easter Day 1933.

In 1934 land in Claygate Lane North, part of Manor Farm, was conveyed as a gift by Marianne Frances Cecilia Litchfield-Speer to the Guildford Diocesan Board of Finance for the building of a new Church and Hall in Hinchley Wood.

The foundation stone of the Church Hall was laid on 28 July 1935 by Bishop Golding-Bird and the building was completed in the same year and dedicated on 17 October 1935 by the Bishop of Guildford. Thereafter services continued in the Hall, the land between the Hall and the public highway being intended for the building of the Church. Doubts arose however (notwithstanding the completion of the Hall), as to the suitability of this land for the site of the Church as it did not enjoy a central position in the Parish, but eventually (all other possible sites having been thoroughly explored and for a variety of reasons rejected) the decision was made to build the Church where it now stands. Progress was delayed by the intervention of the war, and after the war by the scarcity of materials and building restrictions. Finally the foundation stone of the Church was laid on 12 January 1952 by Admiral of the Fleet, Lord Tovey, a Church Commissioner, and the Church was consecrated on 7 February 1953 by the Bishop of Guildford, the Right Reverend Henry Colville Montgomery-Campbell. From that date Hinchley Wood became: "The Parish of St Christopher, Hinchley Wood." The Church of St Christopher was the first post-war Church to be built in the Diocese of Guildford.

The legend of St Christopher

The early version of the story of St Christopher belongs to the 6th Century AD and tells us that Offero, a man of giant stature and great strength worked (as his name indicates) as a bearer of burdens. Wishing to serve a master stronger than himself, he first threw in his lot with an Eastern King; but, finding that the King feared the Devil, he transferred his allegiance to the latter. Then seeing the Devil shudder at the sight of the Cross, he left him in search of a new master. He found a holy hermit who told him to offer his allegiance to Christ, instructed him in the faith, and baptised him. Feeling himself unfitted for fasting and prayer, Offero decided to devote himself to a work of charity and set himself to carry wayfarers over a bridgeless river. One night a little child asked to be carried across and Offero, taking him on his shoulder, stepped into the water. As he proceeded he found his burden growing heavier and he staggered under what seemed to be a crushing weight. On reaching the other bank Offero upbraided the child for placing him in peril. "Had I borne the whole world on my back", he said, "it could not have weighed heavier than thou." "Marvel Not", the child replied, "for thou has borne Him who bears the sins of the world, and so that thou mayest know that I speak the truth set thy staff in the earth and in the morning it shall bear both leaves and flowers." The child vanished.

Offero did as he was bid and the light of the morning revealed his staff adorned with leaves and flowers as the child had foretold. Offero then realised that he had indeed borne Christ. He was no longer known as Offero, the bearer of burdens, but as Christoffero or Christopher, the Christbearer.

St Christopher probably never existed but from early times he had been a popular saint and by the end of the 15th century wall paintings of St Christopher were in

many English Churches. He came to be regarded as the patron saint of travellers, and the fact that the busy Kingston by-pass runs through the Parish and the first service of Holy Communion in Hinchley Wood had been held in the Esher Filling Station made it appropriate for the Church to be called St Christopher's.

The story of St Christopher may be legendary but it nevertheless contains Christian insights aptly shown in a hymn written by a former Vicar of St Christopher's, the Reverend Andrew Warner, and printed at the back of the Church's Ancient and Modern Hymn Book.

The statue of St Christopher

In a niche on the outside of the west wall of the Church is a statue of St Christopher. He is shown crossing the water holding a staff in his hand with the Christchild on his shoulder. The statue, made of fibreglass, is the work of the late Mr. Harry Phillips of Lewes, Sussex, who was Head of the Sculpture Department at Leeds College of Arts and Crafts. Specially commissioned, it was given to the Church anonymously* and was dedicated on 27 July 1975 by the Venerable John Evans, Archdeacon of Surrey.

---

* After the death of Mrs. Nan Lawson, the widow of Mr. Bill Lawson, a former Churchwarden, in October 2002, it was revealed that she had been the anonymous donor; a secret which was kept faithfully during her lifetime, as she had wished.

The statue gives a vivid impression of St Christopher staggering under an almost unbearable burden although the child seems to sit lightly on his shoulder.

Beneath the statue is the foundation stone of the Church bearing the inscription:-

> This stone was laid by
> Admiral of the Fleet, Lord Tovey, GCB, KBE, DSO
> and dedicated by the Lord Bishop of Guildford,
> 12th January 1952
> Churchwardens, W Kerr and J H Jordan
> Vicar, Newton Jones, BA
> Architect, S Beverley, FRIBA

Garden of Remembrance

On the north side of the Church is the Garden of Remembrance for the burial of ashes. It was dedicated by the Right Reverend Kenneth Evans, Bishop of Dorking, on 25 June 1978. At the same time he dedicated the Book of Remembrance which is in the glass topped stand in the Church near the Font. The stone in the Garden bears the inscription:

> "Garden of Remembrance for the Burial of Ashes.
> Set apart in the year of the Silver Jubilee of
> St Christopher's Church
> By Parishioners of Hinchley Wood – 1978"

The seat in the Garden is inscribed:

> "This seat has been donated by the people of
> Hinchley Wood in commemoration of
> The Silver Jubilee, 1977, of Queen Elizabeth II"

The stand containing the Book of Remembrance is inscribed:

> "Presented in Thanksgiving by George and
> Margaret Palmer, 25 June 1978"

And the Book of Remembrance is inscribed:

> "Presented by Daisy K Browne in memory of her
> parents Edward and Elizabeth Browne"

The Windows

There are eight engraved windows in the Church: four on the north side; three on the south; and one in the bell tower.

Proceeding from the chancel the first on the north side is a Nativity Window. It was the gift Mrs. Audrey Watson, the late Principal of Grantchester House School, Hinchley Wood, and is a lasting reminder of the long and happy association between the School and St Christopher's Church where the School's Nativity Play is enacted annually.

The next window depicts Dorcas, the disciple mentioned in Acts 9:36 who did works of charity and kindness and who used her skill with the needle to make tunics and other garments. It was given to the Church by Mr. Stanley Butler in memory of his wife Margaret, a member of the Church, who gave much care to the maintenance of the Church linen.

The third window is the War Memorial window showing St George and the Dragon. It was dedicated on 3 April 1955 by the then Vicar, The Reverend Newton Jones in the presence of representatives of the British Legion.

The last window on the north side depicts the Presentation of the Infant Jesus in the Temple for the observance of the purification ritual. Simeon is seen receiving the child and giving the hymn of praise which we know so well as the Nunc Dimittis. This window was given by Mrs. Pamela James in memory of her mother Mrs. Margaret Lock and was dedicated on 27 September 1987.

On the south side, and directly opposite the Grantchester House window is a window depicting Jesus saying: "Let the children come to me"; it was the gift of the parents of children from Grantchester House School, in memory of Mrs. Watson after her death.

The next two windows are different representations of the good Samaritan: one is in memory of Mrs. L A Try, given by her daughter, Mrs. Joyce Southerton. The sec-

ond was given by the family of Mrs. Celia Cowderoy to the memory of a dedicated parishioner.

In the bell tower, the window (which is set to be read from outside the Church in the memorial garden) shows: "The beauty of creation"; given by the family of Ellen and Victor Langley, in their memory.

There are three stained glass windows in the Lady Chapel. The centre window shows St Christopher from a drawing by a member of the Young Communicants Guild against a stylised background of suburban life. It was dedicated on 25 May 1958.

The left hand window depicts St Nicholas to indicate the connection of St Christopher's Church with the Parish Church of St Nicholas, Thames Ditton. St Nicholas is regarded as the patron saint of sailors; hence the ship in the bottom left-hand corner of the window. His symbol is sometimes three bags of gold (three golden roundels seen on his mitre), the dowry he is supposed to have given to three girls to save them from being sold into prostitution. The inscription below the window is:

1957
Lt Robert Wilson Andrews, RA
Neville Hartley Hawkes
Let Light Perpetual Shine upon them

The right-hand window is a representation of the Madonna and Child. The fleur-de-lys, as a symbol of the Holy Trinity as well as a symbol of the Blessed Virgin, is seen in the bottom right-hand corner. The inscription below the window is:

Ivy Young and Penny Wilson
September 1956
Let Light Perpetual Shine upon them
This Window was dedicated on 9 February 1958

The Pews

With one or two exceptions the pews were donated to the Church. The following early members of the Church presented a pew:

Mr. & Mrs. William Dewe
Mr. & Mrs. H J Wheadon

Mr. J D Cousin
Mr. & Mrs. C J Highwood
Mr. & Mrs. James Tomsett
Mr. & Mrs. E S Castle
Mr. & Mrs. E A Browne
Mr. & Mrs. A G Ingram
Mr. & Mrs. T R A Waterhouse
Mr. & Mrs. R G Burr
Mr. & Mrs. J R Brown
Mr. & Mrs. Lewis Griffiths and Family
Mr. & Mrs. Saytch, Valerie and Vanessa
Grantchester House School

Others were presented by friends or relatives in memory of:

Frederick and Mary Cutbill
Grace M Beddow
Rachel Maria Fraser
Kate Elizabeth Hunt
Walter and Alice Harvey
Ernest Charles Grew
Charlotte L Goddard
Reginald Foden
Lillian Adelina Cordell
Richard J Porter
Adgie Simond
Edward A Holden
Charles James Hutton
Henry Edward Parker
William and Alice Ellis
Charles and Henrietta Eldridge

The front pew on the south side of the Church is inscribed "The Bun Penny and Ship Halfpenny Pew". This pew was paid for by the accumulation of bun pennies (pennies bearing on the one side the head of the youthful Queen Victoria wearing her hair in a bun) and ship halfpennies (halfpennies having a ship on one side) collected locally. The collection was organised by Mrs. Gladys Bentley who improvised collecting jars and delivered them to over thirty householders who had volunteered to take part in the scheme. Every month Mrs. Bentley cycled round the homes of jar holders to collect jars filled with coins and leave empty jars in their place. The coins were paid into the local Post Office and Banks to keep them in circulation. The novelty of the scheme and the peripatetic enthusiasm of Mrs. Bentley ensured a successful outcome. Something like 20,000 coins were handled and checked, and the Church Council placed on record its gratitude to Mrs. Bentley and her helpers. The cryptic inscription on this pew must puzzle occupants unaware of the epic effort which provided the pew for their use.

The Organ

The organ is a two manual extension organ installed in 1970 by George Osmond, Taunton. It replaced a Hammond electronic organ purchased when services were held in the Church Hall. It was dedicated on Trinity Sunday, 24 May 1970, by the Archdeacon of Dorking.

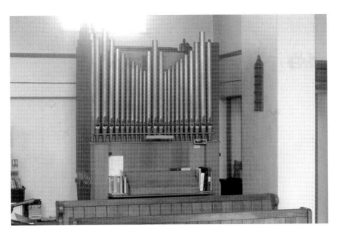

The Font

The font was a gift from the Vicar and people of Claygate Parish Church.

Lady Chapel

In the Lady Chapel is an annulary for the reservation of the sacrament for distribution to the sick of the Parish. A set of bookshelves on the north wall was given in memory of Miss Mary Cuthill, one of the earliest members of the Church.

The Bells

The Tower contains 6 bells supplied by John Taylor and Co., Loughborough, details of which are:

Diameter Inches	Approximate Weight Cwt	Note	Donor
26	3½	E♭	Given in memory of Mr. Cowderoy
23	2½	F	Mr. George Johnson
21	2	G	Mr. & Mrs. Weatherley
20	1¾	G#	Mr, Mrs. and Ian McLaurin
18	1¼	A#	Mr. & Mrs. Whitton
16	1	C	Mrs. Audrey Watson

The Ship's Bell at the base of the Tower was given by Admiral of the Fleet, Lord Tovey.

A ship's bell at the base of the tower of St Christopher's, given by Lord Tovey.

Ornaments, Silver and Vestments

The original altar silver candlesticks and altar cross were purchased from the proceeds of the sale of old silver given to the Church in response to an appeal made in 1951 in the local and national press by Mr. J. H. Jordan, Churchwarden. The candlesticks were stolen in 1967. The present candleholders consist of two silver sconces resting upon slate blocks around each of which are inscribed the words: VENI CREATOR SPIRITUS, the sconces being removable when the candles are not lit. They were designed by John Skelton.

In 1968 a magnificent cope, with a representation of St Christopher embroidered on the hood, was presented to the Church by Mr. and Mrs. Craster Patterson. The needlework and embroidery being the work of Mrs. Patterson.

The Sacristy lamp was a gift from the Parish of Weston.

A glass fronted bookcase near the font was given in memory of Heather Kathleen Silk who died on 21 November 1964 aged 8 years.

A baptismal bowl was given to the church by Mr. and Mrs. Waterhouse and family.

A silver wafer box was donated in 1987 in memory of Mr. and Mrs. Jordan.

A Revised Standard Version of the Bible on the lectern is inscribed: "Presented to St Christopher's Church on the 21st anniversary of its consecration in loving memory of Eveline Florence McLaurin, died 7 February, 1973."

The Authorised Version of the Bible also on the lectern is inscribed, "In Memory of Victor George Rayner, 1893-1954."

The silver alms plate is inscribed:

Sacred to the Memory of Henry Edward Parker
1876-1946
Sometime Treasurer and Sidesman of St Christopher's
Church

The prie-dieu in the Sacristy is inscribed:

Sacred to the memory of Reginald Price

The Doves

There are 17 model doves on the ceiling of the Church flying westward. Mr. S. Beverley, the architect of the Church, when explaining the plans of the Church to the Parochial Church Council said that "the model doves on the ceiling symbolised the word of God being carried from the pulpit to the congregation". A dove however is the traditional symbol of the Holy Spirit. We read of the baptism of Jesus in Mark 1:10, "and when he came up out of the water he saw the heavens opened and the Spirit descending upon him like a dove". There is another single dove flying eastward from the children's corner to the Font.

ST CHRISTOPHER
A. C. Warner
(Vicar of St Christopher's 1971 to 1980)

Jesus Christ who, in the legend,
On our patron's shoulder rode,
Trusting him to bear Thee safely
Where the raging torrents flowed;
Grant that we may likewise bear Thee,
As we tread life's troubled road.

2
Grant that we may likewise bear Thee
In our hearts where'er we go,
So that all we meet may see Thee
In the lives we live below,
That they too by Thee be blessed
With the grace Thou dost bestow.

3
That they too by Thee be blessed,
So that they in turn may be
Saints, who bear in them Thine image
For the rest of men to see,
So may all come to Thy kingdom,
Where Thou reign'st eternally.

4
So may all come to Thy kingdom
And give glory to the Son,
Glory to the Holy Spirit,
And the Father: ever One.
Then Saint Christopher's example
Will bear fruit in everyone.

SPECIFICATION OF NEW TWO MANUAL ORGAN

COMPASS OF MANUALS	CC to A	58 notes	
COMPASS OF PEDALS	CCC to F	30 notes	

GREAT ORGAN

1.	Open Diapason.	8.	Full length bottom octave.	
2.	Stopped Diapason.		Unenclosed	Rank A
3.	Salicional.	8.	From Swell.	Rank B
4.	Principal.	8.	From Swell.	Rank C
5.	Flute.	4.	Unenclosed.	Rank A
6.	Fifteenth.	4.	From Swell.	Rank B
7.	Mixture.	2.	Unenclosed.	Rank A
		3.	Rks.Repeating	Separate Rank

SWELL ORGAN

1.	Stopped Diapason.	8.	Bottom octave unenclosed.	
2.	Salicional.			Rank B
3.	Flute.	8.	Bass from No. 1	Rank C
4.	Salicet.	4.		Rank B
5.	Nazard.	4.		Rank C
6.	Fifteenth.	2-2/3		Rank B
7.	Vol.Calistes 8-ft. Tenor C.	2.		Rank C

PEDAL ORGAN

1.	Bourdon.	16.	24 pipes unenclosed	Rank B
2.	Bass Flute.	8.	12 pipes unenclosed	Rank B
3.	Principal.	8.	Unenclosed.	Rank A
4.	Fifteenth.	4.	Unenclosed.	Rank A

COUPLERS

1	Swell to Great.
2	Swell to Pedal.
3	Great to Pedal.

Electric action throughout with silver to silver contacts.
Drawstop control by modern Stopkeys.
Oak casework with Oak Stool.
Full Scale Radiating in Concave Pedal Board.
Balanced Swell Pedal in central position.
Electrical Blowing Equipment enclosed in the Organ.

**THE
PARISH CHURCH OF St CHRISTOPHER
HINCHLEY WOOD**

DIOCESE OF GUILDFORD

PRIESTS IN CHARGE

1935–1941	ALBERT EDWARD ROBINS. B.A
1941–1945	HEDLEY JAMES VALLINS. B.B.
1945–1953	NEWTON SURDIVAL JONES. B.A.

INCUMBENTS

1953–1966	NEWTON SURDIVAL JONES. B.A.
1966–1971	STEPHEN FRANCIS GUNYON. M.A.
1971–1980	ANDREW COMPTON WARNER. M.A.
1981–1984	ALAN ROY ARNOLD. B.D.
1985–2000	ROY DAVID ROBINSON. A.K.C.
2001	TREVOR DONNOLLEY. B.A.

**A board with the above inscription is carried in St
Christopher's Church**

BIBLIOGRAPHY

BAKER, STANLEY *Milk to Market, 1973*

BARKER, MARION *Esher Memoirs, 1972*

BUTTERS, SHAAN *The Book of Kingston, 1995*

DENDY, MARSHALL, C.F. *History of the Southern Railway, 1963*

EVERETT, HAROLD W. *A History of the Hinchley Wood Residents' Association, 1985*

HARPER, CHARLES G. *The Portsmouth Road, 1895 and 1923*

HEARNSHAW, F.J.C. *The Place of Surrey in the History of England, 1971*

HOLMES, T.W. *The Semaphore, (1983)*

JACKSON, ALAN A. *The Railway in Surrey, 1999*

JACKSON, ALAN A. *Semi-Detached London, 1973*

MASTERS, BETTY (REVISED BY GATES, NIGEL) *The Growth of Portsmouth*

MITCHELL, VIC AND SMITH, KEITH *Branch Lines Around Effingham Junction, 1990*

MITCHELL, VIC AND SMITH, KEITH *Waterloo to Woking, 1986*

OPPITZ, LESLIE *Surrey Railways Remembered, 1988*

PEEBLES, MALCOLM *A History of Surbiton Golf Club, 1987*

PEEBLES, MALCOLM *The Claygate Book, 1983*

ROYSTON PIKE, E. *Borough of Elmbridge*

SOUTHERN RAILWAY *Country Homes at London's Door, late 1920s*

TARPLES, PETER *Industrial History of the Borough of Elmbridge, 1998*

TAYLOR, A. J. P. *English History, 1914-1945, 1965*

THOMAS, DAVID ST JOHN & WHITEHOUSE, PATRICK *A Century and a Half of The Southern Railway, 1988*

WAKEFORD, IAIN *Woking 150 : The History of Woking and its Railway, 1987*

WITTEN, ANITA *The Development of an Outer London Suburban Village, Hinchley Wood, near Esher, Surrey, unpublished, Loughborough University, 1983*

INDEX